Wedge tornado near White Deer, Texas on May 29, 2001

Under the
Whirlwind

*Everything you need to know about tornadoes
but didn't know who to ask*

Jerrine Verkaik
Arjen Verkaik

Whirlwind Books, Elmwood, Ontario, Canada

Whirlwind Books, Elmwood, Ontario, Canada
© Arjen & Jerrine Verkaik, Whirlwind Books, 1997, 1998, 2001
All rights reserved. First edition 1997
Second edition 2001
Printed in Canada

National Library of Canada Cataloguing in Publication Data

Verkaik, Jerrine
       Under the whirlwind: everything you need to know
about tornadoes but didn't know who to ask, 2nd ed. Includes
bibliographical references

   ISBN 0-9681537-4-7

       1. Tornadoes.   I. Verkaik, Arjen   II. Title.

QC955.V47 2001 551.55'3 C2001-901715-4

Printed in Canada on chlorine-free paper

CONTENTS

Photo credits

All photo credits (including cover) are ©Arjen & Jerrine
Verkaik/SKYART except as noted below. The authors would like
to thank the many people listed below whose photos and videos
contributed to this book.

©L. Banks– 52-2; ©I. Birkholz– 166-2; ©R. Coleman– 55-2;
©D. Comber– 23-2; ©M. Courtney– 50; ©R. Elms– 116-3;
©J. Franklin– 24-1, 24-2; ©M. Heslop– 58-2 (from video); ©D. Hill–
45-1, 45-2; ©G. Hostrawser– 121-3; ©K. Idzik– 34, 37, 39, 44-2,
46-1, 166-1, 170-1; ©D. Jones– back cover, 161, 166-3, 177;
©J. MacDonald– 60; ©B. Metzger– 22, 23-1,163-1, 171-1, 171-3,
171-4, 176; ©Ontario Hydro Retail, Owen Sound– 174;
©G. Power– 157-3, 159; ©J. Simpson– 16, 29; ©J. Skanes– 53-2;
©Sun Times/J. Masters– 21, 25, 62, 157-1; ©J. Zyta– 35-1, 35-2,
35-3, 36, 40, 41, 44-1, 61, 150, 153, 157-2, 157-4, 163-2, 170-2,
171-2, 180, 193.

All cartoons are ©J. S. Muir, and we thank him for working
patiently with us to lend the book his touch of whimsy.

Introduction

This book is a labour of love by a couple whose lives have been bound together by a shared passion for the sky. We have travelled many miles, photographing, writing and speaking about the exquisite beauty and variety that inspires our work. We have chased clouds; we have chased rainbows. We have chased snowsqualls and fog. And, of course, we have chased one of nature's greatest furies– the tornado. In chaser's parlance, we have caught a couple of dozen in our time. But it would be truer to say that **we** have been captured– by their power and beauty.

In the many years that we have chased tornadoes we have had one enduring regret. We could not take the time to stop and help people with the devastation that confronted them. We were able to stop long enough to offer a hug or call for help when we were the first on the scene; but our work, photographing and documenting severe weather, demanded that we stay with the storm as it continued its rampage.

We comforted ourselves with the knowledge that good written and photographic documentation of storms was helping to advance scientific understanding of tornadoes, and this would help us all anticipate and respond to tornadic storms in the future. But we wished we could do something more.

This book is that something more.

In the cold April of 1996, when we were making preparations for our annual departure for the Mecca of chasers– North America's "tornado alley"– we were caught off guard by two tornadoes that ripped through Southern Ontario, with snow still on the ground. One of them first touched down 5 km (3 miles) from our home, but where were we? Making one last visit to our family in Toronto before taking off to chase tornadoes in Texas!

Once we recovered from our initial numbing depression (for having missed a tornado so close to home), we realized that this was a rare opportunity to help people learn from an in-depth look at what it is like to go through a tornado. It was a chance to give people "everything they needed to know about tornadoes, but didn't know who to ask."

We wanted to use a detailed recounting of what our neighbours had gone through to focus attention on what everybody needs to know.

So we started with the story– *A tale of two twisters* (Chapter one). We interviewed more than 500 people to discover what they had experienced, what confused or surprised them, and what went right or wrong before, during and after the tornadoes.

We knew that the best way to give people early warning of dangerous weather was to develop their weather smarts, so we decided to include a well-illustrated guide to the stormy sky in the book (*Reading the stormy sky*, Chapter two). It is overflowing with tips, explanations and illustrations that will help you engage in the joys of skywatching and, at the same time, be better prepared to recognize when the weather may pose a threat.

And then, of course, we had to give tornadoes their due, so we walk you through the maze of what is and isn't known about them in *Anatomy of a tornado* (Chapter three). Recently, there has been a North America-wide frenzy of popular interest in tornadoes and tornado chasing, but it seemed to us that much of what was being said just added to the confusion and misinformation that already abounded. We wanted to do justice to what is known about tornadoes, but we didn't want to drown people in all the scientific if's, and's and but's. So we tried to make our explanations as clear and simple as possible without misleading the reader (as simplified explanations often do). We trust that our scientific colleagues will forgive us a few distinctly unscientific metaphors we used to accomplish this.

We knew from our interviews that people were being given conflicting messages as to where to go and what to do to protect themselves from an approaching tornado, so in *Don't just stand there!* (Chapter four) we have brought together the best current advice, along with some background on why it is preferable to some of the tips you may have heard in the past.

But the need for clarification and information does not end with the tornado. For friends and neighbours, the tornado experience often starts with the devastation it leaves behind. Thousands of people may show up on the scene, anxious to know how they can help. But the victims are too shocked, too devastated, to know where to begin. In Chapter five, *Coming to the rescue*, we use the experience of April 20th to make suggestions as to what is and isn't helpful in the aftermath of a tornado.

Long after the surge of community support has subsided, the victims of a tornado are still struggling with a seemingly endless barrage of details and decisions, all of which must be handled while they are on an emotional rollercoaster. *Rebuilding lives and spirits* (Chapter six) looks at important factors that may help them with their struggles: co-ordinating the process; repairing and rebuilding; dealing with insurance; stress and grief responses; and how to get outside help. If it helps even one tornado victim in the future we will feel gratified.

And we wanted to help parents and children work through their fears and emotional stresses– not only those children whose homes have been hit by tornadoes, but also the many others who are terrified every time the sky darkens or the wind picks up. *Helping kids cope* (Chapter seven) gives suggestions based on the stories and experiences of teachers, parents and children, and helps adults understand how their responses and reactions to weather can provide reassurance and comfort to children.

Although devastating tornadoes are much less common in Southern Ontario than in Texas or Oklahoma, it is becoming clear that, even in Ontario, there are preferred areas for tornado development. *What are the risks?* (Chapter eight) takes a look at when and where tornadoes are most likely to happen in North America, recognizing that the odds of being hit are very low, no matter where you are. This is followed by a brief look at how you can renovate or build your home to withstand the winds; and we top off the book with a quick look back at some of the tips that can help you take control of your responses to the weather. We can't control it; we can't change it; but we can prepare for it.

The book ends with an *Afterword* that looks at how tornadoes inspire a sense of community that is rare in these days of harried disconnection from our surroundings. We hope that our brief exploration of how people come together in disaster will inspire you to discover ways of sparking a more lasting, day-to-day sense of community where you live.

The information in this book is brought to life through the real experiences of the many victims, witnesses and helpers we interviewed. Since we had quotes from so many sources, we felt it would be unwieldy and disruptive to the reader to attribute those that were chosen to reflect a common experience. (We have attributed the quotes in Chapter one (the story) and in a few other specific instances.) We hope the reader and our interviewees will excuse us this departure from normal practice. All of the interviewees are listed at the end of the book (page 223).

We have been inspired and humbled by the courage and love we have encountered in the many people we interviewed for this book. To all of them we extend our heartfelt gratitude and prayers for a well and happily lived life.

Thank you,

Arjen and Jerrine Verkaik
Elmwood, Ontario, Canada

1
A tale of two twisters

The tale of the two twisters that took Southern Ontario by surprise on Saturday, April 20th, 1996, is made up of many stories. Every victim and witness has his or her own tale to tell. We have woven many of these stories together to breathe life into this account of what life is like "under the whirlwind," but we could not possibly have included everything we have been told. Instead, we have tried to select elements that allow us to paint a broad and colourful canvas of the tornado experience.

However, every last story, every last detail that people so generously shared with us, has become part of the larger story told throughout this book. In this chapter we have attributed quotes, since the stories belong specifically to the tellers. In the rest of the book we have chosen many quotes to illustrate common experiences, but we have not attributed them.

Although we are starting our exploration of life under the whirlwind with one specific event, our goal is to use this story to draw out all the information anyone, anywhere is likely to need to know about tornadoes. We hope that this attempt to draw the threads of common experience out of the weave of one story will make this book both interesting and informative. And now, the tale begins.

The unsuspecting residents of Williamsford were devastated by the tornado's destruction.

The elements of the book

Under the Whirlwind is a feast of fascinating and useful information – so much so that we offer you a menu to help you find what you want, when you want it. For the reader who is looking for a full-course meal, the table of contents may be a sufficient guide, but there are also several kinds of "snacks" to choose from.

There are tasty tidbits– such as the boxes on **weird** stuff and **myths** that are available in **chapters one and three** respectively. There are also healthy side dishes– such as the **Quick references** and **Checklists** scattered through the later chapters. The main course is also supplemented by **Highlight boxes**– a smorgasbord of close looks at various details that are related to the running text.

And of course there are plenty of desserts– photos, cartoons, diagrams and quotes that make the whole meal more enjoyable.

The kinds of dishes you can choose from are listed below. Dig in. We hope you enjoy the banquet!

weird When a tornado takes on the world, all kinds of strange things happen. Many arise directly from the wind force, some from secondary effects, and a few from coincidental factors. A few more defy explanation and expose our limited understanding of the tornado's exact behaviour. A small sampling of these weird effects are randomly scattered through **chapter one**. (They do not usually correspond with the stories being told on the same page.)

Myth

Tornadoes often leave people scratching their heads, puzzling over what appears to have happened, and it's human nature to try to explain the mysterious. For this reason, myths and misconceptions about tornadoes abound, and the Myth boxes in **chapter three** draw some of them out.

Highlight box

The yellow boxes focus in on the details, reinforcing the information contained in the running text. They are scattered throughout the book after **chapter one**.

Checklist

These are lists of important or helpful details on specific subjects, particularly pertaining to cleaning up and rebuilding after a tornado.

Quick reference

A few boxes of handy or important information– the stuff you need to find quickly– have been scattered through the text, especially in **chapters four through seven**.

Tornado path map

The story of the April 20th tornadoes is told in two places. **Chapter one** looks at the human story and **chapter three** tells the story of the tornadoes themselves, complete with pictures of how they looked at various stages along their paths. There is a map of their paths on page 130, in **chapter three**.

In the beginning

To tell the story of the tornadoes of April 20th, 1996, we need to begin at the beginning– with the men and women at the Ontario Weather Centre (in Toronto) who were our eyes on the skies. They were worrying about what that day was going to bring while the rest of us were out revelling in the first warm day of spring.

The job of forecasting and alerting the public to the dangers posed by severe weather is a tough one. Let's take a look at an exhausting and challenging couple of days at the weather office. The main actors were Rob Paola, who was on the severe weather desk; Arnold Ashton, an experienced severe weather forecaster who pitched in to provide back-up; and Mike Leduc, the senior severe weather specialist, who was off-duty on April 20th, but came in for much of the day.

We join them when the action begins, on Friday, April 19th.

A storm is brewing

As Arnold Ashton told us, "History plays such an important role in determining what's going to happen." Weather doesn't happen in isolation, we only experience it in isolation. It is a progression of events over a broad geographic region. If you want to know what the weather will be tomorrow, you look upwind (usually to the southwest) today.

On April 19th the forecasters at the Ontario Weather Centre had their eyes glued on Indiana and Illinois, where big things were happening. Mike Leduc was not on severe weather duty that day, but he was watching the action with keen interest. "From the day before we saw that it was going to be a fairly active day." There was "a pretty intense system" to the southwest, and it was moving toward Ontario.

According to Arnold Ashton, "It was warm enough and humid enough to generate some pretty wicked storms down in Indiana and Illinois. There were many damaging tornadoes. We knew that on the day [April 19]. We were looking at local radars, current radars, as the tornadoes were on the ground– seeing multiple cells. Initially there were a couple in central Indiana. This is important because the placement of these storms in relation to the synoptic features was quite crucial as to what was going to happen the next day over us."

When Arnold and Rob Paola discussed the situation, "there was a degree of confidence that the 20th of April would be a nasty, nasty day. In fact, we had said to each other that the Kitchener, Guelph, Waterloo area would be the place where there was going to be the nastiest storms. We chose that area because of synoptic correlation– we correlate the features in one scenario [in Illinois/Indiana] and ... translate those features along. And in that forecast setting, this is where all the numbers ... come together and say to you, this is the threat zone." It was like superimposing the Illinois/Indiana scenario on Ontario.

"To tell you the truth, we were of the mindset that there could be the potential for tornadoes 24 hours in advance," Arnold Ashton told us.

The Ontario Weather Centre put out a public forecast that night, indicating that there would be thunderstorms on April 20th, and they advised the other weather offices (London and Windsor, as well as Toronto) that there was a potential for severe weather. Arnold and Rob stayed at work late that night. (Their shift ended at 6pm but they stayed on until 7:30 or 7:45.) They wanted to keep an eye on those "mega storms."

Arnold Ashton said, "I went home and turned on the late news and there was talk of damaging tornadoes– a massive outbreak [in Indiana/Illinois]. That was the expression that they used. And when they use that expression just down the street from us, that's cause for concern. So I was thinking, 'We're under the gun for tomorrow. What's going to happen?' It gets the adrenalin going and that can keep you awake. I was pretty well hyped and ready."

Will it pan out?

But no matter how potent an approaching weather system appears to be, there are so many factors that can change the course of events that it is never a sure thing. As Mike Leduc said, "These things are so notorious for ... the day before it looks like everything's going to be perfect [for the formation of dangerous storms]– and when the day comes up, things don't quite phase.

"All the computer progs from the day before were showing that the low was tracking across Northern Lake Huron, that we would get into the warm sector, and that the instability and wind shear parameters were favourable, quite favourable, for a severe weather event." The models that they were using to analyze the weather were fairly consistently predicting severe storms, but "the big problem for us is ... how do you distinguish these big events [damaging tornadoes] from weaker events" that produce 100km/h winds (60mph), uproot a few trees, drop large hail or spawn a weak tornado.

So when Rob Paola and Arnold Ashton came in to work at 7:30am on April 20th, they were anxious to scan the preliminary data for that day (looking at soundings upstream– at Buffalo and Detroit).The new data come in between 8am and 11am, and are analyzed as they are available. The general pattern still appeared to be potent for severe weather, but it looked like it would be fairly late in the afternoon. Also, as Arnold Ashton commented, "It was impressive, but not overly explosive. And one of the key elements we look for in tornadic storms ... is the presence of low level wind shear, and that wasn't really that clear cut, especially on the Detroit sounding."

For Arnold, the first edge of doubt had crept in. "There were some slight doubts. In our eyes it wasn't completely cut and dried. We knew there would be some pretty vicious storms. There was no question there." But were they likely to be tornadic?

The most painful part of the forecaster's day (also an excruciating part of a tornado chaser's day!) is the long wait between when they finish analyzing the morning's data and when the first storm pops. As chasers, the authors have spent many an hour watching for the first tuft of convection to form, and soon after it does, everything goes crazy. It's a long haul.

"Do you think it's going to go severe?"

As they watched and waited, new doubts started to emerge. "The wind dynamics for a good part of the afternoon were actually out of phase with the thermodynamics, especially the low level moisture. There was a very strong dryline coming across lower Michigan, and it was moving fairly quickly too. It was out ahead of the main dynamics– the cold front and the strong jet maxes and whatnot. As a result, lower Michigan got nothing [no storms]. We were expecting the storms would start to develop over lower Michigan and nothing really happened there until ... between 2 and 2:30 ... so up until then there was some concern that everything might not come together. We were holding off on issuing a thunderstorm watch to see things coming together."

The weather office has to be careful that it doesn't issue watches and warnings so often that they are not taken seriously. They like to have some evidence that a watch is called for first. Because the dynamics were so good that day, they issued a thunderstorm watch at 2:30pm, as soon as the first storms formed over Michigan. Past experience suggested to them that the storms were more likely to produce high winds and hail than tornadoes, so they held off on issuing a tornado watch. They needed some confirmation that the storms had the potential to be tornadic.

But the possibility was still there. As Arnold Ashton said, "The storm developed very rapidly in Michigan and came across Lake Huron, and it didn't lose any intensity coming across [the frigid waters of] Lake Huron. That was a sure sign that this storm was significant." That, combined with the fact that the storm bowed out on its south flank as it approached the shoreline (a sign that it was developing into a squall-line), made them decide to issue a thunderstorm warning immediately. It was issued at 3:30pm.

On severe weather days, Arnold Ashton likes "to get away from the monitors and walk quietly around outside, looking at the sky and contemplating the situation without distraction or pressure. If I could have on April 20th, I would have taken a pause part way through the shift and said, 'Wait a second, don't forget what happened yesterday. Don't forget that there were two dozen tornadoes on the ground. Don't forget what the radar looked like.' In fact, it looked very similar once those multi-cells formed. It didn't at first. It looked like a squall-line, and that's what led us astray. ... In hindsight my mindset might have been a little different, but you only know those things in hindsight."

As experienced storm chasers, the authors have found that when our senses or gut instincts are not supported by the data, we are generally better off trusting our instincts. Instinct is actually accumulated experience, pattern recognition– not sifting dirt through your fingers as in the movie *Twister*.

There should be something out there!

The forecasters at the Ontario Weather Centre knew that **something** nasty should have been happening once the line of storms made landfall near Kincardine. Their analysis told them so. But was it wind, hail or– tornadoes? They needed some eyes on the sky to tell them what was happening. Radar at that distance (from King City to Kincardine) is not reliable enough.

So they started phoning weather watchers and radio stations in the area, trying to uncover any events that were associated with the storm. They got no answer on most of their calls, and nothing to confirm their expectations on the others. Mike Leduc said, "I was expecting to hear about big winds– 80-90 kts. On radar this thing looked like it was big. ... The only thing we could find was a couple of reports of hail. ... Nobody mentioned any wind. ... It is very frustrating to have storms cross that part of Ontario [Huron, Grey and Bruce Counties], because we just don't have all that many watchers up there. ... We were sitting around saying, 'What the heck's going on?' ... If we'd had a report of a rotating wall cloud or some rotation in the cloud we would have said, 'Given the situation and the supercells ... we'd go for a tornado warning right away.' ... If someone had phoned here and said, 'I'm seeing a funnel cloud here,' we would have said, 'What's the odds that that could produce a tornado? The odds are high. Let's get out that tornado warning right away.' But without that, (heavy sigh) that's about all we can do."

By 5:30pm, when Mike Leduc had to decide whether to stay on at the weather office (it was his day off, after all), there were still no confirmations from the public or media that the storm was doing any damage. So he left– and then things started to happen. As Rob Paola said, "This is getting fairly late in the day in April. By this time we expect things to be winding down, so it was a bit of a surprise that as late as 6:00 and 6:30 even stronger storms were developing."

Too little, too late

Although they could see on their radar readings (which were not operating at full capacity) that there was a long line of intense storms barrelling across the Southern Ontario countryside, none of the storms along the line stood out as being potentially tornadic. The storm cell that spawned the northern tornado formed just ahead of the line and took the forecasters by surprise. It developed very quickly. They were receiving their radar indirectly that day and it wasn't being updated as quickly or as smoothly as usual, so, as Mike Leduc commented, "It was not obvious until it was too late." Rob Paola told us, "We were watching the cell that was responsible. By the time we got the report [of a tornado touchdown] it was already in the lifting stage, so we really couldn't do much more with this particular storm. We were a bit surprised that it didn't appear any more severe than the earlier storms that we had put out warnings for and had seen on radar and got very little confirmation out of."

At about the same time as the northern storm was doing its first damage, the action started to build further south on the line (near Listowel at around 5:50pm). There, it was much clearer on radar that there was a potential for damaging, even tornadic, storms. Rob Paola moved quickly and put out a severe thunderstorm warning for Wellington and Dufferin Counties at 6:05pm. He expected it to move between Fergus and Mount Forest around 6:15pm. "There were three storms there and I didn't know which one would go severe. Any one of them could have, so I specified that corridor. I couldn't be too specific."

Here, too, although they gave the earliest warning possible, it was too little, too late for the people of Arthur. As Rob Paola said, "In the case of the Arthur storm, there is very little advance warning we could have given. The storm developed just southwest of Arthur. By the time we got the radar scan for that storm, the tornado was already touching down." They heard of the first damage at Arthur at 6:40pm (from CFTO in Toronto). Their weather reporter had just finished broadcasting her report when she received a call from the public saying that there was tornado damage at Arthur. She called the Ontario Weather Centre and Rob Paola told us, "As soon as we heard that, we issued a tornado warning [at 6:42pm]."

The weather office had not received any telephone confirmations all day, even though they had told all the radio stations they called, "If you hear anything, let us know." But, Rob told us, "Now, the phones were ringing off the hook. It really got crazy at this point. ...We were getting calls on the weather hotline from other observers and weather watchers. And then things got really nuts when we extended the tornado warning for Simcoe County, including Barrie. ... We have a lot of watchers through that area. They are a lot more attuned to tornadoes and messages, and the radio stations will pre-empt programming probably faster than anyone else in Ontario because of their experience in 1985. ... We were also getting calls from people saying they were videotaping the storm right out their windows. They could see it and it was a bit surreal at times."

But, after waiting all day for the action to begin, it was all over within a couple of hours. Rob Paola said, "By 8 o'clock things were dying down. We were still getting reports of funnel clouds and stuff, but no more tornadoes, and by 9 o'clock things were pretty well over."

Not the ringing phones, however. It was time for the media frenzy to begin. The forecasters, nerves frayed from a long and difficult day, were set upon by radio and television reporters, some of whom showed much more interest in looking for fault in the weather office than they had in relaying public sightings to it during the day, or in advising their audiences of information, watches and warnings sent to them by the weather office.

And as Arnold Ashton commented, "There's also a problem on a weekend. Everyone is barbecuing. So how do you communicate, when you don't have sirens, you don't have the OPP [the provincial police] versed in severe weather, cable is hit and miss, and people are outside. How do you scream out that there is a tornado just down the road?"

They had done their level best. As Rob Paola said, "When something like this pops up you run on adrenalin, and I don't think I had anything to eat until I went home. During that whole time you're not even thinking about anything except the radar, the storm, putting out the messages and warnings.

"I think what the public has to keep in mind is how suddenly and explosively these things can develop. Sometimes the meteorologist is waiting for something to happen, and by the time it happens, it happens quickly. And frequently there is little time for getting messages out and getting the warning out to people. So that's why getting communication out by radio, TV, whatever, is so important. We have to deliver that message as quickly as possible. As soon as we are typing it up, it has to be out there."

Arnold Ashton was probably speaking for all of them when he said, "Yeah, it was a tough day. It was one helluva tough day."

On the beach

Sergeant Dave Quince of the Kincardine detachment of the Ontario Provincial Police (OPP) was off-duty on Saturday, April 20th. He was enjoying a relaxing day at his lakefront home when he saw the sky go black over Lake Huron. He watched with interest as the storm's ragged front edge bore down on him. "You could see the fingers trying to come down, pointing out of the back of the clouds." Very soon the shoreline was being whipped by very high winds and marble-sized hail.

? Weird

foiled by the fury—
"Some of the people that were in the cleanup said they tried just for the heck of it to get some of the steel off the trees— and they said that you would need a can opener. Some of it wrapped around twice. It was just wrapped so tight— and you wonder how it could do that."

Just south of Kincardine the winds ripped the roof off a trailer, and an old barn belonging to Wayne Zettler was heavily damaged. A neighbour, Shannon Jamieson, watched it happen and later described it to Mr. Zettler: "The roof of the barn was steel, and the way she described it to me, the wind took it off piece by piece, and it twirled it up in the air and then took it to the north."

This could have been the confirmation of high winds the weather office was looking for, but nobody telephoned it in to them.

The line of storms proceeded across the sparsely populated countryside, receiving little notice, except from a few keen sky watchers. Rick Eyre, near Walkerton, told us later that the sky was dark green, with low cloud. It looked "like intestines being extruded." In Paisley, two shopkeepers— Karen Kimpel and Jim MacNamara— went out onto the street to watch what looked like a funnel cloud, with "twirling cloud bits." Near Chesley people were marvelling at golfball hail, and Marg Manto, at Scone, saw clouds "twirling and twisting together." But the weather office received no reports.

The storm was working up to a tornado touchdown.

Tornado on the ground!

Gail Stoddart acted quickly when she spotted the tornado, snapping this picture.

Gail Stoddart was looking eastward from her home south of Desboro. "I saw all these clouds, and it didn't dawn on me right away what it was. I said to my husband, 'Look at those clouds. Aren't they forming funny?!', and he said, 'That's a tornado!'" The first touchdown was occurring– by Harrison Lake in the Krug bush. Further east, Richard Mountain was looking to the northwest when he saw it. "There was a white, very, very short tornado. It was way high in the air and it was just going down like a slinky ... but I thought it was totally harmless."

But it didn't take Linda and Les Janke long to figure out that it wasn't harmless. Just before she went outside to do some chores, Linda heard a thunderstorm warning on television. Even so, when she first saw "a real strong heavy wind ... taking all the branches and everything up," she wondered, "What the heck's going on here?" Then she saw the funnel.

She ran to the barn to warn her husband, but he was out in the field, so she ran back to the house and said to her children, "I'm not kidding. Get to the basement!"

Meanwhile, her husband, Les, had been out on his tractor when he was suddenly accosted by "wind picking up leaves and stuff. I just put my head down and held on. After it was past me I saw it picking up dirt and stuff off the ground."

Linda ran out to meet Les coming in from the fields, yelling over the roar of his tractor, "I've seen a funnel cloud. I didn't see it touch down." He answered, "It did, it was headed over by Roger's." They knew their neighbours were in trouble, so they called the children up from the basement and drove straight over to Roger and Sharon Martin's farm.

Birth of a home wrecker

Roger and Sharon Martin were sitting in their living room with their young son, Dale, when they first became alarmed at the weather. As Sharon said, "Where I was sitting on the couch I could look out the north window. And there was a hedge there and it was really blowing– more than normal. And then I looked out behind me and there was another little hedge there and it was really blowing. ... Then we heard this noise." Roger told us, "It was like a freight train or like wind in a tunnel– just a big roar, and that's when the windows started flying out. We started running toward the basement."

They had to run through several rooms and it seemed to take forever to get there. Roger told us, "I had gone down two steps [to the basement] and when I turned to see if they were behind me, that's when that window blew in and cut them up in the face." Sharon adds, "It was scary– like, we didn't know what was going on. It blew us back. But then I grabbed Dale. [He had bruises on his shoulders from where she grabbed him] ... The wind just threw us back and I grabbed ahold of him and ... I didn't know where we were going to go and I just stuck down by the stairwell."

Poor Dale was terrified. "I thought we were going to die! All I remember is, Dad yelled, 'Head for the basement!' and everything just went blank. I got pushed back and I felt a sharp pain right here [his shoulder]. That was Mom. And then she let go and she marched along around the corner. And I don't remember putting my foot down on the ground. I just remember grabbing ahold of the stove and me up in the air– and wind. ... And then I pulled myself in and covered Mom's stomach." Sharon Martin was expecting a child any day, and young Dale's first thought was to keep the baby safe.

"[My dad] was still down in the [cellar] stairs, and then I heard a big snap. ... That must have been the walls snapping. ... I felt our plates flying around like flying saucers, and I saw one hit the chimney. ... I saw the chair get picked up and put down, but it never broke. ... And then I felt Dad hug us ... and I saw the tornado leaving."

There was nothing left of the trailers that sat down the road from the Martins' farm.

Sharon adds, "When Dale and I were down in the stairwell Roger was calling for us– calling my name, 'Mom, where are you?' And I remember seeing him coming through the kitchen, and he was walking like you see the men on the moon walking– just floating and grabbing the walls. ... So when I saw him I grabbed ahold of him and ... pulled him around the corner to where we were. And then after it was over it was just really quiet. ... Roger got up and looked out ... and he said, 'Oh my God, one of the barns is gone, my horses!'– and everything was gone– everything! There wasn't a piece of floor [in the house] with nothing on it." The east wall of their solidly built log house had been moved out 60cm (two feet), and the west wall in 90cm (3 feet). It was irretrievably damaged.

Roger told us that on their way out of the house they found "the summer kitchen well busted up." They had left a puppy tied to a leash on the door, "and the wind had taken the door and flung it open. It somehow got the leash wrapped around the doorknob, and that's where he was hanging– upside down." Another dog was staked outside. His dog coop was gone, but he was alive. "Now, he must have done a lot of flying around, too, but we didn't see that." The old dog was all right, but the puppy "was pretty mixed up."

The horses received only minor cuts, and their bodies were painted with mud and straw. The Martins lost a couple of cats. "One of them was mangled up real bad." And although five of the cattle had been pinned down by barn beams, they survived.

The family felt fortunate despite the devastation. As Roger said, "We got all of us together, and that's the main thing." A few days later Sharon gave birth to a healthy baby girl.

"You'd better pull over!"

From the Martins', the tornado mowed through the bush toward Highway 6, depositing a couple of dead deer at the side of the highway as it crossed over to the McNabb and Douglas farms. Velma Specht was driving north when her sister, Marg MacArthur, said: "Velma, you'd better pull over. There's a tornado coming up beside the car." They got to the side of the highway in time to watch the tornado cross in front of them.

Russell McNabb was on the highway, too, when he said to his wife, "Look what's back there, coming up." He told us: "You'd just think it was a

The McNabbs returned home to find their house damaged.

The tornado reached its full force as it blasted through the homes on County Road 24.

bonfire or something. You could see it going up and spinning around, and then everything was coming out the top of it. And my wife said, 'You better hurry up and get home,' but I answered, 'I don't think I'm going home just like that.'"

It's a good thing they decided not to go straight home. When they did, a little later, they found that some of that stuff "coming out of the top of it" was from their house and barn. The tornado carved a path through the cedar bush and took out the next barn north, too.

It was now heading straight for a strip of homes on the east end of Williamsford, as were Barb Hanley and Kim Brintnell, two residents of the housing division.

Keeping pace with the tornado

Barb Hanley was driving east along McCullough Lake Road while Kim Brintnell sat beside her, studying the lowering sky. Kim said, "I think there's going to be a tornado." Barb watched the sky too, until, just as they were passing by the Krug bush, "All of a sudden, we just saw everything starting to come together." Kim yelled out, "It's a tornado. It's right there!"

By the time they reached Highway 6 they realized that the tornado was keeping pace with them. "We knew it was moving right with us because we went a whole concession and a half to that corner and it was still right there."

Kim picks up the story: "Barb was saying 'What should I do? Should I stop, should I go?' I was going, 'Wow!'– I wasn't scared at all. Not one bit. I was fascinated by it. ... Even up until the point that it hit our house, it never scared me. I just wanted to get my camera and get some pictures of it."

Weird? facepack-facelift — It's amazing how a tornado can simultaneously put stuff on and take stuff off at the same location. "At the side of the house, you can't see in any of the windows– like you'd swear somebody had painted the house with mud. But the wood up at the top which was an aged (black) cedar– it's now white, pretty well sandblasted."

They continued their race toward home, watching clouds of flying debris to their south and west as they pulled into the driveway. Barb flew from the car, grabbing the dog (which was tied up outside) as she ran for the house. They looked over to the other side of the road in time to see the trees part. The tornado was coming straight for them.

Barb scrambled into the house with the dog and Kim followed. "I came in behind her and went to shut the door. ... It blew the door right out of my hand. So I reached out to grab it again. Then I saw it take my car." Her car was blown about 7m (20 feet) as she cried out, "It's got my car!"– and they both ran down to the basement. Barb picks up the story: "We never actually heard glass smashing or the roof being ripped off, but everything was really loud– like a loud wind." Kim comments, "It's funny, because I remember the silence more than I do the loudness."

When they emerged from the basement they found that the roof and the east side of their house had been ripped off. Their bedrooms looked like a furniture store display– carefully made beds poised on the edge of a wasteland.

Taken by surprise

Barb Hanley's home was opened to the elements, and Karen Mahon's chimney was neatly decapitated.

Barb and Kim were not the first victims of the tornado as it ripped along County Road 24. It threw several other families' lives into chaos before it reached them.

Karen Mahon was watching television when her chimney was snapped off and her roof was neatly set down in one piece on her front lawn. She had noticed a rumbling noise for several minutes before it happened, but she just thought, "What kind of yahoo ... is out there and he forgot his muffler system?" But as the sound grew louder she reconsidered. "That's not a vehicle. That is a friggin' plane!"

Karen picks up the story: "I finally got my derrière off the couch and looked out the window. ... So I'm looking south into the sky and looking ... for this low-flying plane– and it caught my eye– it was coming at me from the right. Then tree trunks and mailboxes were flying in the air. ... And then I said, "Oh, that's what all this noise is about!" She stood watching for 15-20 seconds and then thought, "Okay, enough gawking here," and got down on the floor. "I had to cover my ears because my eardrums were next to popping. Oh my head! It was so loud that I didn't hear my roof come off and my chimney snap! I stood up after it went by me and said, 'Cool! It missed me– ha ha!', and then I looked out the front window and I went 'Oh, nope!'"

Her neighbours on either side received little damage (except for having their sheds flattened) but others were not so lucky.

Teresa and John Brown were on their way back from Owen Sound when the tornado damaged their home. As they approached their house they were alarmed to see police cruisers and other vehicles crowded near their laneway. Teresa told us, "We thought there was an accident and one of the cars was on fire, and that my sister was killed or something. So we were frantically racing, trying to get through all the crowd." They realized that it was a tornado, not an accident, by the time they reached their home. The area was roped off because

These downed power lines started a fire after the tornado.

the power line in front of their home had caught fire. Teresa said: "Both my sister and my aunt could have been electrocuted. When they came on the property the power was off. It was safe for them to go in and get the dog." They put the dog in the car and walked right by the wires. "My sister said, 'Am I ever glad I didn't hit the wires with my face, because they would still be hot,' and they jumped over it. They were kind of making a joke about it– and they didn't even get from the wire out to the end of the laneway and the power came back on. ... The grass and a board caught fire."

Next door to her, Mary Ellen Caudle had been home with her family when the tornado struck. Once they realized what was happening, "We just grabbed our children and ran downstairs to the basement. ...The whole house was lifted and set back down again. It happened so fast. ... My dog is actually what saved us. She was panting and you could tell there was a thunderstorm coming, but she was beside herself and she just kept nudging us downstairs."

Bruised but not broken

But Ernie Plant and his dog were not so lucky. "I had just put a can of soup in a pot and put it on the stove. ... And all of a sudden this glass started flying around me and I never remembered nothing after that until they were taking me to Owen Sound with the truck. ... I didn't know a thing about it until it hit."

Mr. Plant, his home and his dog were strewn over the fields by the rampaging tornado. Nothing was left of his house, and his small dog's body wasn't found until days later. But the neighbours were out searching and calling for Ernie as soon as they climbed out of the rubble of their homes. When Barb Hanley went upstairs to find her bedroom wall

Nothing was immune to the tornado's force– not even the plumbing.

The Boivins' home was completely gone.

and roof gone, she looked out toward Ernie's and was stunned to see nothing there. "I started screaming, 'We gotta find Ernie!', so that's all we did."

And Mike Boivin, Ernie's neighbour to the east, was out searching the rubble for him as soon as he was able to climb out of the basement, which was all that was left of his home. His young daughter, Michelle, told us, "Daddy was calling, 'Ernie, Ernie!', and Ernie couldn't hear him. And suddenly he found him and he tried to pick him up and he couldn't, because his [Mike's] ribs were really bad."

Ernie told us, "Mike found me out in the field. I don't know how I got there or nothin' else. I've no idea! When it hit here I didn't know what was happening either, and I said, 'Oh my God, what's happening now?!' I was still going over the same thing when he found me in the field."

Arnold Rosenberg, the Clerk of Holland Township, came running to the rescue with his truck, driving up to the pile of debris where Ernie lay. He and Mike were worried that an ambulance would not get Ernie to hospital in time. (He was in his late seventies and badly beaten up.) So, as Ernie told us, "They loaded me in the truck and took me to the hospital at 90 miles an hour. ... I didn't even hear the horn blowing, but [the driver] was just sitting on the horn all the way."

Fortunately, although he was in rough shape, Ernie had no broken bones. "The next morning the nurse came in and she woke me up. The first thing I said to her was, 'How long does it take a feller to die, anyway?' 'Oh, you're not going to die,' she said. And I said, 'How can a man come through something like that and not die?!'" How indeed!

"The baby! The baby!"

But Ernie wasn't the only victim whose survival seems miraculous. Mike and Pat Boivin and their daughters Michelle and Danielle (who were seven and three years old at the time) had quite a story to tell, too. They had noticed the clouds "swirling around," and when Mike took a look out the front window he saw what he thought was a bird flying backward or doing somersaults. But he didn't think too much about it until the wind suddenly grew stronger and the power surged and then went out. This time, when he looked, Mike saw a swirl, like the water going down a bathtub drain.

Pat Boivin tells the story: "He yelled out, "Go downstairs!" three times. By that time we were all downstairs." They chose the best possible hiding place– right under the kitchen sink, where the basement walls were high and the plumbing gave added reinforcement.

Weird? a blast of a wind!—
"The roof seemed to just lift off that barn – it drifted over a couple hundred feet [sixty metres], it seemed to make it do a complete loop and when it was halfway through the loop, that's when everything seemed to just disintegrate. In one second it was gone. You just can't visualize the power – unless you see it."

"It was just like a big black 'voosh' came up from the ground– and I mean there were beams catapulting and you could see all this stuff in the air!"

"And we didn't even have options to position ourselves. I called out for the dog once, and then all of a sudden the curtains were flying and my front window blew out. ... And it just took the whole house then. ... Insulation started flying in the air and ... we had to close our eyes because there was so much debris flying around. ... I thought Mike was holding Danielle and she was up to about his chest, but he was holding onto the water tank, because at one point he felt his arms lifting– he felt he was being drawn up. [The hot water tank stayed but] he could feel it being screwed off the house. We were very close to the furnace, and it was found [far out in the field]."

The hot water tank and the cold water return were the only items in the basement– other than the family– that were not blown away by the tornado. "Mike said, 'The baby, the baby!' and I looked at her. She was crying and she was all full of insulation, but ... I thought he was holding her [but he wasn't]. And then I just grabbed her head and pushed her right down. She was being lifted out. We cleaned out dirt and insulation from our ears for a long time. It just seemed like being inside a vacuum cleaner.

" It got very quiet. Mike said he looked over his shoulder and he saw [the tornado] go over the hill there. And then he found a box to get up on the kneewall. He lifted the kids out and that's when I realized I had broken my wrist."

Mike and Pat Boivin both came out of the tornado with minor injuries, but thankful that the family had somehow survived the ordeal. There was nothing left of their house.

Nor was there anything left of the house next door, belonging to the Greers. Fortunately they were not at home. They might not have fared so well, had they been there. They were senior citizens. (Statistically, seniors are at greater risk in tornadoes than their younger neighbours.)

"Faster than a car"

The next home to be devastated was around the corner and housed an Amish family. Sam Yoder was working outside when he noticed that the sky was "orange at the back and blue at the front." He knew that was a sign of a bad storm coming and continued watching the sky while he worked, until he saw the tornado coming up behind his barn. He ran up the hill to get a better look, then back to the house to tell his family to get to the basement.

The Yoders' home was beyond repair, and the barn was gone.

But his wife was already on alert. One of her five children had been watching out the window and had asked her what the smoke was. She answered that it wasn't smoke and was on her way out to find Sam when he arrived at the house. He told her that it was a tornado and they headed for the basement. Rather than waiting to go downstairs behind them, he decided to go around to the basement entrance at the other side of the house. This enabled him to take another look at the tornado, and he said he saw a column of blue go up to meet the funnel, and it went very, very fast– "faster than a car can go."

After he reached the basement, they huddled there for about 15 seconds, watching as debris and sparks flew through the air. (What caused the sparks in a home without electricity remains a mystery.) Then it was all over. Sam Yoder climbed out first. They couldn't go up the stairs because they were covered in rubble. His wife followed, but the children had to stay behind because they were in bare feet, "and it wasn't fit for them to be out there."

The house was irreparably damaged, the barn was destroyed, and they lost many of their possessions. But they all, even the youngest of them, took these losses in their stride.

Some days later, cottagers to the northeast were surprised and impressed when members of the Amish community arrived, boats in hand, to retrieve the Yoders' sap buckets from the lake. The tornado had carried them from the farm and dropped them miles away, in the water and woods of Williams Lake.

Hailing toys

The tornado now moved out into the countryside, hitting trees and outbuildings, but saving its next significant human impact for Williams Lake.

Not too many people were at their cottages on the lake. It was early in the season. Indeed, Cynthia Cook was surprised and worried because it had so suddenly become hot. "I was saying, 'Isn't this unusually hot?' ... and then, all of a sudden, it was as black as black, and it was purple." Her husband, Bob, and their son, Alex, were

The tornado chewed up large swaths of forest near Williams Lake, but spared the Metzgers' home.

barbecuing supper when the wind picked up quickly. They had heard a weather report with a forecast of hail, so Cynthia said, "Why don't you put your new truck in the garage so it doesn't get dented?" But they just laughed at her.

Bob told us: "It was very windy, very hot, very humid. I was barbecuing steaks and I thought, 'It's really going to thunderstorm. I'd better cook up in a hurry.' I turned around and that's when I saw it, right over the cottage next door. I thought it was coming this way. I threw Alex inside. I saw this huge funnel cloud with all the stuff flying around it. I couldn't breathe."

Alex picks up the story: "I stood by the door and I could feel the cottage shaking a bit, and I saw junk flying around. I saw [the Metzgers'] boathouse picked up and blown apart in every direction." As it turned out, Cynthia was proven right in her concern for the new truck, but it wasn't hail that put a large dent in it. It was a Fisher-Price toy which had probably made the journey from Williamsford.

? Weird car crush—
At one place, a truck was parked out in front of the shed. "It picked the truck up, then it must have tossed it end-over-end the way it was crushed. And it went through the barn and landed over in front of the manure pile. I don't even think a bad car accident, a roll, could crush it as much as it was!"

"Nobody's going to believe me!"

Eleanor Farrow had heard the thunderstorm warning on television, but when she looked out the window at about 5:55pm she figured, "Well, we missed it again," because the warning ended at 6pm, and the sky looked fine to her. (Watches and warnings are given for defined time periods, but the fact that it is nearing the end of that period does not necessarily mean that there is no more cause for concern. It may be updated and extended.)

"I heard something like a jet ... so I went [back] to the window and I could see the sky was all blue, all around it, but there was a huge black cloud, all enclosed ... pitch black, and it extended over to the other side of the point." Eleanor Farrow's cottage was one of several that were along a peninsula jutting into the lake. As she watched the sky it soon became clear that a tornado was approaching her. She thought: "Now, where am I going to go? Nobody's going to believe me!" There was no basement, so she had decided on the bathroom, which was an interior room with no windows, by the time she realized that she had been spared. "If the tornado had decided to take this place, I'd have been in it! I probably would have been in the lake, and it was icy cold." In fact, it had still been frozen over just the day before.

But the storm still held some danger for her. "The lake had whitecaps, not in a regular pattern, but huge whitecaps. They seemed to be coming from every direction. ... And on [the other side of the peninsula it] was all little tiny ripples, just very tiny ripples. And then it was just like someone took a pouring measure and it started at the very end of my flower bed and the water came right across the road and started up this way. ... It was just like those lava things in a volcano, only it was water, and it was right up to the corner of my deck! And I thought, 'Where's it going to go?' [At a nearby cottage] the water was right up to the bushes at her window. Her dock was under water. Our dock was under water ... and I thought, 'What am I going to do?' And just as quickly, it disappeared again and it just washed out." The land from her cottage to the end of the point had become an island briefly, but aside from a residue of mud, gravel and broken docks, little damage was done.

A circle of destruction

Bill and Diana Metzger's heavily forested property did not fare so well. They had company over and were preparing to go out for dinner when Diana asked Bill, "What's that noise?" He answered that he thought it was thunder. Diana told us, "Then I remarked, 'Well, it's not thunder because it's not going away. It's constant.' Then he went to the door and yelled, 'Come quick, come to the door!'– and we could hear the noise all the louder when he opened the door. ... By the time

The short stroll to this cabin became a challenge after tornado-blasted trees littered the path.

we got out on the deck there was stuff flying over us– big sheets of steel from the roofs of places it hit before, I guess, and pieces of wood and tree branches and stuff.

"At that point it really scared us ... so we were saying, 'Where should we go, where should we go?'– because at this point we figured it was a tornado. We had no basement, so we ran into the living room, and Bill yelled: 'Hang onto the fireplace! It's not going to go anywhere.' So we all lay down on the floor, hanging on the fireplace– all four of us. ... Before I lay down on the floor, when I looked out to the back I saw this huge wave. 'Oh, there's a tidal wave!', but I guess the wind picked the water up off the lake behind us. ... I only glanced. I just hung on because I knew something terrible was going to happen. I was sure we were going to go too."

As they lay there they all felt their ears popping. Diana said: "They just felt like they were going to explode. ... All of a sudden it was just still. We got up slowly ... and looked out the back first. All the trees were flattened and we just couldn't believe it because we couldn't hear any trees snapping. ... I was just shaking like crazy. In fact, I shook for about two days afterward– and I don't know what I would have been like if the house had gone like some of the poor people."

The tornado had spared their house. Enormous trees on three sides of it had been laid to waste, and there was very little sign that there had ever been a boathouse on the fourth side. It seemed miraculous that their home had survived while everything around it was devastated. The tornado had begun a long trek through mature forests, laying them to waste. It plowed through Metzgers' woods

The Metzgers' boathouse disappeared into the woods.

and into the Comber bush– a large tract of mature forest that Bob Comber had hoped would become a park for future generations.

"I'm going to get to see one of these things!"

"The tree I was standing by was twisted right off."

Dave and Sue Comber, whose home was nestled on the edge of the woods far back from the road, were cooking supper out on their porch when Dave wandered outside to take a look at the sky. He noticed that the clouds were "boiling and everything. It was just so unusual that I told Sue to come and look."

After she saw that the clouds were "starting to roll and bubble," Sue had gone back into the house briefly to get something. She heard Dave yell for her to come back out. "I went out on the patio and that's when I could hear it– it sounded like a freight train. Then it was really black and there was a lot of debris in the air. When I realized that the debris wasn't paper and leaves, but sheets of metal ... I said to Dave, 'Let's get out of here!' and we ran down into the root cellar."

Dave had been wonderstruck by the tornado. "All of a sudden I could see what I thought was going to be a tornado. I could actually see the circular movement of the clouds. I thought, 'Holy jumpin', I'm going to get to see one of these things!' It turns out I never did, because it was just moments after that that Sue more or less shook me out of my stupor."

When they reached the root cellar they realized that their dog hadn't followed them. Sue said: "Dave opened the door a crack to call her ... but by then we could tell it was right there. ... Then, just as quickly as it started it was over. There was dead silence. ... We figure we were down in the root cellar 30 seconds tops."

Outside, where Dave had been standing transfixed, there had been a picnic table and chair. He was amazed to find that, "Both ended up 200 feet (60 metres) away, down in the bush all smashed to smithereens. And the tree I was standing beside was just twisted right off."

Sue is diabetic and had taken her medication before the tornado struck, so she had to eat– even in the midst of chaos. Dave

Weird? wrap session—
"He found a metal sap bucket that was wrapped around a small branch, smaller than your wrist – and the metal bucket had literally wrapped right around the branch, and you couldn't get it off the branch!"

"I just saw sheet metal wrapped around trees like blankets."

"The granary that was beside the shed – now there's gonna be a fair weight to it – was a half a mile away, wrapped around a lady's van!"

told us, "We're sitting here and eating like nothing had happened, and the boys of the Chatsworth Fire Department came roaring in. They were here within fifteen minutes. ... They came down not knowing what they were going to find. They checked at Vic's (Dave's uncle, whose home was struck by the tornado), and then they came down here not knowing whether there was a house here or whether we were buried underneath the debris or what." Their jaws must have dropped when they saw Dave and Sue eating amid the debris.

"It was pretty impressive how they got here so quickly, because it wasn't easy. You couldn't come down the lane [which was blocked by downed trees]. They came down through the fields. It took 30 people about six or seven hours to open up the lane the next morning."

Dave's parents, Bob and Freida Comber, lived to the north of the tornado path. Bob uses an oxygen machine, and Freida was watching the clouds when she heard an unusual noise. She asked him, "Is there something wrong with that [oxygen] machine?" When he said that there wasn't, she replied, "Well, listen to that roar!"

Archie (Vic) Comber was sick in bed when the tornado struck (top). The Comber bush was laid to waste (below).

Bob tells the story: "I said, 'Oh, it's another bunch of those darned motorcycles going up the road,' and the roaring got louder. ... It was the real roar of a hundred motorcycles going by close to you. We saw pieces of plywood and insulation way up in the sky, and right away we realized they were no birds."

They also realized where the debris was coming from. Freida exclaimed, "Oh my God, that's over at Dave's and Archie's (Vic's)!" She tried telephoning Dave, with no success, and then called Victor, who had just recently come back from being in hospital. He had been in bed when the tornado struck and was telling her that he hadn't noticed too much. "Then, when I was talking to him another man came on the phone. I couldn't understand why somebody else was talking to me on Vic's phone. It was a man by the name of Freddy, from Shelburne. He stopped– saw this thing happen– and came in and turned off Vic's propane at the main tank because the line had been broken at the house. And he said, 'Do you know this man?' I said, 'Yes. That's my brother-in-law.' He said, 'Well you had better get up here as fast as you can because he's in serious trouble.'" But he wasn't injured, just covered with debris and dirt. The house was badly damaged.

If Freddy is reading this book, we are sure that the Combers would like to thank him. Archie was not in a position to look out for his own safety, so his quick action was much appreciated.

weird ? levitation—
"The whole roof from the back side of the barn just went straight up in the air about 5 times higher than the barn— and it just hung there for a minute and then it started to spin, and then just disintegrated and spewed all the way down the field. It just went 'Whoosh!', right up, and it was like slow motion going up. And then it sort of hovered there and spun, and then 'Zap!'– it was all gone."

They tried phoning Dave again, and when he answered his first words were, "Dad, have you ever seen a picture of Hiroshima? That's what it looks like outside my door."

Bob Comber was devastated by the wreckage of his beloved woods. "About three days after this happened, a fella came up to me where I was cleaning up debris and he was from the Hydro [power utility] in Barrie. He said, 'My superiors have sent me over to take pictures because they've never heard of the extreme damage that you've had in the hardwood forest here. ... They're going to determine from the information they get from these pictures how to build a power line and pilons that will withstand that type of storm event.' I said, 'My boy, you'll never build anything that will withstand what went through here!' He said, 'Oh, we can build anything.' ... He came back in about an hour and a half. He stopped and looked at me, and said, 'You know, you're right about that. We can't build anything to withstand what I saw back there. When my superiors see these pictures they are not going to believe it.'"

"We're all quite devastated about the whole thing. It was my hope that one day this would all be a park."

A sandblasted van

Greg Givens, further to the east, was equally devastated. But on its way from Combers' to Givens', the tornado gave Michelle Mitchell a fright. She was driving south on Highway 10 in her new van. "My girlfriend was with me, and we actually thought there was a fire. ... The next thing I know, all the windows were busted in the van and it was turned sideways. Everything was fine one minute, and then there was glass everywhere, and boards coming through the van, and mud everywhere! ... We just thought it was a fire, and boom! All of a sudden the windows started exploding." Her new van looked like it had been sandblasted. The mud had been incredible when the tornado first hit them. "I'd say there was a good two inches (5cm) of mud on my windshield– like, the wipers wouldn't move. That's how thick it was. I was driving with my head out the window."

The van had to be stripped down to the frame and rebuilt.

Mourning the trees

The tornado stripped Greg Givens' forest down to acres of shredded matchsticks. He told us, "When I came down to the barn I heard a sound that sounded like a waterfall in the distance." He could still hear it when he went back to the house, so he was thinking that there might be a chimney fire when his younger son called him to come see the tornado. "Before we could even think about doing anything it was here. We ran and jumped up on the verandah and I closed the door behind me. It took the door right out of my hand. ... As soon as we were in the kitchen we could tell that trees were coming down because they were landing right [outside]." The verandah and part of the roof were also lifted and set back down, and there were broken windows and some damage to the siding, but otherwise the house sustained little damage. But within seconds the barn roof and two driving sheds were destroyed, killing a couple of calves.

"But the sad part of all this is– you can build buildings, but the back part of this farm was– well, I was born here, and my dad and grandparents before me had never cut any lumber out of it. Just

Bill MacLeod stands amidst the wreckage of his mature forest.

mature hardwood bush back there. And I had trails all bulldozed through it– beautiful, just beautiful back there. Just like 150 acres of park– and it's just flat. The whole thing is ruined."

"We don't get tornadoes around here!"

Across the road from Greg Givens' farm, Cindy Harrison was prepared for the worst. "I always watch the skies. Everyone around here teases me, 'We don't get tornadoes around here! What are you worried about?'" But Cindy grew up near Windsor, Ontario, where tornadoes are a more serious threat, and she wasn't taking any chances.

"My oldest daughter had two friends over who were supposed to ride back home to Holland Centre." Cindy wouldn't let them go. One of them objected, "My mom's going to be mad," but she stood firm, saying, "Well that's too bad. This is bad weather. This can become serious weather. You're not going anywhere." She insisted that they put their bicycles in the shed and wait.

And earlier she had forewarned her husband, "It's even tornado weather," but he had laughed at her and he went to town to gas up his truck– against her objections. At about 5:55pm Cindy's oldest daughter, Janis, saw a funnel cloud. Cindy took a look and told the children, "They always come out of the west. It could come our way. It may miss us by a mile; it might hit us dead on." The kids wanted to gather precious belongings together, but she said, "No. You get yourselves downstairs."

Once they were safely downstairs in the cold storage, she asked her oldest son, David, to watch the tornado to see which way it was heading, and she went up to warn her neighbours by telephone. "We had a good five to seven minutes before it hit and we could raise nobody on the telephone. Then [my son] said, 'You better come down now. It's coming our way.' So when I went down I could see [the tornado] coming up the road. You could see the debris. You could see it starting to pick pieces of trees up. You couldn't actually see a funnel at that point. You could just see a big mass coming your way. ... Then, when it came to the corner we saw the other one. [There were two funnels.] One was a big grey mass; then we saw one that looked like a long dirty piece of rope. ... The last thing I watched it do was take a tree apart. Then I thought, 'That's close enough for me.' I went into the cold storage."

The kids thought it would be a good idea to get the video camera so they could film it, but Cindy said, "We're watching these two coming, but we don't know if there are any above us that are going to come down," and she made them wait until ten minutes after the tornadoes had passed.

Cindy's neighbour, Terri Griffin, got a closer look at the smaller, ropier funnel. After her kids were safely in the basement, she went to the back door to look out. "That's when I saw it dance around [in the back] where all the trees are bad. It was sort of bouncy. It would bounce up and back down. ... But it wasn't the big one. The big one you could see over at Greg's [Givens]."

Cindy's and Terri's husbands were both away from home when the tornado went through. John Griffin, Terri's husband, stood watching it through the window of his friend's drive shed. "The walls were moving a foot, wobbling in and out."

? Weird

clean sweep—
"It sucked **every single fly** out of my house! I've had cluster flies ever since I moved here. Up until the moment of the tornado I was vacuuming them off the windows. I've **never** been without them – and I don't have a fly in the house now, ever since the tornado!"

"Their boathouse was totally wiped – you'd just swear somebody had moved the whole thing – like, there was no debris around it whatsoever. From here there wasn't any sign really that the boathouse had been there – like there weren't boards sticking up, beams or anything – it was just **gone**."

In one stretch of forest, the tornado swept the floor completely clean – leaves, soil, everything – exposing and leaving behind only the new green shoots of leeks which now stood naked, 15cm up (6 inches), where normally they would have been barely breaking the ground! "The only thing that was left in most places was the leeks – just all of a sudden I had leeks that high!"

Dave Harrison, Cindy's husband, came back from gassing up his truck and couldn't get onto his road. People parked at the corner explained that a tornado had gone through, but he didn't believe them. He finally found a back way in, but when he got as far as Greg Givens' place and saw the damage there, all he wanted to do was get home. Cindy said: "He couldn't see our place from there, so he backed up, floored it, and went over all the trees [that were blocking the road]. He made it home."

The longest eight seconds

Everyone was at home at the MacKenzie farm, although they may have wished that they weren't.

Gloria MacKenzie was in the house with her grand-children and one son that evening. She wasn't paying much heed to the weather, but she had noticed that the animals were behaving strangely. The horses and cattle were acting "a bit funny," but even more strange was the fact that there were crowds of birds down on the ground, under the trees. "The whole back [lawn] was just covered."

The MacKenzies' shop collapsed with two men inside it, but neither was seriously injured. But John MacKenzie was swept around his barnyard by the tornado.

Gloria told us: "There was a wee bit of wind, and then, all of a sudden, it got quiet— and really warm. We were in the dining room when I saw the trees go." She scurried around, gathering up the children, and was headed toward the living room when she saw the patio doors "sucking in and out." She changed her mind and started heading for the basement, but they didn't make it that far.

"The basement trap door was blowing up and down ... and when I went to the door, everything was coming up through the cellar– grass, gravel and insulation from the basement. ... So I got on top of the trap door to pull John's [her husband's] saw over it, to keep it down. And the door flew open. The [wind] pressure was so bad it put me right through the ceiling. My hands went right through the insulation. [There was no drywall on the ceiling, only insulation and a vapour barrier.] And then, when I came down ... I landed on my knees and got to the door and slammed it. [The children had been standing terrified in the doorway while Gloria was thrown into the ceiling.] I slammed it and we just lay on the floor. The tornado was still going. ... We could see it all go by the window– we saw stairs, we saw boards, we saw beams, we saw my barbecue set.

"It went very quiet, and as we got up I walked to the door and opened it. I saw that the barn roof was gone. At that time, John was supposed to be in the drive shed with Glen and Troy [Glen Gamble and Troy Harquail], but when I went out they were getting him up [off the ground.]"

Glen and Troy had been in the shop, however, when it started shaking and twisting. Glen dived for cover under the truck. Troy lay down beside it. Gloria was astonished when she saw the crushed remains of the building: "I was amazed how they got out. I still don't know how they got out from that little hole that was open. It must have

?Weird get a grip— "You look at fenceposts and there's nothing for the wind to grab hold of – but we had fenceposts pulled right out of the ground."

been adrenalin." They had wasted no time because they knew John MacKenzie had been outside during the tornado.

John had gone for a wild ride. Before the tornado, he was coming back from an errand at the barn when Troy came over to him. John tells the story: "I said, 'It's always calm before a storm,' but I was only fooling around. And then I turned around and looked at [the western sky]. I said to Troy, 'Look at that. That's a tornado!' He told me where to go, he said, 'No, it's not.' I said, 'Well look, look again boy!' He just took a look and I said, 'Get Glen out of the shop!' Well, it wasn't very far. He ran into the shop and they never came out.

"I thought it seemed like a long time, but it wasn't. ... I was heading to see why it was taking them so long to come out of the shop." But he changed his mind and turned back toward the drive shed to let the dog loose, "and when I turned and went back that way, things were just flying." And, in a moment, so was he.

John was whisked up by the winds and taken on a 90 metre (100 yard) spin around the barnyard, travelling in a loop. He flew through the air about two metres (six feet) above the ground (He was carried over a 1.2m (four foot) fence). "I had a tractor cabin ... and I saw it coming toward me. It was just picked up straight into the air ... and it was just swinging around like it was coming at me." There were many objects being spun around with him, including large truck tires.

He said that as he was being carried back around the loop toward the barn: "I could hear this ripping and tearing of the building. ... I figured the whole barn was gone. I figured I was going for the stone wall [of the barn]. ... Then I don't know what happened for a while right after that." John crash-landed before he reached the barn, breaking the rail off a fence as he went through it. He came to his senses, clinging to his favourite (but battered) hat, with Glen and Troy leaning over him.

It was a ride he wouldn't choose to repeat. "I used to be in rodeos professionally for a long time, and that eight seconds [riding rodeo] was never as long as this eight seconds. ... I was wondering about travelling around without a steering wheel in my hand!"

"The wind just threw my voice back"

The Saunders' farms are run by a large, close-knit family– the children and grandchildren of Ed and Eleanor Saunders. Brothers-in-law Dave Smith and Bruce Saunders were working in the barn when their teenage nephews, Matthew and Steven came in to tell them they had seen a funnel cloud. Dave told us: "When we looked out ... it was just coming over the hill from MacKenzie's. ... We got everybody into the dairy barn and they went into the milking pit. Matthew and Steven's dog was outside ... so I tried to get him to come in. ... I was on the other side of the screen door, in the barn, watching the tornado."

"I was unable to see the house [his father-in-law, Ed Saunder's house, across the road to the southwest] but I could see the big bank barn. ... All of a sudden there was a lot of noise, like a loud roar coming from it, and tin blowing by, and then Ed's barn just blew straight up in the air– just a big cloud of dust and tin and timbers. ... Then it went to [Vern] McCauley's barn. It just blew the top off. At that point we ran out to find Ed, because he had ... left to go down to the drive shed [before the tornado hit]."

Marg Saunders had tried to stop him. She was in the house when a neighbour called to warn of the tornado. She had gone to the basement with her son, Jay. "We looked out the cellar window. ... Ed was calmly backing out of the garage [on his tractor] and I could see the funnel. He wasn't aware that it was coming. So I ran back upstairs to try to get him to come into the house, but the wind just threw my voice back so he couldn't hear me."

Ed said that when he finally saw the tornado: "I just jumped off the tractor and lay down beside the wheels. I chose that spot because in wartime you were hurrying to get as low as you could, wherever you could get. ... I knew it wasn't normal to see that stuff coming through the air. I just thought it was a terrible wind."

Back at the barn, Dave tells us: "We had to scramble around for a few minutes to see where everyone was– a sort of head count. I thought maybe [Ed] had walked back home, so I ran out to the road. I didn't see him on the road, so I ran back and that's when Bruce [Marg's husband] got in the tractor and went over and found Eleanor [Ed's wife]."

Eleanor Saunders had been alone in her home when the tornado struck. She said: "The wind picked up and the window was not locked, so I went up to try to lock it. It was shaking ... and it wouldn't lock. I knew then that there was something, because I saw it over the hill. ... Then the window blew apart and the bathroom window went. I tried to go down cellar. [The cellar entrance was in the shed.] ... I looked out and the door was gone off the porch to the woodshed, and I knew I couldn't go down because the roof was off the woodshed. So I came back in and before I got the door shut there were twigs in the kitchen and a big [tree] limb had come down and opened the outside door. So I just stood there."

Looking down on the scene after the tornado hit the Saunders' farm.

The next day, the family was shocked to see that a roofing nail had impaled the wall right over where Eleanor's head must have been when she stood in the kitchen. There were also viciously sharp shards of glass embedded in the walls and ceiling.

"I stood there, and when it ... stopped, everything seemed to be still. But everything was gone by that time. ... And I remember going in the living room ... and I looked out that way and our barn was gone, the two drive sheds were gone, and I just wilted ... and Bruce jumped through the big window [which was out]. He came to me and took me over to his house. They took me to the hospital just to check out my heart."

"The birds started going in a circle"

The Dakin family were all together that evening. Linda Dakin was watching the sky with her children. "My son was very fascinated. The clouds were white and they were going in a circle– really, really pretty– big fluffy clouds. And the birds started going in a circle and were flung out ... Then we saw the thing ... a tail [the funnel]."

Twin funnels move off to the east after leaving the Dakins' barn in ruins, and damaging their house.

Her daughter Salina's fiancé, Jason Rusnak, had been on alert since he first saw what looked like "a bunch of smoke". He had experienced the Grand Valley tornado of 1985 and knew enough not to take the risks lightly. "I just kept saying, 'That doesn't look too good out there.'" He asked his fiancée's uncle, Dennis Novasad, to come out on the porch and verify whether it was a tornado. He said, "Yeah, I think that's a tornado," but nobody else believed Jason.

Jason tried to get everyone to go to the basement, but they were slow to respond. "Nobody decided to go downstairs at that point! Anna Marie [Salina's younger sister] ran outside to get her cat, and Salina was upstairs– she didn't even know what was going on. So I just kept yelling, 'We should get downstairs ...' I was ready to go."

Finally, when Anna Marie went to get her cat, the Dakins realized that they were in imminent danger. Linda said: "So I grabbed her and pulled her back in the house, it was seconds. We went in and as soon as we closed the door the windows all shattered. We ran to the basement and when Anna Marie looked out the window she said, 'Oh, there goes our barn and our drive shed.'" The house sustained some damage, but they all made it to safety. Anna Marie's schoolbag was later found 40km (25 miles) away, near Collingwood.

"I went into warp overdrive"

At the Phillips' fish farm, buried in acres of bush and wetland, they were given the first hint of what was to come when the power went out. Losing power to the fish tanks is cause for alarm, so Scott, the youngest of the Phillips men, drove his truck over to the pumphouse to power up the generator.

Scott's father, Mike, had just arrived home from Toronto. "All the way home I thought, 'I don't like the looks of those clouds.' ... I had gone upstairs to change. The sun was shining– beautiful– and [when the power went out] we just thought somebody had hit a Hydro [power] pole down the line.

"It was very still. There was no wind and a bit of humidity. And then, all of a sudden, the wind just kind of went 'whmmm', all at once, just as if you turned a switch. ... It stayed there– it didn't fluctuate at all. ... I picked up my shirt and it came up again, the very same way, but one level higher. As soon as I heard that I thought, 'That's not normal!' It was

"Let's see … a little here, a little there"

coming from the [far side of the house], so I ran out of my bedroom across the top of the house and looked out the far bedroom [to the west]. And it was just completely funnel right from the corner of the laneway to here. It was just one great big funnel with a hollow spot in the very middle. And everything in the middle was smashing together as it was going.

"Well, soon as I saw it, I thought, 'I'm dead'– because I could have sworn it was going to come right through the yard. ... I was headed down to anything with concrete walls. Where I was it was all wood. Just as I turned [to go downstairs] it came up to the third velocity. The house was just faintly shaking– you could feel a small vibration [when the second level of wind gust came up], like a real, high wind blowing against the house. ... Well, when it came up to the third level– again, it was just like boom, boom, boom– the house started to vibrate like you had a 50 ton capacitator idling in the basement. And the whole house was shaking, the plaster was cracking and it was twisting off. ... Then, just as I got to the door [at the top of the stairs] there was a whole chunk of barn roof, all intact, and it just missed the house by inches.

"I didn't slow down. I think I went into warp overdrive when I saw that chunk of roof come by the corner of the house. I remember I kind of hit the wall– I never hit the top step. I just jumped at the wall and went down it like a cat and frog, trying to get to the bottom. Actually, I almost had to push myself off the wall– launch– because the wind coming up [the stairway] was probably 50-60 miles an hour (80-100kmh)."

Mike's father, Nelson Phillips, was outside throughout the tornado. He had been out behind the garage. "I was walking with a couple of gas cans and this gust of wind caught me from behind and threw me on my face, I'd say about 50 feet (about 15 metres) anyway. It came and was gone in 15 or 20 seconds."

When Mike ran out to him he was disoriented. "He didn't really know which hand was up or down. He was just like the dog." One of their dogs had been "rolled along by the tornado and was dizzy as a bat." Its eyes were rolling and it was completely disoriented.

Scott, too, had been caught by the tornado. But he was in his truck. He had just returned to it after powering up the generator. "I just realized that there was more wind all of a sudden, and [thought to myself], 'Where the heck is this coming from?' Then I started to see the trees really bending. I never even heard anything until it was right there. ... I saw two of them [funnels], side by side. One was a little bigger. It came right over me. The other one went right alongside. The truck was really moving [from the wind] when I stopped. I felt the tornado ... just start to pick it up a bit, and it kind of rolled from one corner to the other. That's when I put the hammer down [to get out of there]. I couldn't go anywhere. I was boxed in [by fallen trees]. But I was in my truck. I was glad for that."

Weird? rock exchange— "Well there's a rock back in the bush that's not ours! Might be as high as five hundred pounds tops. It's not our rock because it's kind of just thrown down. I had put an ATV trail up there and I had picked up all kinds of little rocks – and they're all gone from where I had chucked them off to the side of the trail."

The damage pattern on the Phillips property was very intriguing, and could probably keep tornado researchers scratching their heads for some time. Mike said: "It went through like a big giant– the two funnels taking alternate steps. And then it was like he was running and then skidded about an eighth of a mile, and then both of them just flattened everything."

"Like grey lightning"

And the giant seems to have been somewhat playful. At Blantyre, eleven-year-old Kimberley Crews saw it take a barn apart "like Lego." Her mother, Ruth, had arrived home from work just before the tornado struck and the family was in the kitchen for supper. Ruth kept asking, "What's that sound, what's that sound?" It kept getting louder and louder, and when Kimberley went over by the window to get her plate she saw the tornado coming over the barn behind their house. She said, "That's the sound!"

"The barn came apart like Lego."

Kimberley told us: "It was cone-shaped and it was the colour of a reddy kind of mud. It came in with its tail behind it and it was on an angle. ... I couldn't see the top of it because it was so humongous. ... It just barely touched the barn and then a board flew off. And then it ... covered the barn and all the boards started coming apart. It was taking the barn apart like Lego."

They all ran for the basement. Her father, Gerry Crews, said: "I could see nothing except mud and water as it hit the house. The house seemed to go under a vacuum. My ears were popping. It almost drove me to my knees, it was so severe. Once it hit, it hit real fast, and then everything just settled down. And that's when I came back up and looked out my far window. That's where we saw the two twisters going side by side."

But now they were off the ground. Kimberley recalls: "It had skimmed the bluff and gone up. It turned around and looked like grey lightning, and turned around and touched down somewhere else. And all of a sudden, it just took off."

But not before it had damaged another house, acres of woods and a couple more barns. Jack Marshall watched it make its last strike– on Ed Seidle's barn. He said: "The whole roof from the back side of the barn just went straight up in the air– about five times higher than the barn– and it just hung there for a minute and then started to spin. Then it disintegrated and spewed all the way down to the field."

With this last pirouette, the northern tornado was gone.

? weird

one good shove—

"The window frames in the barn were blown right out of the foundation— and they were mortared right in solid. They were intact, inside the barn about 25 feet from where they had been. They looked like they were taken out by human hands and set back in the barn somewhere– I couldn't believe it."

"I had a very heavy-duty well-built manure bucket with steel tangs that'd be 2 inches by 1 inch– like very rigid– and it picked it up and it threw it through one of the trees that was about 16 inches in diameter, and right through it, just speared it like an arrow into a bale of hay. Never bent the tang."

One person had a vintage car parked in the garage. He found little sticks about the size of toothpicks shoved into the rubber tires so far that he had to use pliers to pull them out. "There's no mechanical way you could ever do that!"

Another one!

But another tornado had already made its entrance well to the south of Blantyre. One of the supercells that Rob Paola and Arnold Ashton had spotted developing near Listowel had mushroomed into a tornadic storm and begun its furious progress over the landscape of Wellington and Dufferin counties.

"Wow! Look at that thing!"

At Parker, Doris Hagarty and her son had watched "finger-like things" forming out of the edge of the clouds, wondering, "Is it threatening?" By the time she saw her husband, John, pull into the driveway it was becoming clear that a tornado was being born. "We stood on the front deck and just went, 'Wow! Look at that thing!'" Doris went inside to telephone a warning ahead to her mother.

Meanwhile, a little further to the northeast, quite a number of people were watching in awe as the tornado formed along Concession 16 of Peel Township, just southwest of Arthur. Jerry McKinnon was watching it "hailing like crazy," when, "all of a sudden it just sucked all the hail to the south ... and there it was! The tornado was only 200 feet (about 60m) away from my shed. It went right beside us. It bounced right over to the neighbours' and took their shed. Then it came back and took the roof off the little outhouse there and then away it went down in through the [Conestogo] river."

Stanley and Susan Hogencamp had their eyes fixed on the sky, too. As Susan told us: "We actually saw the funnel form. The first thing we noticed was the hail– very large hailstones coming down. And then we looked up at the sky and the clouds looked unlike anything we had ever seen before. They were moving very, very quickly and then going right up, straight up into the sky. And as we were looking out [to the southwest] we didn't see a funnel cloud yet, but we saw our neighbour's drive shed blow apart. The drive shed looked as if a bomb had gone off inside it– it blew outward. And then everything fell

Diana Krul shot this picture as her family watched the tornado.

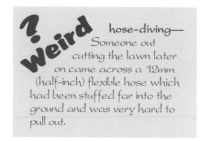

? Weird hose-diving— Someone out cutting the lawn later on came across a 12mm (half-inch) flexible hose which had been stuffed far into the ground and was very hard to pull out.

down on itself. The wind started picking up pieces of debris and bringing it around in a big loose circle. And then it all came together and the funnel formed. It was quite skinny at that point, and right to the ground."

The Hogencamps weren't sure where the tornado was going, so they decided to take cover away from the window, lying on the floor. When they looked out a window on the other side of the house a bit later, Susan said, "It looked like it was going to head right toward Arthur, which made me think, 'Should I pick up the phone and call someone? What should we do?' We could tell that everything looked wider than when we first saw it. It must have been building force."

Engulfed in mud

Indeed it was, and the people in its path along Highway 9 had no idea that it was coming. Jim Sannes was driving west along the highway, heading out of Arthur, when he noticed "this funny cloud formation" and stopped the car to look at it. He was surprised when the cars behind him stopped too, and he decided to drive on a bit further ... "It was still non-threatening. I had no clue that that thing was going to do [any real damage]."

But, as he watched, the tornado descended upon two houses and a barn and crossed the road in front of him to strike yet another farm. "That was the end of anything I saw. I was completely engulfed in mud and hail. ... All I remember is things going all over the place, and I thought, 'Oh, I went too close!' It passed in front of me about 200 metres (about 650 feet)."

Still, Jim Sannes didn't realize how serious the danger was until a farm gate landed on the road beside him. It was all over within 20-30 seconds. He climbed out of his mud-slathered car and walked over to one of the houses that had been hit. He tells us: "I saw a man there with his head all bloodied. His house– the whole roof had gone and everything. I didn't know what to say to him."

The man was Paul Hald. He had just finished up the supper dishes and gone in to relax in front of the television when the power went out, and before he knew it, he found himself lying on the floor with the house gone from around him. Something had slashed him in the face, but other-wise he was unhurt. But he had lost everything.

Paul Hald was taken by surprise, and his house disappeared from around him.

But the sun was still shining!

The other house that Jim Sannes had seen the tornado hit belonged to Brian and Sherry Henry. It was a stone house, solidly built, and had withstood the weather's worst for a century.

Sherry Henry was at home with her young children, Brittany and Jacob, and some friends who were visiting from the city. She had no idea what the day was to hold for her. There had been hail, "but after the hail came, I thought the storm was over. It looked fine outside."

The mortar was stripped from the Henrys' stone house.

Fortunately, she happened to look out her kitchen window. "I saw a black wall. There was still no wind at the house, and the sun was still shining, [but] there was debris. I think it was the other side of the barn." Just shortly before the children had been playing outside, but now, "Everybody was in the kitchen, thank God," Sherry said.

"The tornado was smoky looking. There was no funnel– I never saw the top, the bottom or the sides of it– just a black wall. I said, 'Get to the basement!' and grabbed the kids."

Nobody doubted the urgency in her voice. They ran to the basement immediately– Sherry, her children, and her friends, Linda and Brenda. Sherry said: "Brenda's really the hero because she showed [Linda] where the basement was, and Jake kind of got tossed down. Just before I hit the top step the power in the house went out. It hit so fast, and it was dark down there. I was yelling for [the others] because I knew they were down there, but I couldn't see them. They came to me and I grabbed their hands. We just stood there and waited." They listened to the sounds of the house being demolished above them, "but it only lasted 5 or 10 seconds. Then it went silent. We were scared to come up."

But when they did venture forth they were astounded by what they found. "It looked like such a war zone," Sherry told us. Although the walls of the house still stood, the mortar was gone from much of the stonework and most of the house and its contents were destroyed. The barn behind the house was gone and there were cattle roaming everywhere. Several had been killed and more had to be destroyed later. One calf miraculously survived after being found hanging in a tree. Sherry said, "It had a dislocated back leg, but they just sawed the branches off the tree and it plopped to the ground, and away it went."

The tornado put on a powerful show of strength. Heavy concrete well lids were found 3 metres (10 feet) from the wells. A horse from the demolished barn was carried 60 metres (about 200 feet) and was found in a pile of debris, with cuts, but well enough to give birth to a foal in the bush that night. There were two full freezers on the porch, side by side. One was found across the road at Paul Hald's; the other was still near the house, but was badly mangled.

Cars and heavy equipment were thrown into heaps of crushed metal, a car on top of the tractor, a trailer and a truck carried long distances. Sherry was taken aback, to say the least, when a police officer came up to her, in the midst of such devastation, and asked "What did you lose?"

"I couldn't answer him. I was– what a ridiculous question! I'll never forget that question," she told us.

But her husband, Brian, had no idea his house had been hit. He was driving on the Conn Road,

Everything– house, barns and vehicles– was destroyed.

northeast of Arthur, when the tornado devastated that area minutes later. Sherry told us, "He didn't come home. He didn't think it hit here." Brian was tracked down at a friend's house and told to come home. As Sherry said, "I guess they were pretty upset when they got to the bridge [just east of the Henry house]. But [Brian] said that when somebody told him that everybody was all right, he was okay."

"I'm not leaving this window!"

Norm and Joanne Kidnie had a bird's-eye view of the tornado as it struck their home. They were visiting Norm's brother, Jack, about one kilometre (half a mile) down the road, when they realized that a tornado was approaching from the direction of their own home. They had been marvelling at how the water on the pond seemed to be lapping straight up and down, even after the hail stopped, when one of the family noticed what she thought was smoke, "bubbling and going higher and higher." Norm took one look and said, "That's no fire. That's a tornado!"– and the family gathered at the window to watch. Norm thought about heading to the basement, but the family remained glued to the window. Joanne said: "I'm not leaving this window until I see where it hits. ... It was just an awesome sight– the stuff inside it whirling. It was really amazing."

They watched it skim by Brad Clarke's house (behind Paul Hald's). They wondered as they stood there whether it would hit their son Paul's home, which was between where they were and their own home. They watched it hit Henrys' place. Joanne said, "By the time it picked up Henrys' stuff it was huge at the top." But when they saw their son's house still standing after the dust settled, they thought the family had escaped unscathed. They had misjudged the distance. It was their own home, further down the road, that had taken a hit.

Joanne said: "When the dust had cleared I could see our house, because it was a light green. I said, 'It seems to be there,' but someone said, "Where's your barn? I don't see your barn.'"

So they took off down the road to see what had happened. "It was quite a shock when we entered our driveway." They had lost about thirty trees in their yard and, although the house was still standing, there was a lot of damage inside. Nearly all the windows were broken, the door was gone, chunks of plaster had broken off and the walls were out of kilter. And everything was covered with mud and glass. The barn and drive shed were gone, and much of the remains of Hald's and Henrys' homes were scattered on the Kidnies' land. Their son discovered what he thought was a dead baby bird, but when they examined it they discovered, "That's no baby bird!" It was a full grown pigeon, defeathered by the tornado.

But overall, the Kidnies responded to the tornado with awe, not terror. "You just can't believe it unless you see it." They were mesmerized.

The Kidnies watched from down the road as their farm was struck.

36

On the north end of Arthur, Ray Baker was not nearly so inclined to stand watching when he saw the tornado approaching his gas station. When he first saw it he thought a factory had caught fire, but then he saw debris going around in the "smoke." He told us: "I wasn't waiting any longer. I knew what it was! I left and headed home. When I swung onto my street I looked back. I could see it was going away from town, so I just came back up." The tornado had spared the town of Arthur, destroying a couple of barns on the north side of town. But it was building power for a renewed onslaught on the Conn Road.

Not again!

It's a wonder that Bruce Eden was able to "grin and bear it" when the tornado destroyed his immaculately maintained equipment.

Midway between Highway 6 and the Conn Road sits the Eden farm, and Bruce and Judy Eden were veterans of the 1985 tornado outbreak. Even so, Judy Eden told us: "[A tornado] was the farthest thing from my mind. Even though the dog was acting funny– following us all over. ... And that gets quite annoying because, in the barn, everywhere we turned we would almost trip over him. This went on for two or three days before. I said to Bruce, 'Oh, something must be going to happen.' You know– there's something wrong but you're not sure. If somebody had said to me there was a chance of tornadoes on Saturday I would have thought they were crazy! Because how often do you get them in April?! And on Wednesday we had snow."

So despite (or perhaps because of) her prior experience and her dog's strange behaviour, Judy was taken by surprise. She had heard that there was a chance of thunderstorms with strong winds, but "I never thought anything of it." She said: "The kids were sitting by the window. We had just finished our supper and the way it was hailing I thought it was going to crack the glass. Then it seemed to calm down– it quit hailing. But it looked bright enough from that window that I thought, 'Well, it's going to pass over. We're not going to get much.' But I saw a white wall of rain ... and I said to Bruce, 'Is it ever going to pour rain!'

"Then Bruce got up– he must have sensed something. Something didn't seem right. He got up from the chair and he said he could see the trees just going like this [being blown over]. So he knew it wasn't rain– it was a really heavy windstorm. So he just clicked and

?Weird pile driver—
"There was a 2x4 that landed in the front here. I thought it was just a little piece of wood– like, you know– I saw the butt of a 2x4 sticking out. But no, I couldn't get it out of the ground. It was in the front lawn– it went down a good 3 feet (about 1m)."
"Some of those boards were drilled 3 feet (about 1m) into the ground. I saw them pulling them out days later with not even the big tractors, but with highhoes with chains wrapped around them!"
"The pond still had ice on it and we had a floating dock in there. Now I don't know what height it must have pulled it up to, but it buried into the front lawn about five feet (one and a half metres) off the front of the house and I had to use a front-end loader to pull the boards up– so it must have dropped from a fair height!"

said, 'Get to the basement!' But even then– the whole thing was white– it wasn't registering [with me]. It just wasn't clicking in that there was a tornado coming– because this one was white! The one in 1985 was black. ... This is what amazed me. I was standing right there when [the 1985 tornado] happened, looking out the door. It was pitch black and you could see the swirls going around the house."

They barely made it downstairs with their children, Stephanie and Craig, when the tornado blew the doors off. Judy said: "You could hear the glass breaking. You could hear the timber breaking. It sounded like it was– again– lifting the roof off and breaking the windows, but you don't know how bad it is until you go upstairs."

Within 15 seconds they were greeted by an eerie silence– no noise at all, even from their cows. "My husband said to wait a minute because we were in a soft seat and there was so much glass on the stairs and stuff. He wanted to go up first to see if the barn and everything else had been hit. He walked out– he just said, 'Everything's gone!' So I thought 'Everything?– is that *everything* everything, or just the shed and the barn and stuff?'"

In 1985 the Eden's stone house had taken a more direct hit than it did in 1996. At least half of the roof was gone and there was much more damage upstairs. But although the damage to the house was less extensive in 1996, the barns, outbuildings and farm machinery were hit very hard. Bruce was disheartened when he saw the equipment and buildings he had cared for so meticulously destroyed.

They would have to rebuild again, but the house still stood. Judy told us: "Someone said that if they ever get enough warning [of a tornado], we're going to have a lot of neighbours here in the basement, because they know it's strong enough to stand it. [But] if it ever hits us again we will not rebuild. Enough's enough! Just the idea of having to rebuild again– well, it's hard. It takes a toll on your nerves because you get to the point where you cringe every time you hear a crack of thunder or storm warnings. You just can't live in that fear all the time. ... How many times can you plan on rebuilding your life?"

A sense of humour can do much to carry people through disasters, however. There was a picture in the local paper, taken at the end of the Edens' driveway, which demonstrated their fighting spirit. It said, simply, "Caution, Tornado Crossing."

"I got mixed up"

The Edens were not the only people to be hit twice. The "tornado crossing" included their neighbours, Ralph and Betty Gorvett, too. It then moved eastward to the Martin farm, where the large family of Paul and Rose Martin were about to have their first brush with nature's greatest fury.

When Rose Martin looked outside to see hail, she thought, "Oh well, there's no garden planted, so it doesn't really matter," and went upstairs to bathe her youngest daughter, Reann. She didn't pay much heed to the loud wind

The Martins' barn was lifted and set back down intact.

sounds she heard while she was upstairs. She was more concerned about getting everyone ready for church. As the wind sounds grew louder she thought the children might be making the noise, until her husband, Paul, came bursting into the bathroom in alarm.

Paul was in the barn, doing chores with Darrell Weber, when he first saw hailstones, but they kept on working. He said: "We never thought of a tornado, of course. Darrell yelled over and told me there was a fire out the back window. ... I ran out the back barn door because I thought he meant our barn was burning. I didn't know where the fire was. As soon as we [went] out the back door we saw it coming. It would have been half a mile away yet (about 1km). We ran into the house before it hit Edens'. We never stopped running– he was right at my heels and I just yelled, 'Basement!' That's all I said."

The tornado had grown very wide. "It was a couple of farm widths wide right down to the ground. I could see tin, steel roofing and timbers. ... The sky was right full of it. I just saw it for a split second when we took off. We never stopped to look at it more."

Paul tore into the house, looking for his family. Rose said: "He figured that everybody was going to be in the kitchen or dining room because he knew we were all getting ready to go away. And then he couldn't find anybody. I think he kind of panicked, because all at once the bathroom door just burst open and I thought he had lost his mind!" She said that when he told her to get to the cellar immediately because a tornado was coming: "I just wasn't thinking tornado. I really thought I should at least look out the window to see if it was really true, but Paul wouldn't let me. I said, 'I've got to wrap Reann up,' and he said, 'No, you don't,' but I did

grab a towel and we ran for the cellar. We just got inside the furnace part [of the cellar], that's as far as we got when we felt it driving over."

Meanwhile, Darrell, following hard on Paul's heels, had saved eight-year-old Laura Martin from running straight into the lap of danger. Laura tells us that when her father exploded into the house, yelling "tornado!": "I started running. I got mixed up with the fire drill and the tornado drill so I started running to the door. When I was almost at the door our hired hand [Darrell] just scooped me up and dragged me down to the cellar. But when I was almost at the door I could see [the tornado] through the window. It was black, and it looked like it was quite huge."

Darrell remembers running in from the barn. "I was yelling, too. But then the two boys went down into the basement, Paul went upstairs, and Laura ran out past me– back [outside] again. I asked: 'Is one of the kids in the van, or what does she want out there?' She was just totally stoned. She didn't answer or anything. Then I just grabbed her and ran down in the basement."

Rose picks up the story: "I really don't know how long we were in the cellar but I don't think it was that long. All at once everything was really quiet, and then Darrell looked out the south window and said, 'The drive shed's flat.' Then Paul opened up the window on the north side and jumped back. He stepped back and told Darrell he was supposed to look. He just couldn't bear the thought of looking outside."

The barn stood (although it had been lifted and set back down), but the silo and shop were gone, along with the drive shed. The house was relatively untouched: the chimney blew off and there was a mess from broken windows, mud and debris, but the family was fine. Rose said: "If we had known that the house wasn't going to be taken, then we would have stood at the window and watched it. It would have been something to see." But you never know how much– or how little– time you will have to take shelter from a tornado.

"I couldn't believe it!"

Across the road from the Martins, Lee Swallow was thankful for the warning call she received from her boyfriend, Dennis Alderman. She might not have been here to tell her story if he hadn't called.

Lee's children were away visiting their father and Dennis had gone home to get ready for their date when Lee found herself captivated by hail falling outside her home. She thought, "Wow, is that ever neat!" as she watched the quarter-sized hail, which lasted for a good 15-20 minutes, and then she went upstairs to get ready for her evening out.

As she was getting dressed the phone rang. It was Dennis. "He had gone out of his house [southwest of Arthur, and close to where the tornado started]

Lee Swallow was lucky to get down to the basement before the tornado struck. The room where she had been was destroyed.

and gotten into his truck to leave. The clouds looked very strange to him. He actually watched it touch down from over there. He watched the first explosion when it hit the barn over on Highway 9 [Henrys' barn]. He watched all the stuff fly up and then he watched it pick up speed."

He had driven a short distance by this time and he picked up his cellular phone to call ahead to Lee, warning her of the tornado. "Lucky he had the car phone, because if he had had to drive home and then phone me, he probably wouldn't have phoned me in time," said Lee.

Lee ran downstairs and outside to see what was happening. "I could see the [Edens' and the Gorvetts']. It hit the one and then it hit the other one. I watched them blow up. It looked like the sky was coming down and blowing everything up, and then everything was flying all over the place. ... And it was wide. When it went past their houses [which are not close together] it was almost like it took them both at the same time. ... Paul [Martin's] place was about 1000 yards [900 metres] up the road, and it took out part of his place and all of mine. That's how wide it was."

She had been outside no more than five seconds, and had put her dogs in the van in preparation to make a run for it, when she realized that she only had time to run for the basement. "I realized there was no way, because by then it was already hitting those farms. So it was, 'Okay, get the dogs and go to the basement.' I got one, but the other wouldn't come out so I closed the door and left her there. It was only about 10 feet (3 metres) from the outside into the basement. ... I got down there and I had about two seconds to figure out where I wanted to be in the basement. ... I just barely got against the wall when the windows came in."

Lee Swallow's house was two stories, with brick and siding. The second floor, where she had been just minutes before, was destroyed by the tornado. "I knew that the glass was going to fly, but I had no idea when I came out the things that I would see. [When I was down there I felt] fear, complete and total fear. It was very noisy. And the wind– and glass and everything. There were a few boxes and stuff, and they were flying around in the basement. There were shavings on the floor that were flying around, and mud. One minute the wind was blowing in the basement, the next minute it was still. I was probably only down there half a minute at the most.

"I had no idea how much damage it could do. I watched the barn explode across the road, but it wasn't registering. When I came out of the basement I just wanted to get out of the house and find out if the horses were all right, because they were in the barn. I don't even remember turning around and looking in the kitchen when I went to leave. I got the basement door fine, but when I went to get out the back door ... the inside wall of the bathroom [had fallen] in so it was jamming the door to go outside. And I opened that door! Still, to this day I don't know how I got that door open!

Lee Swallow's dog rode out the tornado in this van.

? Weird *slipping between the cracks—*
In one bedroom, a curtain was found hanging outside through a crack even though the window there didn't break. During the tornado, a space opened up between the window casing and the window frame, through which the curtain was drawn before the space closed up again.

? Weird *no licence to steal—*
"We had some licence plates that were nailed onto the implement shed ... and they were just hangin' on a nail on the wall. They were left and that implement shed's gone! And you'd wonder why something that light wouldn't take off too!"

? Weird

a ton of garbage—
"There was another one-ton truck in the yard— like one of those construction trucks, 4-door— it picked it up and just turned it right up on its roof and slammed it down on the ground. Completely wrote it off, just absolutely garbage!"

"The extra room that was on the back of the house was okay other than the windows being blown in– the roof was still on it– so I thought, 'Oh well, this isn't so bad!', but I hadn't turned around to look at the kitchen– to see the ceiling on the floor and the mud and everything all over. So, kind of quickly, I opened that door to get out, and then when I walked outside I just couldn't believe! I just couldn't believe! The first thing I saw was the Hydro [power] pole– not like the ones they use today, [a wider one]– it was snapped right in half and lying across the driveway. The wires were everywhere, just everywhere. I looked toward the barn that was behind the house and it wasn't there! And there had been three animals in it. It just wasn't there. It was gone. There was nothing but cement. So the only thing I wanted to do was find [the horses]."

Lee spotted one of her horses standing about 900 metres (1000 yards) from her, and had started out toward her when Dennis appeared on the scene. He had raced all the way, driving over downed wires to get to her. (The lines closest to her house were dead, but those at the corner were still live. As a volunteer fireman, he was aware of which would still be carrying power.) Lee told us, "He was just so glad to see me, and it was just a time to calm down and get over the shock of it [while they hugged]." But they were jolted out of their reunion when they saw the horse running down the middle of the road toward the live power lines at the corner. "I started hightailing it up the road [in white fancy dress and cowboy boots!], but by the time I got halfway up there were about 10 people. These people saw [the horse] coming down the road and got past the power lines to stop her. By that time a vet was there. I couldn't believe it! He was already there and had given her steroids to calm her down, and was starting to work on her wounds."

All three animals suffered injuries, but they survived with the loving attention of Lee and her daughter, Mandy (who nursed her pony, Magic, back to health). The dog that had ridden out the tornado in the van had gone for a wild ride too. "[The van] was actually picked up and turned around and then a grain bin from across the road [the Edens'] was wrapped around the outside of it." But the dog was fine, even though the van windows were smashed.

Lee was safe too, but shaken. "I had everything together until I saw that horse, and then I was gone. Somebody was holding me, some lady I don't even know. I was bawling on her shoulders."

The circus of television cameras and reporters had already begun by the time she walked back to what had been her home. "I walked into the front door of the house– which wasn't there, it was sitting in the hallway– and

? Weird

cabinet shakeup—
"It left a glass hutch that's made out of wood surrounded by glass full of porcelain dolls. We had lost the key and couldn't unlock it– yet the tornado had the door wide open, had opened the door and blew all the insulation into the porcelain dolls– never cracked a doll and the glass was still intact but the whole hutch was full, just full of insulation– completely covered with insulation."

the movie camera was right there behind me as I walked in. I was really mad and I walked out." The police cleared the house of reporters, but they were there again the next day, when Lee's children came to see the destruction for the first time. They captured Mandy in tears. As Lee told us, "This kid is twelve and a half, almost thirteen. That's her whole life– that house and what was in her bedroom– and it's gone, just gone. And they had to get her reaction on tape." As Mandy told us later, "I don't think there are any words that will describe how [the tornado devastation] made me feel. Only– horrifying."

"Hair up, lips back, barking, growling, snarling"

"Something's wrong …"

One block north of Lee Swallow, Kim and Audrey Straker had been forewarned by their dogs. Audrey told us: "We have five dogs, and they were all in the kitchen because the weather was bad [it was hailing]. ... All of a sudden it sounded like there was a massive dogfight in the kitchen." Audrey ran to the kitchen expecting to find a mass of brawling dogs, but they were all lined up, "looking out the back window– hair up, lips back, barking, growling, snarling. They were just going crazy." Audrey peered out the window, expecting to see an intruder, but what she saw was the churning, black tornado to her south. Kim snapped a couple of pictures and they ran for the basement.

? Weird mud slinging—
"The wildest thing for me was the mud and the straw and everything just thrown across the walls. It looked like kids had gone in there with a spray gun and mud and just decorated the whole house."

"I'm not getting trapped in there!"

But on the next road east, Lloyd Hutchison wouldn't go to the basement. His wife, Hazel, told us that their son was the first to see the tornado. "Bill saw it out the window and told us to vamoose. He said it was coming straight over our shed [but from a distance]." Hazel went down to the cellar with Bill and her grandson, but Lloyd wouldn't budge. Hazel told us: "He said, 'I'm not getting trapped in there,' because it's an old-time cellar with a little window– you couldn't even crawl out it. He thought he might get trapped in there with junk if the house went. But our son in Arthur– he saw the tornado. So he jumped in the truck and picked up our youngest son, and when we came up out of the basement they drove into the yard. So we wouldn't have been trapped long." Fortunately for Lloyd, the tornado missed the house, although it damaged their barn and went on to do more damage at another son's home, across the road.

But it was saving its full force for a much more violent strike, by the Damascus Road (Wellington Road 16).

On the road to Damascus

Earl Lane was lucky that his attention was drawn to the outside by the hail, because otherwise he might not have seen that a tornado was ripping toward him, heavily damaging the home of Ruth and Kenneth Gilder and a tract of mature pines en route. Earl and his wife, Alberta, just barely made it down the cellar stairs before their home disappeared from above them. He reported having seen daylight when the house was lifted off its foundation. They spent a harrowing few

? Weird hit and run—
"I was at the bottom of the basement stairs and it blew a square hole in the wall above the stairs which I was lying underneath. No-one knows what caused it, and it was perfectly square. And Dad said it was never patched there. So there must have been something that hit it– it blew through this window and into the wall [and went back out again]."

seconds, watching as the contents of the basement were whisked away by the wind. Even the furnace whipped around the cellar where they were huddled. But it was over as quickly as it started, a lifetime's accumulations blown to the winds. Soon after, Alberta's sister, Joan Shaw, arrived on the scene to find them standing barefoot and in shock on the front lawn. Even though they had emerged unhurt, as seniors, the prospect of rebuilding their lives from scratch was more than they could take in.

The tornado had hit the home of Henry and Gisela Sieger (beside the Lanes' home) at the same time, but they were spared living through the experience because they were away for the day. When they arrived home at two in the morning their son, Andrew, was there to help ease them into the pain of their losses.

The Lanes hid under the cellar stairs and came up to find their home a tangled ruin.

The Hill family chronicle

Around the corner, the Hill family pulled together to ease Melvin and Lila Hill into their losses, too. But for the Hills there was one big difference– they had all suffered through the tornado themselves. David and Candy Hill's home and outbuildings had been utterly destroyed; Trevor and Graham Hill were working at Melvin and Lila's home when it was destroyed; and Robert was working outside at his farm when his wife, Charlene, drove into the lane, the tornado's winds battering her car and causing minor damage on their property.

"Why don't we pretend there's a tornado. We'll have a drill."

David Hill's hat marked the spot where he lay as his house, barn and silo were destroyed.

The first to be hit were David and Candy Hill. Their teenage daughters, Jennifer and Angela, had been outside playing in the hail when Jennifer saw a suspicious looking cloud over the hill to the west. She said, "It was black and boiling, and there were two little things coming out of it."

The girls asked Candy if it might be a tornado, but she said no and went back into the house to continue working. Angela asked if they should close the windows, and Jennifer asked, "Should we go down to the basement?"– but, as Candy said: "My first reaction was, 'No.' Then, all of a sudden I thought– I guess we feel it was the Lord speaking to us– just go downstairs. What hit me was, I shouldn't be like that. The girls want to go down; I should go down, because then if they are ever alone they won't think: 'Well, Mom thought it [wasn't necessary] last time. We won't do it this time.' So I said, 'Well, why don't we pretend there is a tornado. We'll have a drill.'

"So we went downstairs and we looked at three different spots to sit in the basement because they had had tornado drills at school. We were discussing what wall we should sit on. We finally settled on the west wall, as far away from the windows as we could go. To us it was just a drill. I kept thinking, 'David's going to laugh at me for this one!' We put [some] coats down and got into position. There wasn't room for all three of us, [so I put the girls against the wall, but] by the time we were getting into position we realized it was starting to get windy again, and we started getting worried."

Angela and Jennifer said, "We were trying to get up [to find David, their father], but my mom kept us down." Candy goes on: "We figured he was in the barn. We knew he was outside somewhere, but we had no idea where."

The power had gone out when they were on their way downstairs, and now the glass started to fly. Candy said: "I remember hearing a 'swoosh' at one point, and I could see when I turned my head that it was all light up behind me. I said to the girls, 'The house is gone!', but the whole time they were worried about their dad. I saw they were determined to go find David and I said, 'All we can do is pray about it,' and we did a lot of praying, didn't we?!"

Their prayers must have been answered, because soon after, when the winds had died down but they could still hear things falling, they started to look for a way out. The stairway was blocked, but they heard David calling for them. He started clearing the debris near where they were and they climbed up over the shattered remains of their home. They were together again.

But David had, indeed, been out in the middle of the tornado. He was in the barn when, "the first thing I saw was the hail coming, and then the high winds and ... the barn snapping– the whole structure. I knew that it was a tremendous wind, but I never thought it was a tornado. There were two sets of hail. The first set came in about four minutes before the next set of hail. In between there was a calm for about three to five minutes– a deafening calm. I was outside, looking around and that's when I went back into the barn ... and all of a sudden the hail was coming again."

When he was outside between the hailfalls he had not looked to the west (toward the tornado) but he had looked over

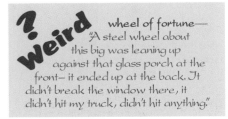

? **Weird** wheel of fortune— "A steel wheel about this big was leaning up against that glass porch at the front– it ended up at the back. It didn't break the window there, it didn't hit my truck, didn't hit anything."

Melvin Hill (left) looks out on the rubble of his home.

at his brothers across the road. He couldn't understand why they were moving machinery out of the yard. They could see the tornado coming from their vantage point, and thought David could too, but his view to the west was blocked by a hill.

Once he was back in the barn, the wind grew wild. Hay started to blow around, and as he started to run out the roof lifted. "I just knew I had to get out of where I was standing, because I knew it was dangerous. But then, where I ended up was no better." David was knocked to the ground between the collapsing barn and the silo, with wood debris on top of him. "I knew what was over my head. When you have a 60 foot (18m) slab silo over your head and you get that kind of wind taking barns down, what's it going to do to the silo? I was five feet away from it. It came down, but it went north– and I was on the east side of it.

"I realized where I was, lying on the ground. ... I got up on my hands and knees to get going again, [but I said to myself], 'I'm not getting up,' because at least I had something on top of me [wood] to protect me. That's when I watched the house get hit. With that kind of speed of wind it should have been instant. It wasn't, because I watched the house swirl. I saw the swirling bricks. ... I thought there was no way they [his family] were going to come out of what I saw! This swirl looked just like a bonfire. ... It was just overwhelming.

"[As the tornado passed] I got up off the ground and had to find out if I could find my two daughters and Candy. I ran to the house– they said I must have flown to the house, because things were still falling when I was yelling. I stood on top of the house and started yelling for them."

Meanwhile, Trevor and Graham Hill had taken shelter in Melvin's house across the road. They had been watching the storm's approach for five or ten minutes, but ended up having to run for cover in a hurry. Trevor said: "We literally ran down the stairs, ran over to the window, and then we just hit the floor and [the tornado] was there. It was there and it was gone. We knew that it was over, but when I was still at the bottom of the stairs I never dreamt of seeing what I didn't see or saw! We went right up. There was a door at the top of the steps and that door should have taken us into the kitchen. The kitchen was there and we walked into it, and the next door should have taken us into another room– and we were standing outside!"

It was not until they went to check the barn that they turned and saw that David and Candy's place was gone.

Robert Hill, who lived next door to the east of David and Candy, was the first to show up at their farm. As Candy told us, when he drove in, "I grabbed him to hug him because I was just so glad to see somebody, but he was just like a board– until I could make him realize that David was okay. All he could see was the devastation, and that he couldn't find his brother." She was thankful that her son, Cameron, was away at the time. He would have been frantic about David's plight had he been there.

Trevor Hill's birth notice was found 80km (50 miles) away, near Barrie.

The Hills were all dazed and disoriented as they surveyed the wreckage of their homes. But they quickly rallied together to provide strength for their parents, Melvin and Lila. They were on their way home from Florida where they had been visiting another of their sons, Douglas. As they had crossed the border that evening they were alarmed to hear on the radio that a devastating tornado had hit the Arthur area, but they comforted

themselves that it was a big area and they wouldn't be affected. When they reached Fergus, south of Arthur, they asked where the tornado had hit and were told, "Out Highway 9, west of Arthur, and up the Conn Road and Damascus."

Melvin said: "Then we were really concerned. But still, you try to think positive. And all the way out to the corner [of their road] the lights were all on. Of course, the Lanes' house was in darkness. We couldn't see it was gone. And then we saw the Hydro [power] trucks. There were two of them blocking the road and they were pulling lines. One of the Hydro men walked over. He wouldn't let us down the road and I said: 'Well, we want to go down the road. We live down there.' He said, 'Are you the Hills?'and when we said, yes, he said, 'Well, there's not much left." So we knew we were in trouble then." The Hydro worker added. "And David Hill– they were wiped out too."

Meanwhile, the family had acted quickly and flown Douglas, the son that Melvin and Lila had been visiting in Florida, up to meet them on their return. They all came out to greet their parents as Melvin and Lila pulled into the laneway of their demolished home. "So we had a little pity party," said Melvin, and their children said: "Listen. We could be making funeral arrangements because David was pinned down. We could be making funeral arrangements and still have all this to go through"– so, Melvin said, "that made me feel so much better. I just went from way down there up onto a different plane. We have so much to be thankful for, and we are. ... There's blessings through it all. I think we are going to come out of it stronger than we were before. I really believe that."

The survival of David Hill's family seems nothing short of miraculous, but there were other uncanny details of the Hill family's story that stand out, too. Trevor's wife, Kathleen, has a cousin who lives near Barrie, and the cousin found Trevor's birth record on his farm– carried about 80 km (50 miles) by the tornado, yet landing on the property of someone who knew the family. And Jennifer, David and Candy's daughter, told us: "A picture of my great-great-grandpa was found in Barrie. My grade seven teacher– his friend was in his garden one day and he saw it. He saw the last name and he showed it to my teacher. He said, 'Oh, I had a student that had that last name, and she went through the tornado.' So he came and showed us, and it was my great-great-grandpa." A cancelled cheque from Melvin Hill's home was also found north of Barrie, by a geography teacher who used it to liven up his classroom discussion of tornadoes.

"Did you hear the roar of a train?"

Emerging from the marsh

The tornado itself continued its progress toward Barrie, plowing through the Luther Marsh after it hit the Hills', having damaged a couple of other buildings on their road, too. Guy Jolicoeur, on the east side of the marsh, just happened to look outside. "Holy smokes! We've got a twister!", he called out to his wife and teenaged sons. They all trooped into the room and plunked down to watch the television. "No," he exclaimed, "It's not on TV, people! It's right there!"– pointing down the road at his neighbour's home.

The whirlwind brushed by the edge of his neighbour's house and zeroed in on the home of Liz and Charlie Bryan around the corner. The Bryans were in their kitchen when Liz noticed the hail coming down. She had asked Charlie shortly before whether the wind might portend a tornado, but he answered, "No, not this time of year." However, she was on alert when she saw the hail.

No sooner had Liz wondered aloud whether they should go down to the basement than they heard glass breaking. She said, "Let's go!" and, since she was standing right by the cellar door, she opened it. Charlie grabbed the children from the kitchen table and they ran downstairs, closing the door behind them. All they could hear was shattering glass. They didn't realize that it was a tornado. Charlie said, "I don't really know what made us move so fast."

It was all over in seconds, and when they came up from the cellar it took a while for the extent of the damage to sink in. Charlie looked out to the east and saw that the trees and his neighbour's drive shed were gone. He told us, "We could see other people's mess, but not our own." But Liz, noticing that she could see the sky through a crack in the wall, opened the door and turned to him, saying, "Charlie, your barns are gone!" Their solid brick house was still standing, but it was irretrievably damaged– twisted and cracked to the point of instability. It took days, weeks, even months for the extent of the damage to sink in completely. Charlie told us that he often stopped as he was working, looked around him and thought, "Shoot! What kind of power does that thing have?!"

It wasn't until he was alone for the first time after the tornado that the emotional impact of his losses hit him. He fought off depression as he did his chores, thinking, "What am I going to do– because as long as the barn was there I could make a living, but if I had to build a barn, I would have to go further in debt. ... This wasn't part of the plan."

? Weird gathering the little ones— A wide swath of damage cut through a mature forest. To the sides of the main path were several smaller strips of damage. Each began all by itself a short distance away, then drew in toward the main path and merged with it like tributaries to a river.

"We live it every day"

But for Charlie and Liz it was at least possible for them to start making new plans, dreaming new dreams. They were still young. For their retired neighbours, Bob and Betty Dale, the tornado was only the beginning of a long and painful fight to get back to normal. At their time of life, dreaming new dreams couldn't carry them through the struggles. Although their house still stood, it showed many signs that it had been structurally damaged. There were cracks in every room; it was clear that the roof had been lifted; the plumbing pipes had been lifted out of joint and put back down off kilter; the chimney had fallen through the roof; and the brick wall had separated from the foundation in the cellar. They felt

unsafe and unhappy because they had to fight so hard to repair and rebuild. Rebuilding can be a long and painful process under the best of circumstances. As Betty Dale told us many months after the tornado, "We live it every day."

"Constant rolling thunder"

The Courtneys– Mark and Jane, and their children Brandon (17), Brock (13) and Cory (8)– had worked together over many years to restore and renovate their home, an old church. No insurance settlement could adequately compensate them for the hours of loving attention they had poured into it. But they, too, were about to embark on a long struggle, just to get back into their beloved home.

On the evening of April 20th, "constant rolling thunder" had drawn Brandon outside while the family played Ping Pong in the basement. He was fascinated by lightning and didn't want to

Even this sturdy brick converted church– the Courtneys' home– sustained heavy damage.

miss anything interesting. Soon, he called his family excitedly, "Come here, you gotta see this!"

Clouds were swirling around each other. Mark said: "It was like two cloud systems were coming together, and they would swirl and break apart. ... We thought we had really seen something just with them swirling around each other, and were going, 'Wow, did you see that?!'... and the next thing we knew ... they started getting bigger and bigger, and it turned into the whole incredible size of a head. As we watched it I started thinking, 'If this is a tornado, what are we going to do?'"

It soon became clear that it was a tornado. "It formed a huge, huge head, and then the funnel started to form downward. ... At that point it didn't feel like it was coming toward us. It just looked like it was getting bigger. Our eyes were glued to this thing in the sky and my wife was saying, 'What are we going to do– what are we going to do?'"

They decided that, if they had to, they would hide in the laundry room. But then they realized that their cat, Smurf, wouldn't be safe in its home in the garage, so Mark went to try to lure her out. As he tried to coax the cat, he became aware of a mounting roar, coming from the west. He told us, "You know what it's like to stand close to Niagara Falls– it was that loud ... and getting louder. I had to give up on the cat, because I knew– the way this thing was roaring, my heart was pounding. It was so loud and so huge, and obviously coming our way. We had no idea whether we were going to live or die! I ran from the garage– my family was still watching it from the doorway. I said, 'Get in! Get in!' I kind of pushed my family in front of me, 'Quick! Quick! Get in the laundry room!' "

As he pushed his family downstairs he worried what they would do if they were trapped, so he ran back up to fetch the cellular phone. When he got back down to the laundry room, slamming the

The cat hid under the Courtneys' car and the chimney embedded itself in the ground.

doors behind him, "Cory [the youngest] was starting to cry a little bit, and then he quit. It was scaring him but he didn't lose it– none of us did. I put Cory on the floor and got on top of him, and my oldest son, Brandon, just took over. He put Brock and my wife on the floor and he covered them. ... We just didn't know what was going to happen."

They were there only briefly when their ears started hurting and they started to have difficulty breathing. Soot had come down the chimney and was choking them as they huddled in their shelter.

Mark said: "Even at that point I didn't think anything had happened. I thought, 'Okay, a strong wind has passed by us. It threw some soot down the chimney'– we were all starting to choke and gag. My wife became concerned that something was on fire because of the sooty, smoky smell. I stepped out of the laundry room when I knew we had to get out of there, because we were having trouble breathing. [I thought] that it had missed us and was hoping that we were safe, that it had gone. I opened the laundry room door and immediately could see light through one of the windows in the rec room toward the front of the house. I thought, 'That's strange, the kids must have left the front doors open."

In fact, the front doors were gone, and glass, mud and debris littered the cracked and twisted interior of the house. The roof had been lifted and set back down, trapping large tree branches inside. Mark said: "We were having to climb over trees and rubble everywhere to even look around our house. It was incredible. ...There was no trace of the garage left at all. It was completely gone, and immediately my heart sank because I thought for sure the cat [was gone with it]. ... And I yelled out to everybody, 'We gotta look for Smurf. Wherever she is, she may need our help.' That's all we did for the next 15 or 20 minutes– branched out and called her."

? Weird

left behind—
"He said everything was gone, like all the silverware– **every-thing** was gone off the table– except the centrepiece. And it was still sitting there and there wasn't a thing wrong with it!"

After raking the lawn, someone put the trimmings into the back of a pickup parked right beside a picnic table. The table disappeared– they only found one piece of broken leg in the field– but the grass and trimmings were still sitting undisturbed in the pickup.

"Strange how some things were left and others weren't. In the drive shed the walls were completely removed but the bikes that were leaning on the walls were still there."

"There would be two trees right beside each other, virtually within, let's say, 4 feet (about 1m)– and one would just be rubble and the other one was standing there like it had been a nice sunny day."

But they did find her, coated with mud, but safe under the van. The whole house was covered in mud, too– the tornado's gift from the Luther Marsh.

Mark said: "We were all in absolute wonder and shock. When we found Smurf and knew that our pets were okay and that we were okay, I had a feeling of profound joy. ... Everything else was in ruins, but to think that we had lived through that, and some slightly different circumstance could have meant death for one or all of us. ... It was a great feeling– weird. Ironic, I guess."

A big ball of fire

The tornado proceeded eastward, having blasted its way through numerous farms, a conservation area and a major power corridor in East and West Luther Townships. George Draper was watching as the tornado was coming through the bush. "We could see all the debris blowing up and I said: 'Holy– it's going to take down the Hydro [power] wires!' As it hit there was a big ball of fire, and then it was just like slow motion. As it went through it was just like the

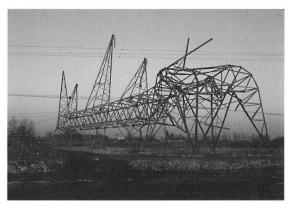

The crumpled remains of these towers bear witness to the power of the tornado's winds.

tower was crumbling." Three high capacity towers were mutilated by the tornado. It also did minor damage at a home on Highway 25, but its next significant impact was on the farm of John and Wilhemena Kottelenberg.

"Nobody warned us"

John Kottelenberg told us: "We never saw the tornado coming– it was partly hidden by the barn. ... The neighbours watched it for about 15 minutes, [but] nobody warned us. I'm just as glad they didn't because, you know, what are you going to do?" He was in his chicken barn when, suddenly, a few shutters flew out in front of him. He looked outside but saw nothing, so he thought it was just a gust of wind. And then the power went off. He told us: "The young lad came upstairs in the barn looking for me. I saw him but he didn't see me, so he tore off again– and I started thinking maybe something happened in the barn with my grandson with the cows. ... Maybe he fell in the gutter or a cow kicked him. I went outside and saw the silo lying down. ... I didn't know if it was a tornado or what it was."

Wilhemena was taken by surprise too. She was in the house with her granddaughter and hadn't noticed anything other than some rain until she saw debris flying by outside. Realizing that what she was seeing was off their buildings, she decided to take shelter downstairs, but by that time the tornado had probably passed by. Fortunately the house sustained little damage, mainly to one side of the roof and eaves. She didn't realize just what had

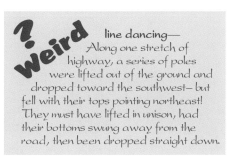

? Weird line dancing— Along one stretch of highway, a series of poles were lifted out of the ground and dropped toward the southwest– but fell with their tops pointing northeast! They must have lifted in unison, had their bottoms swung away from the road, then been dropped straight down.

happened until a neighbour called to say, "The tornado just hit you!" The top half of their silo broke off and there was damage to other outbuildings, but the tornado had spared them much of its fury.

Strange things are done

What the tornado lacked in violence it made up for with weird effects over the next few miles. At the home of Philip and Janice Hawkins it left a disconcerting damage path, skirting the house on both sides, but leaving it with largely superficial damage (although painted with mud). It lifted a large layer of ice several inches thick off the top of the pond, putting it back down like a crooked lid on a jar. The dock that had been on the pond was hurled and embedded in the lawn– so solidly that it had to be removed with a front end loader. Begonia bulbs that were planted in pots by the window exploded, even though the nearby windows didn't break. And Janice and her son Christopher were surprised when the toilet in the basement bathroom where they had sought shelter flushed itself. They had felt intense pressure changes in their ears, but they hadn't expected the toilet to respond!

Across the road, at the Fernbrook Natural Spring Water Company, the tornado lifted an empty tractor-trailer so it leapfrogged over a full one (which was knocked over, spilling its load). The airborne trailer then hit the northeast corner of the barn, crushing the beams and taking out the side wall, and continued through the air for 24-30 metres (80-100 feet), rolling when it landed until it came to rest as a twisted wreck 122-152 metres (400-500 feet) from where it had started its journey. A farmer two kilometres (one and a half miles) to the south watched it fly through the air.

Shrink-wrapped skids of bottled water in the basement of the barn were left intact, but after the tornado there were leaves and dirt wrapped in between each layer of wrap. Bottles from Fernbrook landed in the laneway of one farm several kilometres to the east of the bottling plant, and the lids landed at another farm.

The ice on this pond was lifted by the tornado.

The tornado hurled a tractor-trailer far into the field, heavily damaging the Fernbrook building on its way.

"We're going to die today!"

But the tornado still had more than tricks up its sleeve. It held terror and devastation for the Evans family, just down the road from Fernbrook. Francine Evans was in the bathroom with her boy, Nicholas, who was taking a bath. She had been consoling him because he was frightened by the thunder. She told him that the thunder was just noise and he said, "So we're safe, Mommy?" and she answered that yes, they were safe. But as they were leaving the bathroom and Francine's husband, Larry, was going in to wash his hands, Larry glanced out the bedroom window across the hall and saw the tornado.

The Evans' stone house was destroyed before they could reach the basement.

Francine said: "All Larry said was, 'Tornado!– Run!' We ran down the little hall and by the time we got to the dining room [halfway through the house toward the cellar stairs] Larry yelled, 'Stop! The rest of the house is gone!'– and then he froze. He went into shock. He saw the roof go, he saw everything go– I didn't see anything. I was just told to run and I was trying to save my little boy.

"He froze in the dining room, so I grabbed him and my son and we went back into the bathroom and shut the two bathroom doors. We could hear it going through the house like a freight train and could feel the house vibrating. My husband whispered in my ear, 'We're going to die today,' and I whispered back, 'No, because I don't feel my life flashing before us.' ... Then all of a sudden– I mean within seconds– it was over, quiet– there was no more noise. There was not even a bird chirping– nothing. Dead silence." And their home was destroyed.

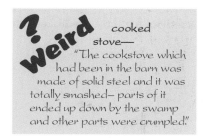

? Weird cooked stove— "The cookstove which had been in the barn was made of solid steel and it was totally smashed– parts of it ended up down by the swamp and other parts were crumpled."

Flying trees and doorknobs

Wayne and Jackie Jones, on the next road east, had bought their home for its beautiful setting in a dense grove of trees, so– even though it was spared– the devastation of their woods broke their hearts. But it provided quite a spectacle to the Bospoorts across the road. Isobel Bospoort said that, as the tornado passed, "a bunch of trees went by– [it] looked as if they had gone through a Christmas tree lot– marching across the sky. I thought I was dreaming." They had seen the tornado in time to get to the basement, but their home and trees were undamaged.

Their neighbours, particularly Melvin Muller and Janice Wyville, were not so fortunate. They had been working outside that day, and although Janice thought it was "kind of a strange day," she didn't think that it looked like an abnormal spring day.

She said: "I came in and turned on the evening news. We were watching a station out of North Carolina, and it was funny– they had just said on the news that there were tornado warnings for 10 states in the U.S. The television went off and the noise came. That's how quickly it happened. And then all the windows started to go in the house. The strangest thing was that the doorknob from the front door [at the west end of the house] ... blew

Pine trees marched through the air.

straight out of the door. It came right down [the hall] and hit the kitchen wall like a bullet. We couldn't run to the basement because it is at the front of the house. We attempted to get from our family room to our office because there's a huge closet there, and we made it to the doorway. By that time [the tornado] had taken down our shed and I watched it go off over the field."

But the shed and windows were not the only damage their property sustained. Melvin and Janice were just at the beginning of a long struggle to clean up and rebuild damage that twisted and shifted their home, but left it standing. Melvin said: "It actually took the front wall and bowed it in about five inches (13cm)– the whole wall. ... And a four by six foot (1.2 by 1.8m) dormer window was taken out and disappeared– frame and all."

Janice added: "In the back upstairs bedroom the window didn't break, but the curtain blew between the wall and the outside siding. It just went out [between the frame and the wall] and got stuck." The tornado also picked up Melvin's brand new truck, leaving it with $5,000 damage. He said: "Yeah, I saw that happen. It went right up in the air and just came right back down. [The tornado] just bounced it like it was a yo-yo." The paint was sandblasted off Janice's car.

They were afraid to leave their home that night– fearful of looters and sightseers. So Janice and Melvin moved a couch into the back end of the house (where the damage was less severe) and stayed there that night. "All night, all we could hear was more parts of the house falling down inside." They no longer felt safe in their own home, and it was to be a long struggle determining whether it was safe to repair rather than rebuild from scratch.

Diving for cover

To the east, Bill and Lynne Anderson's home was not significantly damaged, but Bill was at the barn with the vet and his children, Kelly and Scott, when the tornado demolished it. "We were just coming out and I looked out of the window. I saw this stuff flickering in the wind. I said, 'Holy geez– a tornado!' and I shoved my son back through the door of the grain barn, and yelled to grab Kelly and [for] the vet to hit the floor right behind the stone wall. There was a big post that came flying through the hayshaft– but we never heard the barn come down. Why I said, 'tornado' I don't know. I had never seen one before."

But Larry and Linda Andrew's view was blocked by a hill to the west, and the first thing they saw after friends phoned to warn them of the tornado was "a blob of wind. ... It was a white debris cloud. I couldn't see the funnel. I guess if I had been looking up I might have. [The sky] didn't look weird. It wasn't windy at that moment," Linda told us.

But nonetheless they decided to get the family to the basement, because "there was something coming."

As they huddled in the basement they heard crashing sounds, but Linda didn't really think there was much damage as it was happening. The next day she could not understand why her chest and back were so sore, until she realized that "It was from hanging on. I clenched myself, and that's why. And in the morning, my jaw– I went to chew some gum and I couldn't even chew." Those few moments in the basement had been tense indeed.

"There's something wrong with the horses."

But it wasn't just tension that pained young Kelsey Butler. Her older sister, Erin, was the first person to raise the alarm. She had looked out toward their horse barn and yelled, "Dad, there's something wrong with the horses." They were running wildly, at high speed, in the pasture. Then she noticed that there was something coming off the roof of the barn. Her father, Gary, said: " I looked at the barn and there was a piece of plywood in the air. I said to myself,

The Butlers' home was beyond repair.

there's something wrong. There's no plywood on that barn. I looked behind the barn, and that's when I saw the funnel cloud. ... I yelled to the girls [Erin (15), Kristen (13) and Kelsey (7)] to get to the basement. Then I saw the roof come off the barn."

Kelsey saw the barn roof go too. Rather than running to a corner of the basement for cover, she stood mesmerized in front of a glass door. Gary told us: "When I came down to the basement Kelsey was still looking. She was still about one metre (1 yard) from that door. I yelled at her, 'Get away from that door!' As I said that the door came off ... and she was tossed about 10 feet (3 metres) into the wall."

She ended up with a huge lump and a black eye, but otherwise all right. But although the house and barn had both been hit, the family didn't realize the extent of the damage right off. Gary and Erin ran to check on the horses. Erin said: "I don't think I even heard [the tornado] stop, but my body knew it stopped. Then I ran outside. I didn't even notice the house was damaged– all the glass and everything– until I was going out the door. Then I saw glass because the door had fallen in. I didn't even see how the garage was wrecked. I didn't know until everyone was crying at the house."

After taking care of the horses Erin returned to the house and walked around to see the damage. She was shocked. "I felt mostly kind of screwed up, because ... it all happens in a minute." In that minute she and her sister, Kristen, had put their school tornado drill experience to good use. Erin took cover in a protected part of the basement, cushioned by horse blankets, and Kristen hid under a heavy sewing machine.

For miles around people watched the Butlers' barn roof float through the air.

Their mother, Ann Butler, was at work when the tornado hit, but she didn't miss out on all of the action. "I was working in Violet Hill ... and heard really loud thunder, ominous thunder. ... I got a call from the owner [who was across the road], and as I picked up the phone she just said: 'Lock the door. Get to the basement. There's a tornado.' By the time I got to the back stairway I could feel a difference in the air pressure– it was like a 'whoomph'– a very odd sensation, and the building felt like it trembled. And all of a sudden it was gone.

"So I went back to the front of the store, unlocked the door and looked outside. Our display items were all over the place. They were smashed. Across the street, where there were quite a number of cars at the restaurant, there were big limbs of trees down ... on top of the vehicles. I immediately went to the phone to call home and the line was busy, so I thought, 'Oh well, of course, nothing's happened there. It was just here.'"

She had just gotten down to the business of cleaning up some of the debris outside the store when the phone rang. It was Gary. He said: "You've got to get home right now. The garage wing's down on top of the truck, the windows are in the house. I don't know where the horses are. Kelsey's got a horrendous bruise on her head. I don't know how bad it is. Come home!" Fortunately, her car had been parked down the road, away from the area where the other vehicles had been damaged.

She drove home, "concentrating on the road and trying to get around the debris," to find her husband and children in shock. Gary said, "The girls' expressions reminded me of pictures I'd seen of Vietnam– young kids [in shock]."

Dazed and confused

Irmgard Leimbrock was also in shock. She had been sitting on the couch, watching television with her dog, when she first noticed "little black pieces flying around in the trees." She thought: "Oh, that must be my roof ... but then the antenna came down and was twisted around the big tree. Then I got scared."

Before she had a chance to run for shelter she heard a loud crack and the chimney crashed through the ceiling and onto the living room floor– right in front of her. She told us: "The dog took off and I got scared, 'My house! My house!'– I was screaming– not crying– screaming." She ran for her bedroom, and seeing that the window was open and the drapes outside, she climbed up on the window sill to retrieve them. That's when she heard a stranger's voice, saying, "Take it easy– we are coming," and the police and fire department were soon there, trying to get her to leave the house. But she said, "Not without my dog!"– so they all

Bricks flew and garages tumbled as the tornado approached Violet Hill.

set about searching for it. She eventually found it herself, frightened and hiding in a corner.

Irmgard, too, was emotionally distraught. One man who came driving up soon after the tornado had passed was taken aback when she wandered out onto the road in front of his vehicle, unaware of the danger. She was dazed and confused– in shock from her experience.

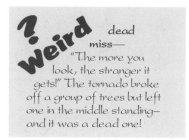

Weird? dead miss— "The more you look, the stranger it gets!" The tornado broke off a group of trees but left one in the middle standing— and it was a dead one!

"Have you got a basement?"

On Highway 89 many of the cars had drawn to the side of the road as the drivers saw the tornado approaching. Some of them didn't know whether to race forward to get through before it crossed in front of them, wait it out where they were, or take cover.

Rudy and Dina Coleman thought they would outrun it, but gave up and waited when slower traffic got in their way. They watched and photographed as the roof of the Butlers' horse barn danced circles through the air nearby– completely intact throughout its flight.

Norm Keith was surprised when a stranger came running in for shelter. He was just coming up from the basement to fetch a flashlight when a man in one of several cars stopped on the highway spotted him. "He came running– charging up– and he said, 'Have you got a basement?' I looked at him and said, 'Yeah, we have a basement.' He said, 'Well, let's go!' I thought the guy was crazy or something. ... He was scared, he [had been] driving into [the tornado] for about 20 minutes and didn't know what to do. He said if there was nobody in [our] home he was going to go into the milkhouse."

Weird? taking aim— "The one curtain rod in the kitchen where the patio door is was stuck right into the wall like a spear— yet it never broke the patio door!"

"He just peeled out of here!"

In the old town of Violet Hill, near where Ann Butler was working, Cheryl Mason watched in surprise as her cat went sailing through the air. And the patrons at the restaurant had finally heeded the owner, Maureen Baufeldt's, urgent command that they get down to the basement.

She told us that soon after the dinner guests had arrived they noticed the weather. "They were saying, 'You should see that funny cloud!' So we all stood at the window and looked at this cloud. And you could see [that] when it touched down debris would come flying out of the bottom of this cloud. So people went outside to watch it."

The musician who was playing that night was from Indiana (where tornados are more common), and when he saw the tornado he began to panic. He said, "Maureen– it's going to hit us!" but she told him not to alarm the guests. He was beside himself, saying, "You're not listening to me! It's going to hit!"

So Maureen's husband went outside to take a look. He told her, "It's not moving. It's not coming here," so no action was taken for another

Weird? tidy twister— "It had taken the roof off, it had taken parts of the room away, but sitting on their dresser was a glass candle perfectly where it was. I mean, the whole room is in shambles but here's this little glass candle sitting on the dresser that was left. And the bed's made, and his slippers are sitting under the bed where he left them!"

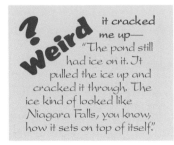

ten minutes or so, when Josh, the musician, explained to her, "The reason that you think it's not moving is because it's coming **at** you!" Now she recognized the danger they were in. She said: "We forced all our 38 guests into the basement. ... Two men were emphatic about standing outside and watching it, and they had to be physically thrust down the basement."

Not everyone had waited that long, however. Maureen said: "There was a couple who had been through the tornado in Barrie 11 years ago. He grabbed his wife [and ran for the car]. He was in the car, she had the door open, and she didn't even have her fanny on the seat or her purse inside the car or the door closed or anything! He just peeled out of here. ... I could not believe it! He was that frantic!"

Maureen stayed on upstairs with the chef, one waitress and one guest– who she found out later was a Toronto firefighter– rushing around to extinguish all the candles in the restaurant. The last thing they needed was for the tornado to start a fire! She said: "All of a sudden this man [the firefighter] yelled, 'Dive!' and we just dived under the tables."

When it was over and the guests emerged from the basement to shattered glass in their cars, Maureen tells us: "It was just a very emotional thing. Everybody just left. We said, 'Nobody has to pay for anything– just go.' We had no [power] so I had my dish-washing department sweeping glass out of people's cars. ... The parking lot was just covered in glass and tree branches." Some of the cars had been sandblasted by gravel, too.

And to top it all off, Maureen had to stay open for a party with a later reservation. "We told them, 'We have no [power], we cannot cook for you. We're very sorry. We'll try to arrange another restaurant for you,' but this one party of 25 didn't [care], they were going to party. ... I was not in the mood to socialize with anybody."

"I figured it would take a while"

Down the road, Lloyd Sawden had been warned by his neighbour that a tornado was coming, "But I figured that would take a while yet so I went ahead with tea and making supper." While he was fixing his meal he saw the corner of his trailer home shake, but didn't think too much about it until moments later. "Before I had a chance to open my mouth, I landed on the ground [inside the trailer, which was blown over]." His barn was destroyed, and his cows were on the loose– but Lloyd was fortunate to be alive. Because his trailer home was nestled below a knoll it escaped being flung great distances, with him inside.

Lloyd Sawden lost his barn and trailer, and many homes in Violet Hill were damaged as the tornado blew through.

"This is getting serious"

Atop the knoll was a subdivision of large homes, and many of the residents were out watching the tornado's approach, some with video cameras in hand. Gabe Scavone watched as Lloyd Sawden's barn exploded before his eyes, thinking, "This is getting serious!" He told us: "It's not like you could see a funnel cloud or anything. I couldn't see anything. I didn't know that it was right on top of me. I was standing on the deck outside and I opened the door. It just ripped the door right from my hand. Then I tried to close the door with my shoulder. I finally got it closed, and by that time it had hit the Maletta's house, across the road."

Saverio Maletta had been watching the tornado's approach too. He was at home with his wife, Vedia, his two sons, Frank and Chris, and one of his nephews. He said: "We were watching TV and outside it wasn't cloudy. It was sunny, basically a nice day. And we saw a big flash of lightning to the west. I told my wife that was unusual, so we shut the TV off. I had never seen lightning unless there was a storm or it was cloudy. The weather really didn't look that bad. I walked around the house to the kitchen and looked out the window. I saw there were dark clouds out there to the east. [By this time the storm's anvil had stretched out toward the east so that most of the cloud was well ahead of the tornado, which was still approaching from the west.] ... It didn't really look that bad. It looked like it might just pass over and be clear within half an hour. When I looked out the front door to the southwest I

could see dark clouds moving in ... and I could see just a little tail on the bottom of the clouds. I thought that was unusual so I just kept looking at it, and all of a sudden I thought, this could be a tornado– so I [video]taped it almost from that point all the way up until just before it struck the house."

The Malettas' home received the first severe damage in the Violet Hill subdivision.

In fact, Saverio didn't even get all the way down to the basement before it struck. He stayed up at his front door, camera in hand, until the last moment. His wife kept asking him to close the door and go downstairs, but he didn't want to miss anything. "When I saw that it was getting too close and I felt it was going to strike the house, I told [my wife] to call the kids downstairs. They all went down and I stayed up here because ... at this point I still thought it was going to miss because it kept going up and down. When the damage was done down the road I was looking for a trail or a breeze, or something on the ground to see how far it was from my house still– and never saw anything, until I panned up [overhead] and it looked like it was right above the house. ... Then I could see the little pine tree in the front starting to wiggle and shake and I knew it was right about here. So I backed up from the curtains and made a run for the basement. ... By the time I got downstairs [we] could see the grass [being whipped by the wind] and hear the noise."

He kept the tape running all the way down, capturing the family's pandemonium and the view of debris flying by the soon-to-be-shattered basement window as he went. Saverio told us: "My sister is always saying, 'You should have taped this, you should have done that.' I think that was going through my mind when [the tornado] was coming. I said [to myself], 'Boy, is she ever going to be proud of me!'"

Vedia hadn't believed Saverio when he first told her it was a tornado. "I thought, 'Yeah, right!'– because he's always trying to trick me." Once she realized that he was serious, however, she was torn between making sure the kids stayed safe in the basement and running upstairs to plead with her husband to come down. "It was very frightening," she said.

After the tornado passed, the Maletta children came up from the basement.

We asked Saverio if he would do the same thing again– videotape an approaching tornado– and he answered: "Oh, yeah. Somebody looks after us. We've been through quite a lot together. ... I think I'd be traumatized if [someone was hurt or killed]. Because I wasn't physically injured, I really don't know how to fear it. I know to respect it, but I don't know how to fear it. If I was hurt, then I'd be terrified."

The kids **were** terrified as they huddled in the basement, waiting for their father to come down. Frank (7) said: "I was scared because I thought he was going to die. He was taking a video! He was right near the window!" When we asked his younger brother, Chris (5), how he had felt, he answered, simply, "Lonely."

Receding into the clouds

Nothing remained of the Grattons' barn.

The tornado continued to rip through the subdivision, damaging roofs, brickwork and windows as it went. One family lost everything because they were not insured and couldn't afford to repair or rebuild. Another couple had just returned north from their winter vacation– passing through tornado warnings and watches in the U.S. tornado alley– only to have their horse barn destroyed by a home-grown tornado once they reached supposed safety.

But the tornado was near its end. Russell and Colleen Gratton had just turned on the news in time to hear a report that a tornado was near Shelburne. Russell said: "I just ran to get the video camera at that point, and ran outside. ... It didn't look terribly crazy. ... The wind started to get stronger ... I started seeing something form up in the sky– more like a big round cloud coming down. It wasn't like a funnel or anything like that. That's why I didn't think it **was** the tornado. I was thinking I was going to see it on the horizon. ... And then I started seeing little chunks of stuff up in the air. At first sight I thought they were birds. And then I focused and I thought, 'Hey, that's a **big** chunk of something!' ... As it got closer, material was starting to come toward us."

Colleen had gone to the basement with the two Gratton children as soon as they heard the news report on television, but she hadn't really believed anything would happen to them. She said: "It was more like a joke. ... It was Saturday. We had nothing to do, so I made it kind of like a game. And then my son [George] went upstairs to look for his teddy bear." Russell continues: "When I started seeing stuff flying, George had come outside a couple of times [and I told him] 'Go downstairs!' But I just stayed out there." By the time everyone but Russell was settled in the cellar the tornado was almost upon them.

Russell started seeing large pieces flying overhead and thought: "'Holy mackerel!' First of all, that's pretty close– those pieces are pretty big. And then I noticed the surface stuff started coming. ... That's when I started to back up and come back into the house, because I was afraid of being hit by something."

And just in time, too. Russell backed into the house, video camera still running, and as he ran past a picture window on his way to the basement, he stopped to film the barn behind his house– or what had been the barn behind his house. It was being whisked into fragments by the tornado as he stood there, flabbergasted. By that time the danger had passed, and the family came upstairs to watch the funnel disappear into the cloud after one last swipe at a couple of farms on the next road over.

The people of Barrie (which was directly on the path, had the tornado stayed on the ground) were to be spared the ravages of another devastating tornado. They had endured more than enough in 1985.

A smorgasbord of tornadoes

These two twisters were far from the most devastating that had hit Ontario, and certainly not up to the vicious destruction of an F5 "mile-wider" in Oklahoma. But those are rare– even in "tornado alley."

Although the April 20th tornadoes are estimated to have been F2 and F3 on the Fujita scale of tornado strength– strong enough to be very dangerous– they killed nobody. But they had given the unsuspecting people of Southwestern Ontario a smorgasbord of tornado forms and effects from which we can all learn. They had also put to the test what people **thought** they knew about tornadoes.

How much do **you** know, and how much of it is wrong? Read on.

The tornado left many haunting scenes in its wake.

"...of course, I was reminded of
Godsfinger. Godsfinger— what a
strange name. What an exotic
place, yet on the map so ordinary,
so normal, and mundane.

One thing I noticed about coming
face-to-face with even a small
portion of God's power is its
absolute neutrality— not good, not
evil— just there. Existence. Being.
Raw unadulterated power cruising
across a farmer's field in the
clever disguise of a twister.
Bullfrogs quiet in anticipation.
Tomorrow's heartache and debris
caught in a whirling Doppler-like
mantra.

They say that one is never the
same after being touched by the
finger of God. Even a slight brush
on your cheek can drop you to
your knees in wonder. There can
be no wasted moments now. Only
the present. Pregnant with
imagination. Bound with the
sinews that make dreams
manifest. A translucent jade
gargoyle. A Jacob's ladder of fine
lace. Life, love, and death in the
forest."

Ken Dunn

2
Reading the stormy sky

We all live with it and we all talk about it– but do we really know what's going on out there? The weather plays out its daily drama in a never-ending, ever-changing display of beauty and variety. Weather allows the redistribution of heat and moisture over the planet's surface and most of the time this happens in an orderly fashion. But once in a while the imbalance becomes very great and Mother Nature counters with a burst of extreme, sometimes dangerous events in the atmosphere. Though rare and brief, it is these moments that grab our attention and sometimes turn our lives upside-down.

Is there nothing we can do except sit back and let it happen? At the very least we should be prepared and become "weather-smart" so that we notice the conditions that foretell danger and can act upon them. Many people affected by tornadoes say that they did not have as much warning as they would have liked. And the reasons are obvious: we are all busy doing things and can't always catch warnings on radio or television. Storms become severe quickly and often only in a small, localized area, so even the weather office has its hands full assessing the situation and relaying that vital information to us. So what **can** we do? We can all be our own warning system by developing a weather-eye to help us become familiar enough with the characteristics of stormy weather that we aren't surprised by them.

When you know what to look for, what to expect next, there are no surprises. Meteorology is a complex science, but the laws of physics operate in a very orderly manner– and nothing happens by accident with weather. Everything has a purpose and an explanation. The changes we see or sense are part of that day's weather plan– all we need to do is learn to read the sky like a manual. Whether it's clouds, wind, light, or changes with time, everything out there is a part of the language of weather. With a little basic knowledge and attention to the sky, we no longer need to view storms as a "foreign language." We will also be aware of what **not** to worry about, and can sit back and enjoy the pleasures of watching stormy weather without a needless fear of the unknown.

 ## Do we need a weather war zone?

The media likes to dwell on conflict and confrontation as a source of entertainment. Weather is no exception. Severe weather is often attributed to clashing air masses or a struggle between hot and cold air. Such simplifications don't do us much good because they imply that grand schemes and faraway forces are behind a severe event– forces that lie beyond our understanding. In the most general sense it is true that advancing cold air masses help to initiate storms. Abrupt temperature changes accompany passing fronts and the same active weather pattern which brings us these fronts also brings us stormy spells. But weather is not at war– it's on a perpetual quest for balance, for equilibrium. And a storm, with all its dangers and inconveniences, is a brief, energetic burst of activity that stirs up a local imbalance for the sake of balancing the atmosphere globally.

We could turn the picture around, instead, and say that a storm **causes** a hot-cold clash. Initially the "hot" is near the ground and the "cold" is above us, providing the means for strong convection. After a storm forms, its downdraft delivers a return supply of cold air down to the ground to replace the rising warm air. The much denser cold air slips and slides around, pushing into and under the lighter warm air until a balance is restored. What we experience as a storm is really an eloquent peacemaker between the opposing forces of nature.

Weather basics

Before you can understand a severe storm it is helpful to know a bit about the atmosphere. All of our weather and clouds happen in a thin vail (16km, or 10 miles thick) which envelops the Earth's surface. This lowest layer of the atmosphere is called the troposphere. Near the ground, day-to-day changes are brought along by weather systems– highs and lows, cold and warm fronts– which bring us regular fluctuations in moisture and temperature. The winds in the lowest kilometre or so are always changing, as each high or low

Sunset illumination helps us distinguish the separate cloud layers in this mixed sky. The highest cloud, still brightly lit, is a waning shower in the distance. The closer clouds are in shade but look dark against the brighter sky or light against darker clouds.

pressure system passes by. But above this, winds are mostly westerly (from southwest through northwest) and they are generally stronger as you go higher, reaching speeds of 50-100kmh (30-60mph) and more above 5km (3 miles) over the Earth's surface. This means that the highest clouds are the earliest indicators of an approaching weather system (or thunderstorm) to reach us.

A storm needs instability in order to develop. Much of the process of weather-making depends on the simple fact that warm air rises and cool air sinks. A cross-section of the troposphere shows that air temperature decreases with height. When the atmosphere is

What makes a cloud black?

Something looks black because it sends little light to your eyes. With clouds, the light is either reflected off the cloud from the surrounding sky or has passed through it. When a cumulus cloud grows tall, it is very dense with tiny water droplets from rapid condensation, and it blocks the light from above. Its base is like a shadow, and the taller the cloud, the darker the base. In addition, the anvil of a large storm throws an extra shadow over the lower clouds, making many of them look black even though they aren't that thick themselves.

When you see a large, solid black cloud bank connected to a storm, you are looking at the main updraft feeding into that storm. It is within this column of rising air that the rotation leading to a tornado can form. This rotation, when present, almost always shows itself by forming a roughly circular lowered part of the cloud base (the wall cloud). It is lower in the sky than the rest of the storm and has a different shade of black when seen up close– anything from a brown-rust shade to a lighter grey. This colour variation comes from distant skylight getting in underneath the storm, reflecting off the lowest cloud portions.

Clouds look black when they are thick or shaded by other clouds. Their blackness by itself need not worry you. Instead, look for a connection between dark clouds and the nearest storm you see. If those clouds are part of that storm– like a bank extending south or southwest away from the rain area– it deserves to be watched for signs of lower cloud fragments or rotation. With no storm nearby and no obvious signs of organization, dark clouds are nothing to be concerned about.

stable (which it is, most of the time) this decrease is modest, and any bubble of rising warm air quickly becomes cooler than the surrounding air and stops rising. But if the temperature decrease with height is steeper, rising warm air bubbles do not cool down enough to make them cooler than their surrounding air. They continue rising to great heights, forming large convective clouds. This is an unstable atmosphere.

A warm, moist air mass can become unstable in two ways– by becoming warmer at the bottom, or by becoming cooler above. The sun heats the air near the ground, making it more unstable in the afternoon than at night. Weather systems bring with them cooler air aloft, which makes an air mass unstable by "top cooling." Either or both of these can tip the scales, triggering strong updrafts. But we need one more ingredient– moisture. If the air is too dry, convective clouds will not form or they will be too small. In very humid conditions the air only has to rise a small distance to condense, forming lower cloud bases. Condensation also **releases** heat into the air inside a cloud. So once a cloud becomes large enough, this extra heat lends it a built-in ability to survive and grow even larger.

The right conditions for stormy weather depend on just the right imbalance, in which warm air is able to rise to great heights. A storm needs a "trigger"– usually provided by cooling aloft– and a "push", often from an approaching cold front. It also needs "fuel" in the form of a moist air mass. Once it has formed it needs one more thing to flourish– good ventilation. A storm's intensity depends on wind shear, or the extent to which stronger winds aloft help the cloud system breathe, by carrying precipitation forward, away from the warm updrafts feeding it. (With poor ventilation, a storm's inflow– the warm air that feeds it– can be "choked off" by rain.)

What clouds can tell you

If you want to know what's up in the weather, just watch the clouds! Clouds trace the motion of air at different levels. Low clouds are soft and lumpy, and move across the sky at a good clip, often from the same direction as the winds you experience outside. Middle clouds are more detailed, textured, and travel with the prevailing flow aloft that carries weather systems along. The highest clouds are white, fibrous streaks or sheets of ice crystals, and they give us the earliest indication of a change to come.

When you are out on a drive you may notice that some clouds come toward you quickly while others seem to take forever. High clouds can be seen up to 150km (90 miles) away (assuming you have the visibility); but a low, dark cloud that wasn't even visible a moment ago will traverse your view in a very short time. Clouds with low bases are only visible for a distance of 10-40km (6-25 miles)– much less when haze or rain is present– and this may only give you about ten minutes to notice and assess what is coming. Low clouds only **appear** to move faster because they are closer to you– the higher clouds are usually moving much faster.

Most of the time the atmosphere is relatively stable and clouds do not develop much vertically (growing upward). But when conditions are unstable, even small cloud elements may sprout turrets, and the building cumulus clouds will boil and tumble as they grow larger. When strong updrafts are present there are also compensating downdrafts, and it is this up-and-down motion that gives the sky its jumbled, contrasty look. As the day progresses, these random-looking clouds gradually begin to draw together into larger, more organized cloud masses and structures. You will see a clear evolution from many small cumulus to fewer, larger ones as these clouds fight it out for the available heat and moisture. Eventually only a few large storms reign over the region and everything in the sky is part of their realm of influence.

The thunderstorm

Every storm starts somewhere as a large cumulus cloud. The characteristic flat, black base and boiling top continue to grow and expand for 10-30 minutes until a shower begins. At this point the cloud may be 2-5km (1-3 miles) in diameter, and its top has reached a height of 8-12km (5-7 miles). This "cell" now shows up on radar as a small round dot. What happens next depends on how unstable it is and how strong the winds are high up in this cell.

Seen from the outside, a thunderstorm cloud is a magnificent mountain of moisture. The air rises in a strong, sustained updraft which appears as a boiling crown at the top of the storm. This air then spreads out in the anvil, part of which hangs back (seen at left) while the rest flows forward (ahead and right, out of view). The air enters the storm at the lower right (inflow) forming new towers with dark, flat bases. On the backside (left), downdrafts prevail and the clouds are less defined and drier looking. At the meeting point of the forward-side inflow and the backside outflow is a small lowering, right below the main updraft.

A large amount of rain forms quickly within a thunderstorm cell and begins to descend toward the ground. In light winds (in a sultry mid-summer spell) the descending burst of cool rainy air crushes the updraft and the cell collapses. But when the winds aloft are strong, the upper parts of the cloud blow forward and carry much of the falling precipitation forward as well. This forms the familiar "anvil cloud", a high greyish streak or sheet of cloud that stretches out ahead of the storm. You see this anvil approaching first, and as it thickens and lowers, the rain and thunder intensify. What you experience is still a single cloud– a large three-dimensional hunk of moisture, overshadowing everything else in the sky. If the storm is distant, you will see it as a cream-coloured wall of cloud with some towering parts and a flat, fibrous top. But if the storm is moving your way, the anvil fills the sky and obscures your view of the storm's structure until the core comes nearer.

A severe storm first needs to become a sustained thunderstorm in which a procession of new updraft cells keeps it going. Each updraft pulse enters the cloud system and merges with it. After a short time, it matures to form a new burst of precipitation which temporarily becomes the new core of the storm. (The "core" is the storm's centre of power.) That portion of the cloud drifts forward, weakens and joins the anvil– and new updrafts take its place. In this way, the storm regenerates and survives. The cloud we see and experience is not a single, static entity– it is an evolving system, an efficient rain machine fueled by a steady inflow of warm, moist air.

The storm environment

The area around an organized storm is a busy place. The sky is in a state of perpetual flux– updrafts, downdrafts, clouds at various levels moving in different directions, dark parts, light parts– and all of it happens for a reason, as part of a loosely connected circulation of warm and cool air. To make sense of all this we first need to survey the scene.

We need to remember where that day's clouds are moving from, where the nearest storm is (see how a storm is structured, page 71), whether that storm is approaching or passing by, and whether there are other elements (rain, lightning, a cool wind) to consider. Use the changes in your local wind conditions to spot nearby areas of rain or cool outflow. Take note of where the dark and light areas are. Watch the darkest areas to see if they begin to produce lightning bolts or new shafts of rain. The darkest areas are regions of rising air (building clouds) while the lighter parts are downdrafts– which you might see either as clear gaps between clouds or as a region of thinner cloud within an overcast sky. You may also have noticed that areas of rain are often lighter than the surrounding clouds. This is because the rain drags cool air down with it, thinning out some of the lower clouds. The boundaries between these pockets of cool outflow from a storm or rainy patch are marked by darker clouds– sometimes mere fragments with no real shape (scud) and at other times a bank of heavy, dark, growing clouds that often becomes a new storm a little while later.

An organized severe storm takes control of the wind pattern around it and the clouds are controlled by this flow, giving the scene a sense of order. High above, the anvil spreads out like a grey blanket. Below it are darker clouds at the main condensation level. They thicken as rising, condensing air approaches the heavy rain core in the distance. The lowest clouds move with the winds near the ground and often, as here, line up with the inflow blowing toward the storm.

The storm environment

This storm is sustained by a procession of new updrafts entering at lower right. Each one rises and joins in to add its portion to the anvil cloud at the top. Before the anvil ages (top left) it shows the separate updraft pulses as steps flaring out like waves against an imaginary ceiling.

One of the stranger sights under some storms is mamma. These are bulges or pouches hanging from the underside of the anvil. Here, glancing sunlight makes them very prominent. They can look menacing and have often been equated with threatening weather. But the mamma themselves are harmless and only indicate small downdrafts in a part of the storm that's far from its more potent core region.

Somewhere under every storm is a place where the warm inflow air meets the cool outflow air. This is where you will find the lowest clouds and sometimes a lowering, or lowered cloud mass, attached to the storm's main cloud base. The small lowering here shows us that the warm air coming from the left is forced to rise suddenly when it meets the cool air coming out of the rain at right. A storm's lowering is like a facial expression— you can tell what's going on inside by watching it change.

Clouds in the storm environment occupy all the levels of the troposphere. As the day becomes warmer, billowing cumulus carry moisture skyward where it spreads out in various layers and slowly evaporates. If the updrafts go above the freezing level, the clouds freeze into ice crystal anvils which are blown forward and take longer to evaporate. This sky has both low cumulus and high cirrus clouds (from distant anvils) in it.

Towering convective clouds often trail to the south of an organized storm. This axis is the rain-free base– a dark, flat cloud base with no rain falling under it. All the forming precipitation is still aloft here. As the towers mature into showers, they add their rain to the storm's core of heavy precipitation, seen here at left.

This is a closer look at a young storm's rain core. A single heavy downpour is surrounded by the storm's crinkly cloud base. The darkest parts of this rain-free base are where the strongest (tallest) updrafts are. There are slight signs of lower cloud scraps here too. When a storm propagates, or "grows" forward, the dark bases mature into new showers and more dark bases form adjacent to the new rain areas.

In the first photo, the darkest cloud bases indicate rising air while the lighter parts– including the distant rain curtain– are where the down-drafts and thinner clouds are. In the second photo, a disorganized jumble of light-dark elements means that no single part is very strong. Compare this with the scene on pg. 67.

There are three main groups of clouds that are worth noticing in the stormy sky. The **lowest clouds** are fast-moving and are pushed along by brief, local wind effects. They exist only as long as there is rain-cooled air pushing into warmer air to force condensation. They evaporate if the cool flow weakens or warms up. These clouds are very transitory and are not usually attached to the larger, darker clouds nearby. Above this is the main condensation level, where all the **growing cumulus clouds** reside. The bases of these clouds are black– almost bluish-black when compared with the other clouds in the sky. When the larger ones pass overhead, brief downpours with big droplets are likely. Above everything else is the **anvil cloud**, if there are storms around. This sheet of cloud has a smooth, leaden-grey appearance that darkens gradually in the direction of the storm. It generates steady rain and some soft thunder, but sometimes the rain evaporates before reaching the ground.

You can learn to read the clouds like a map of air motion– both up-and-down and sideways. If the overall picture is a messy one, the chances are that the weather near you is disorganized and nothing to worry about for now. Some of the most turbulent-looking clouds

Weather words

We have tried to stay away from unfamiliar weather words as much as possible in this book, and we have provided definitions and explanations for terms along the way. However, there are a few words that are a natural part of talking about the weather, but may feel unfamiliar to you. Don't let them stop you in your tracks!. They usually mean exactly what they sound like, and if you read on, the context will provide the meaning for you. Here are a few.

Aloft– just means "up higher in the sky." It may not be a regular part of coffee table conversation, but it's hard to talk about weather without going "aloft"!

Updraft– Air moving upward. The interplay of warm air rising and cool air descending is the very stuff of weather. So when we say updraft, we are just talking about an area of the storm where warm air is rising into it (and giving the storm its oomph).

Downdraft– That's right- air moving downward. Cool air descends out of a storm, and where this happens you have a "downdraft".

Inflow– The part of a storm where warm air (that updraft again!) flows into it.

Outflow– Cool (sometimes downright cold) air flowing out of a storm (through downdrafts).

Core– Where the action is- like the core of an apple, but potentially much more hazardous to your health! Severe storms have highly focused areas where the storm is fed by warm air and large cumulus towers grow and join into the storm.

There are other weather words, such as cumulus and virga, which may look like Greek (actually Latin) at first sight, but they often have humble or poetic origins. Cumulus just means "heap" and refers to the clouds that heap up into the atmosphere (convective clouds); and "virga" is from the same root as "virgin". In effect it is "virgin" rain, rain that never touches the ground- it evaporates before it gets there.

are harmless. Skies that appear jumbled and chaotic, with a confusion of light and dark patches, may look ominous, but they are simply the result of sinking air (weak downdrafts) poking holes in the darker clouds. Although the entire sky seems threatening, no one part looks serious by itself. By comparison, a sky with large, discrete, focused elements is probably well-organized and bears watching. This kind of stormy sky will leave you with an impression of purpose, of an orderly, sculpted appearance that points to large-scale forces shaping the weather. What we want to do is learn to spot these "organized" situations and anticipate the changes that they foretell.

The severe storm

There's something different about a **severe** storm. You might think it's only a matter of degree– bigger, stronger, even blacker– but it's more than that. It takes a special, near-perfect situation to make it possible. Even with all the right conditions in place, a storm has to maintain a delicate balance between the warm air feeding it and the cold outflow air it creates. Too much cold air and the system chokes. Not enough and the warm air entering the storm (the inflow) lacks that extra little push it needs to maintain strong, focused updrafts. A balance– and you have a very organized, self-sustaining system that can survive for many hours and attain its maximum potential.

The balance can be disturbed too, causing the storm to weaken for awhile or even collapse. The most common cause is a lessening or cooling of the inflow. This can happen if the storm moves into an area already filled with cooler air, near a large lake or another

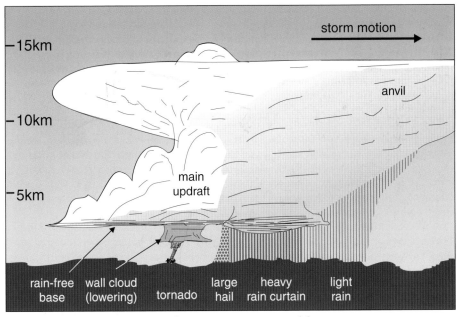

storm motion

15km

anvil

10km

main
updraft

5km

| rain-free base | wall cloud (lowering) | tornado | large hail | heavy rain curtain | light rain |

Severe storm structure and features
A simplified depiction of a single, intense thunderstorm cloud. To the right (north-to-east) are the anvil, rain and downdrafts, while to the left (south-to-west) is the the main updraft base, leading away from the storm's core. The updraft base, seen at a distance, is called the rain-free base because you can see under it. Lowerings form under the rain-free base near and to the left of the rain core at the warm-cool boundary between the outflow and the inflow feeding the updrafts. Most of the anvil streams ahead of the storm but in many cases a hang-back anvil shield is also present.

Other winds

Most of the wind damage you are likely to hear about will be related to one of the following words which you may encounter in the media or in a weather forecast.

Straight-line is the description given to any wind or wind damage when that wind was blowing in one direction. It refers to all wind effects except from tornadoes.

The **gust front** is the leading edge of cool air that comes down inside a thunderstorm and moves forward along the ground. It is present with most storms and is marked by a line of dark clouds, a sudden wind shift, and an abrupt drop in temperature. A very intense gust front can contain brief, weak tornadic effects from gustnadoes (see *Tornado types* in **Chapter three**) but these are rare.

A **downburst** is a strong, damaging wind caused by an intense downdraft inside a storm which reaches the ground and spreads out very rapidly. It can range from less than 50m (160ft) to over 16km (10 miles) wide and can persist from a few blocks to many kilometres before diminishing in intensity. Downbursts are usually accompanied by precipitation but can also occur without any, if the air under the storm is quite dry.

A **microburst** is a small downburst (less than 4km (2.5 miles) wide) and it is not likely to last more than a few minutes. Brief, localized pockets of straight-line wind damage are most often caused by microbursts. A large severe storm can contain many microbursts which re-form repeatedly. Each one may have several short swaths of damage with it. Damage is most likely with microbursts in a fast-moving worst-first storm (see page 75). Typical wind speeds are 80-130kmh (50-80mph) but can reach as high as 240kmh (150mph). Debris from these winds can show some twisting effects but is never carried more than a kilometre downwind.

A **derecho** is a special kind of long-lived intense storm in which repeated downbursts leave a long damage swath. Damage is often widespread and the storm may also contain all the other severe effects, including brief tornadoes.

storm. It can also happen because the storm is too successful– when a particularly strong phase is followed by a very large surge of rain and outflow, which undercuts the inflow source. Even local landforms can have an influence, sometimes aiding and at other times inhibiting a storm's smooth progress by distorting the low-level wind pattern. And even with perfect conditions down below, there is always the risk that general atmospheric conditions will not remain optimal for long.

Severe storms have several characteristics in common. They have long anvils, a clearly-defined core of heavy rain or hail, and a line or bank of clouds trailing away from that core. This "tail", as some people have called it, represents the axis along which warm air is channelled quickly and efficiently into the system. It is also the dividing line between the warm air ahead of the storm and the cooler air in its wake. Severe storms are also tall, but not necessarily large in extent. Instead, they are compact and energetic, with quick updrafts-downdrafts and a rapid cycling of air through the system. When you have a distant view, you can watch a single tower rise, merge, flare out, then drift downwind as part of the anvil plume in as little as 20 minutes.

Another interesting feature of most severe storms is the way they move. While the anvil streams forward with the flow aloft, the core of the storm will appear to shift constantly to the right (south) by comparison. This "right-turning" is the result of a very rapid rate of growth– so rapid, in fact, that growth toward the warm inflow outpaces the regular forward cloud motion. Storms are only able to do this if they have explosive updrafts (very unstable). This accounts for their ability to become and remain severe with minimal impact from nearby cold air.

A stormy day

The right day to watch

The best way to be prepared for a stormy day is to start the day before– by watching television!

Although individual thunderstorms can't be predicted as easily, the general conditions which make them likely are usually apparent beforehand. Tomorrow's weather in your area may well be on the news from localities to your west or southwest. Damaging storms and tornadoes are big news nowadays and you can turn this media obsession into something useful.

Many weather forecasts on television show the positions of fronts and low pressure areas as well as a bird's-eye satellite view of the cloud patterns. These patterns advance 300-500km a day (200-300 miles) in mid-summer and 500-1000km or more a day (300-600 miles) in spring and fall. In summer, most of the stormy days are initiated by cold fronts from the west or northwest. In the spring, however, many of the year's most destructive storms form as part of a deep low in mid-continent. Typically, the low draws warm, humid air north from the Gulf of Mexico, deepens rapidly and moves northeast toward the Great Lakes (usually near Lake Superior). You can see it on the satellite photo as a pronounced

Severe weather watches and warnings

Watches and warnings are issued by the weather office to help us anticipate and prepare for severe storms. **A watch** is issued if conditions are favourable for such storms, and it covers a large area for an extended period (often 6-8 hours). During this time, you should watch the sky and listen for updated information or warnings. Don't automatically assume that an expired watch means the threat is over– the timing may be off slightly or a revised one (that you didn't catch) may have been issued. **A warning** is issued when a severe storm has already formed and is approaching a locality. It covers a smaller area for a shorter period, usually around an hour or so. A **watch** means to keep a watch out for a storm or tornado and a **warning** means to take immediate action. Media reports frequently confuse the two and use them interchangeably.

Severe thunderstorm watches are more common than tornado watches and both include the threat of a severe weather event. The definition of "severe" varies slightly between Canada and the U.S. but generally includes hail larger than quarter-size, winds exceeding 90kmh (55mph) and/or wind damage, flooding rains, and tornadoes. Although tornadoes aren't mentioned specifically in a severe thunderstorm watch or warning, you should still consider them possible. If you are under a **tornado watch**, tornadoes are likely somewhere in your region later on. With a **tornado warning**, a tornado has been verified (either by a confirmed sighting or by a clear sign of rotation in the storm on a radar image) and you should take action. If the warning is for your specific location this means that you should seek shelter immediately. If it is for another location nearby it would be a good time to prepare ahead (see **Chapter four**) and watch the sky more carefully.

The media can't always be counted on to give us timely watches and warnings. It helps to own a Weatheradio receiver, an inexpensive unit that picks up the three weatherband frequencies used to broadcast watches and warnings as well as regular forecasts. Most localities have Weatheradio coverage now and the unit can be set to tone alert so that it only comes on when something important is being broadcast. Weatheradio is a great way to keep on top of fast-changing stormy weather. Let's all hope that this valuable service is not compromised by inadequate government funding!

"comma cloud," a long arched band of cloud with abrupt clearing behind it. This classic satellite pattern is often accompanied by a tornado outbreak and happens regularly each spring. The weather conditions that you will experience with its arrival are equally familiar– cool followed by rain, strengthening southeast or south winds, then abruptly warmer, changeable, and more humid.

The April 20th outbreak, for example, was preceded by **two** days of tornadoes across the Mississippi Valley and into the States of Illinois and Indiana. Anyone watching those news reports should have guessed that a big storm day might be in the offing a little farther east. This type of spring system is common to the eastern half of North America, especially the central and northeast regions. Northern regions also experience more summer severe weather resulting from cold fronts. Areas farther west, nearer the Rockies, are less dependent on large-scale weather systems for their storms and the causes are more diverse.

Getting a feel for the circumstances that can result in severe weather takes practice and attention. The clues are scattered here and there and it's up to you to put them together, because the forecast doesn't give you much to work with. If the morning forecast doesn't mention "severe" but includes words like "thunderstorms, possibly heavy" or "strong" or "with risk of hail and high winds," the potential exists and you should watch the activity later in the day.

Before the storm arrives

You don't need to be in the dark about stormy weather. Check the forecast regularly for updates. Watch the sky occasionally so that you are aware of the overall trend or anything unusual. Keep an eye out for the first signs of an anvil cloud overspreading your locality. Remember the typical cloud features and what changes you can expect. If you have a Weatheradio, check it to see if a watch has been issued and put it on tone alert in case something important is broadcast.

There's one other thing you can do to receive the very earliest indication of developing storms in your area. An ordinary AM-radio can become an inexpensive lightning detector if you tune it to static. It's as simple as turning the dial to the bottom or top end (wherever there are no stations) so that the only thing you hear is the occasional crunch from a lightning discharge. We (the authors) have used this handy monitor for many years to judge the distance and strength of storms– with incredible results. The interpretation is easy. A storm's distance from you is indicated by the loudness of the static, and a large amount of it means that there is lots of action around. Lightning bolts come across as short but harsh crunches, while the longer anvil flashes with thinner filaments sound softer. If all you hear is long, smooth static, the storm is well-aged and probably not very intense. You can't always count on lightning to tell you that a storm is severe (especially in spring, as the April 20th event showed) but when you do hear steady, rapid crunching or frequent short flashes with a sense of urgency to them, it's a sign that strong storms are out there.

An anvil cloud spreading ahead of a storm. The clarity of this western sky lets us see what's coming.

The sky darkens

It's a nice warm windy day outside. You feel good– relaxed– carefree. A prediction of rain later on seems very far off– maybe even unlikely. But then you sense the light changing inside the house. The brightness withdraws, slipping quietly from blues to whites to greys. A change is on the way and you sense your mood changing with it. A glance out the window to the west now reveals a darkening sky, and the first twinge of concern imposes its unwelcome presence. The weather has entered your private world and its outcome becomes your destiny.

A darkening sky. It's still too soon to tell what kind of storm is coming– but what emerges from the darkness will show you the answer.

Will you know what comes next? Despite all the possible variations and exceptions to the rule, there is a way to generalize your experience of a severe storm into two quite different progressions of sky change. They can be thought of as either "worst-comes-first" or "worst-comes-last", with "worst" referring to the potential for a damaging effect rather than how bad it looks. The one tends to arrive suddenly while the other comes on more gradually. Both are preceded by a thickening anvil (and often other lower clouds) before you notice any rain or thunder.

Worst-first storms carry the threat of damaging winds from **downbursts** or **microbursts** and large hail, but rarely tornadoes. When tornadoes do occur in them, they are usually brief and weak, and are located on the south or southeast side of the storm, right along the darkest clouds. A wall cloud structure is sometimes evident and there are often large chunks or rolls of very low scud trailing back into the rain from this lowered cloud base (see photos, page 78-79). These storms are more likely in the evening or at night, and during very humid conditions.

Worst-last storms are capable of producing very large hail and strong, long-lived tornadoes. When there is a tornado, it is usually preceded by hail, but not necessarily much wind. The tornado/wall cloud part of the storm may be separated from the visible precipitation by as much as 5km (3 miles), so you might be fooled into thinking that the tornado is not connected with an obvious storm and has arrived without much warning. Worst-last storms are most likely in the late-afternoon into the evening, and are not as likely at night.

A microburst lifts a plume of dust off the ground. A "rain foot" or a "dust foot" like this one can form at the leading edge of an advancing rain curtain and indicates brief, very strong winds.

When worst comes first

Worst-first storms are much more common, especially in summer. They account for the majority of non-tornadic (straight-line) wind damage events. When they approach, the sky darkens quickly as an ominous black cloud bank races toward you. Lightning bolts are common along this cloud bank, or just behind it in the heavy rain curtain. The largest hail, when there is any, occurs near the beginning of the storm. Winds are breezy southerly, and then become briefly calm. As this low cloud bank (the **gust front**) passes overhead, the temperature drops abruptly and a cold west to northwest wind sweeps in. When the gust front is separated from the rainwall, very strong winds may occur **before** the rest of the storm gets to you. At other times the strongest winds accompany the arrival of the heavy rain and the greatest risk for damage occurs within the deluge.

A powerful gust front surges to the right. The edge of the cold air has a very low bank of clouds along it, made lighter by skylight reflected from its forward surface. Behind this bank, after a short distance, is a wall of dust and heavy rain.

These winds originate inside the storm as a powerful downdraft that plummets to Earth and spreads out along the ground. When the entire downdraft is involved it is known as a downburst and can tear roofs off or topple trees in an area 1/2-1km (up to half a mile) wide by several kilometres long before weakening. In rare cases a storm does this repeatedly, creating a series of downdraft pulses which spread intermittent damage along a much longer path. Meteorologists call this a **derecho** storm. A smaller-scale wind effect, the microburst, can do the same type of damage over a smaller area– a few houses to a few city blocks in length. Once the first few minutes of heavy wind and rain have passed, conditions improve quickly. The thunder becomes more rumbly and protracted, and the steady rains peter out within an hour. There may be other storms later but they are not nearly as likely to be severe.

A squall-line is often made up of several such storms in a line, and a long gust front may join them all, dividing the warm air ahead of it from a large area of rain-cooled air behind it. If the gust front is wide and dark, with lots of lightning, a new storm is developing along the forward edge of older parts of the system. Cold air surges forward, plowing sharply into the warmer air. The system "grows" forward and the peak intensity is always near that forward edge. A severe storm maintains a balance along this boundary, but when it weakens the cold air becomes too dominant, pushing the gust front forward well ahead of the rain. Some of the most interesting cloud formations occur during this transition. (See the photo spread on pages 82-83.)

The highest winds along a gust front often form hunks of low cloud that look like teeth under the advancing cloud base.

This is a typical gust front in humid weather. It is a low cloud bank with smooth front edge, ragged base, and heavy rain and lightning right behind it.

When worst comes last

There is a certain logic to a worst-last experience– it feels so normal for a storm to begin gradually and wind up to a climax. That's because it happens regularly every summer with ordinary thunderstorms. But in the rare case when it is a severe storm, the worst-last scenario is much more dangerous– it may end with a tornado.

In worst-last storms there is a slow but steady increase in everything– the darkness of the clouds, the lightning and thunder, and the rain. As you watch these changes, keep tabs on how quickly the storm is approaching– some spring tornadic storms travel at 50-80kmh (30-50 mph)! When the rain begins it is light or moderate, but steady. The thunder is long and rumbly, but you may hear an occasional distant bolt too. Winds may be a bit gusty at first (during the rain), and they may turn briefly to the northwest or north, but they lighten up again soon after.

The next important change comes when the rain becomes heavy, possibly intermittently, and mixes with or changes to hail. This is a warning that the updraft region is getting nearer and you may now see a more concentrated darker area of cloud coming toward you. In very hot, humid conditions, large quantities of rain and hail may fall; but if you are in line for the storm's core, the rain eventually decreases and changes over to mainly hail. If the hail becomes larger and larger it will also end soon– but this is no time to become complacent! You are right at the strongest part of the storm, where most of the air is rising above you– to as much as sixteen thousand metres high (the top of the troposphere). Although the cloud base is black, you can probably see brighter sky beyond it. If a tornado risk does exist, a wall cloud will show you where the rotation is. (See *The wall cloud*, page 105) The air will be dead calm for this last few minutes. After the darkest clouds pass, the sky brightens rapidly– often becoming completely clear– and winds freshen from the southwest or west.

Put your weather knowledge to work for your community

Storms form, move, and change quickly. Their damaging effects are often too small-scale and brief to be accurately picked up by radar. The forecasters at the weather office need timely visual observations from the public to help them complete their task. To accomplish this they have set up a network of trained volunteers who provide a vital link in warning the public of threatening weather. Anyone with a keen interest in stormy weather and some basic training can participate. With the enthusiasm and weather knowledge you gain from this book, you may want to get involved. Weather can be exciting and rewarding. We have given you a start. You can build on it, try out your wings, and do something for your community while you are at it.

If you are interested in knowing more, your closest weather office can give you more information. In the U.S., ask about the Storm Spotters program, which is administered by the National Weather Service. Places with frequent severe weather have an active spotter network in which local sheriffs play an important role. When spotters are activated they are posted around communities, watching for signs of threatening weather. In Canada you can contact the Severe Weather Watcher Program, which is run by Environment Canada. These programs are administered locally or regionally and your enquiry will be forwarded to the right region. Representation from cities is already quite thorough but there's a great need to expand coverage in rural and remote areas.

Another very valuable volunteer contribution is provided by CANWARN (Canada) and SKYWARN (U.S.), independent networks of amateur radio operators. They conduct their own training and co-ordination and provide a professional weather-spotting and communications service for their communities in co-operation with the weather office. Their organized contributions can become crucial in severe weather outbreaks, during which they set up and maintain contact with emergency response groups.

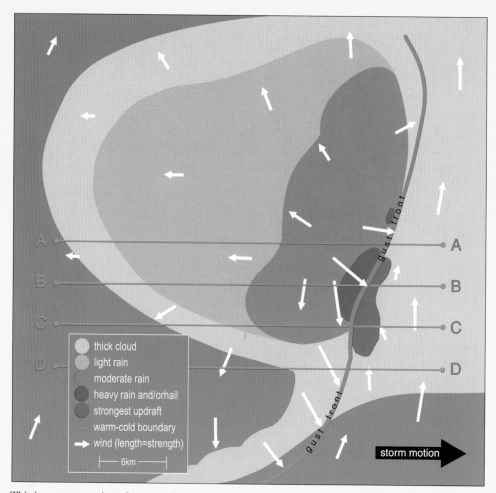

This is a representation of a worst-first storm, seen from above. The four paths through the storm, 3km (1.9 miles) apart, yield very different experiences.

A has few surprises.— The sky darkens as a line of clouds (the gust front) approaches quickly. As it passes overhead, a cool wind surges in. Within minutes, rain and thunder overspread you– but it's not too serious. Winds abate and the steady rain and rolling thunder persist for awhile, then peter out. It remains cooler but cloudy with light winds until the sky brightens in about an hour. This progression is typical of weaker storms as well.

B is a direct hit on the storm's centre.— This time, the gust front is wide and dark, with frequent bolts of lightning and a leaden wall of precipitation just behind it. The air goes calm briefly, then a cool wind sets in as the darkest cloud bank passes overhead. Winds may become very strong for a few minutes. Hail, large raindrops and lightning are soon followed by a blinding deluge. After about 5-10 minutes, winds abate and rains begin to ease and slowly wind down as it gets brighter. This is the classic example.

C is a near-miss nail-biter!— You see most of the storm's rain and lightning passing to your north– but a wide black base is coming toward you. The winds go dead calm as a large updraft base (sometimes with a lowering) passes directly overhead. Then a cool north wind arrives, along with a brief shower of large drops. Moderate rain and some lightning do follow but it's not as heavy or dark as you might have expected. Winds will turn and lighten, and rains will end fairly soon, followed by brighter sky. This example can resemble some tornadic storms and is capable of producing brief tornadoes or gustnadoes– so watch that lowering!

D is on the outside looking in.— A high anvil overcast gives way to a bank of darker clouds leading away from a storm passing you by to the north. All the blackest clouds and lightning are in the distance. Winds will lighten a bit, then turn and increase as the gust front passes, accompanied by a few drops of rain. The wind may precede the cloud bank. If this cloud bank is moving south as well, you may be in cool, windy conditions for a short while. The sky will clear quickly and winds will soon become lighter. Along this path you have a clear view of all important cloud features without any of the risks!

A typical worst-first storm in which the heaviest rain falls just behind the gust front because the newest updrafts (creating the heavy rain) are lined up along the forward edge. Farther back, rains thin out quickly. Notice the low scud forming where the moistened outflow begins to rise into the black updraft base, as well as the curved rain edge where strong outflow winds plow forward.

Compared with the small storm above, this massive severe gust front had a multi-tiered cloud wall followed closely by a damaging downburst and heavy blowing dust. Behind that there was baseball-sized hail and a torrential squall.

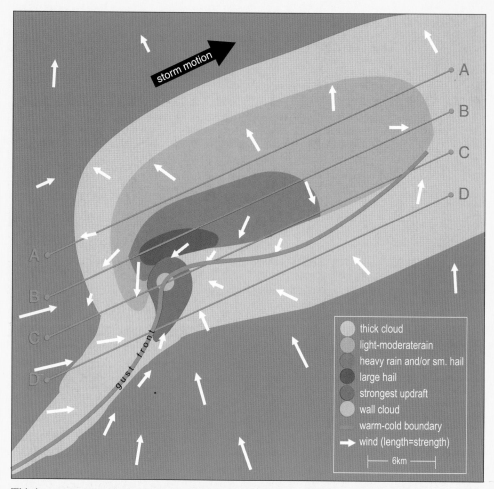

This is a representation of a worst-last storm, seen from above. The four paths through the storm, 3km (1.9 miles) apart, also yield very different experiences.

A is a no-nonsense encounter.— Rain and thunder begin gradually, level out at a moderate pace, then wind down. You won't see any big changes in wind, temperature, or dark clouds and will not be aware of what's passing to your south. You have no sense of severe weather nearby.

B is a classic progression with the works.— Rain and thunder increase gradually but steadily, from light to moderate to heavy with hail, then hail getting larger. After a bout of heavy hail, bolts, and a gusty wind followed by some residual rain, the sky brightens rapidly. You may see a dark area pass to your south but will not recognize it unless the precipitation is thin.

C will be the surprise of your life!— The storm begins the usual way, but you will soon notice that most of it is passing to the north. You may miss the precipitation or skirt it, getting into a brief shower of rain or hail (this part can range from nothing to heavy hail, depending on the storm's degree of right-turning). Winds are all over the place, becoming initially lighter, turning to the north briefly (sometimes gusty), then going calm. This calm should alert you to approaching danger. A pronounced dark cloud and lowering arrives next, and if there is a tornado, it will be here. Right after this lowering passes, a gusty north wind arrives, sometimes accompanied by light rain. (This part is also quite variable– some storms have nothing while others can have a brief, heavy deluge at this point.) The sky clears rapidly and after a brief quiet period, the wind strengthens from the southwest.

D is closer than it seemed.— A storm passes by to the north but there are initially no changes at your location. You see a dark sky pass by and have a clear view of the storm's lowered updraft base. Extending south from the storm is a dark cloud bank and, as it nears, the winds become lighter. They may go briefly calm when the line is overhead. The line passes, the wind shifts and increases, and the air cools a bit. It clears immediately afterward and becomes sunny, windy and drier. Without an awareness of storm structure, you will have no sense of severe weather nearby– unless a tornado was visible!

A worst-last storm is hard to illustrate because most of the earlier stages aren't very interesting or visually dramatic– all the action is on the back end! Here, looking north, the anvil, rain, and low clouds are at right while the newest updrafts at left are at the very back of the storm. Under the rain-free base (lower left) is a small lowering, indicating the site of the main updraft feeding the whole system.

In this view to the west, the anvil pokes out above a dark rain-free base on the south side of a heavy rain curtain. There are slight indications of cool outflow pushing forward at right, but the main area of interest is in the distance where a developing wall cloud sits under the cloud base. This is a close match to the diagram.

The gust front

This is the southern half of the gust front at the bottom of page 78. It is moving at about 100kmh (60mph) with winds almost twice that high. A slit between two of the forward-edge bands lets an odd light green colour through.

When the air is drier and/or the gust front moves along slowly, the cloud bank along it will not have a ragged bottom edge because the air is not forced upward quite so sharply. The bank is still lower and darker than the storm's base above it and can still be followed by heavy rain, but without strong winds.

This pair of photos shows a gust front before it arrives and after it has passed. Before its arrival you will see a dark cloud bank with a rough bottom edge coming quickly toward you. In the background is a wall of heavy rain to follow it. After a couple of minutes, this dark cloud line races past and you will briefly be in cool, windy conditions before the heavy rain

arrives. Looking at the backside of the gust front, you see a turbulent sky with a distinctly vaulted shape. This is because the forward (now distant) edge is the lowest part of it and the cloud base slopes upward behind it. This slope matches the shape of the forward-moving cool outflow air and the dark crinkles form in the warm air lifted along this boundary.

This low cloud bulge formed in response to a surge of cool outflow from the rain at right. It is lined with little "teeth" where the updrafts along the gust front are condensing some of the cool, moist air. These lower cloud tufts can be caused either by enhanced condensation (small patches of moister air drawn up into the cloud base) or by localized pockets of stronger lifting of air. The lower and thicker the teeth, the more likely a damaging microburst is.

Many gust fronts also extend well away from the heavy rain in a storm. Here, the storm in the distance has left a pool of cool outflow in its wake. This cool air is slowly moving to the right, preceded by a multi-layered gust front that has almost no convection (rising air) along it. The sky is clear ahead of and behind it, but the temperature will plunge as this cloud bank passes over.

Some gust fronts arrive unexpectedly far from the storm that formed them. Here, in dry air, only a thin line of clouds (at two levels) marks the arrival of cooler air. It wasn't long after this, though, that larger clouds grew quickly into new thunderstorms along this same innocuous axis!

What if you can't tell for sure?

This supercell storm is twisted around so that the wall cloud is close to the front of it, hidden just under the very low flange. It looks like a gust front, worst-first situation but has tornadic capabilities.

One of the wonders of skywatching is that there is infinite variety. But this means it's also difficult to set down hard and fast rules. We can give you guidelines, but please remember that for every rule there will be exceptions and use the knowledge you have gained from this book to interpret what you see in an open and flexible way, allowing for the exceptions to the rules.

A notable exception during very humid conditions is typified by the "Barrie tornado" (May 31, 1985) and by other strong tornadoes each year in the U.S. In these hybrid storms, high humidity causes very low cloud bases, which make the storm unusually dark and hard to see in. Also, large amounts of precipitation cause strong downdraft winds inside the storm, a bit like the worst-first case. However, it is structured like a worst-last example that has been twisted around, and the progression you experience changes. When these hybrid storms occur, the following tips may help you read them. If it only rains heavily where you are (no large hail), the main danger will pass to your south. But if you are destined to receive the tornado, it may be shrouded in low clouds and rain or hail. This can occur when powerful rotation drags some of the precipitation all the way around the tornado, blocking your view of it. When this happens, storm chasers say the tornado is "rain-wrapped." Fortunately, it is not very common! In the absence of clear signs of rotation or a tornado, be on alert if the winds become calm and the lowest, darkest clouds are on the south or southeast side of the rain and lightning.

The worst-first and worst-last distinction is far from perfect, but we hope it helps you observe and understand storms better. Regardless of what kind of storm is present, you can't go wrong if you pay attention to a few basic points that will apply to all storms. You should be most concerned about a severe weather threat when you see or experience the following (assuming no tornado is visible): the lowest, darkest clouds are rotating; or the air is calm underneath a large black cloud base attached to a storm nearby, especially if large hail has just ended. In addition, remember that the tornado often happens separate from the rain and lightning of a storm and is not preceded by wind as a warning sign. By contrast, a tornado is very unlikely when it is storming out in the usual sense– when heavy rain, wind, and lightning are under way.

A closer look

What can you learn from...

The common, recurring aspects of storms are usually harmless and we don't need to view them with fear or apprehension. Each one gives us another piece of the puzzle. The more we know, the better we can see the larger picture and recognize a storm's structure and potential dangers. The context of what we experience points to the trend in a storm and suggests what may come next.

The temperature

Around a storm, the only time the temperature drops is when there is cool outflow. This means that there is a large downdraft nearby. It may be right over you (raining hard out) or many miles away– but you will almost always see a gust front when the outflow arrives. On the south side of a storm, this transition to cooler air can happen with only a line of clouds and a brightening sky behind. Closer to the storm's core and to the north, it is usually accompanied by heavier precipitation.

When you feel the cool wind arrive, take a look around to see where most of the rain and lightning are. If they are well to your west, the storm is still coming, and you only need to watch it for worst-last clues. If they are to the north and you are underneath a dark base that doesn't seem to be moving through quickly, look west or southwest for any signs of a lowering on the base. In any case, if the air is much cooler than it was before the storm, the only threat possible is a few strong wind gusts from microbursts within the heavy rain.

Wind

There are two kinds of wind around a storm. The first is just that day's regular wind– which is usually southerly (from southwest through southeast) and warm. If you are closer to the storm's core, what the wind does depends on where you are relative to both the inflow (air rising into it) and the outflow (air descending out of it). The regular wind often strengthens as a storm approaches, becomes gusty, and backs slightly (turning from south to southeast, for example). This is because the storm's inflow turns the winds toward it a bit– a common occurrence just ahead of severe storms with rotation. The air flow over a region is altered by the presence of a strong storm and the closer it is to you, the more obvious it is that the wind is "pointing" to the main updraft. When this part of the storm comes nearer, winds slacken quickly and there is an eerie calm. Unless there is no wind anyway (as on a stagnant summer day), a calm under a storm– especially when accompanied by a broad black cloud above you– means that you are under the main updraft. If there is any rotation it will show up here! The danger passes again as soon as a cool breeze sets in.

The second kind of wind is the cool outflow that spreads out under the rain and moves away from the storm in every direction. On the forward-moving side of the storm it forms the gust front, and can be very gusty from the west or northwest. Inside the rain the wind constantly changes

When you see a line of scud or very low clouds under a stormy sky, it's most likely being pushed along by a cool outflow wind. The outflow can spread far from a storm too and arrive as a line of clouds in a clear sky.

direction, since it is pointing away from the main downdraft. The wind becomes lighter and moves gradually back to that day's regular wind when the storm's influence pulls away. A more persistent west to northwest wind prevails once the cold front passes, within a few hours.

Hail

Strong updrafts carry water droplets high up in a thunderhead, where they freeze. Many blow downwind in the anvil, but a few fall back down and grow larger by adding more layers of ice on the way. This forms a small hailstone, which usually melts by the time it reaches the ground, giving us a big cold raindrop. If the downdrafts are large and strong or it's a cooler time of year, the stones can survive all the way down. Small hail– whether you see the stones or not– is common in most storms.

If the updraft is stronger and more persistent, so that the small stones can cycle up and down a few times before getting too heavy, the hailstones may be larger. Once in a while this can be achieved by a storm with an intense, tall updraft but not enough organization to cause rotation. Areas near the Rockies have many of these tall hailstorms that do not contain tornadoes. But farther east, large hail is more directly associated with a well-organized storm and should be seen as a warning sign.

The only thing to consider with large hail is the progression from smaller to larger stones. The small ones are carried forward aloft and arrive earlier. The largest stones fall last, usually without any rain at all. The air will be calm. At that point you are already under the storm's main updraft and should check the dark base for any signs of rotation. The tornado can occur where a few stones are still falling, or it may come after a few minutes of nothing falling at all. Almost all tornadic storms have quarter-size or larger hail in them, but that hail may not always fall where you are. Your neighbour up the road could get the hail and miss the tornado while you miss the rain and hail and get the tornado!

Worst-first storms are most likely to have large amounts of small hail accompanied by rain and wind. On rare occasions they become violent storms– with very large hail and damaging winds. When this happens they can cause extensive crop and property damage. As with other worst-first examples, the greatest effect is early on and only lasts a few minutes at its worst.

Heavy lightning and thunder

Most of the intense lightning in a storm occurs just downwind of the main updraft, where a rapid transition from water to ice particles is under way high up in the cloud. The amount of lightning is proportional to the temperature that day, as well as the storm's size (height) and strength (rate of growth). Mid-summer storms may have more lightning than spring storms of the same size, but this doesn't mean that they are more severe. Many storms with lots of lightning are nothing more than flashy, noisy rainstorms.

The lack of lightning may lead you to assume that a storm is harmless– but that's not … wise. Highly organized severe storms are often characterized by a powerful updraft and very strong winds aloft. Both of these help to carry most of the effects of freezing well downwind before they begin to produce lightning. And because the lightning is so high in the cloud, much of it spreads as horizontal anvil flashes, rather than going to the ground as bolts. All these things may give you the impression that there is not much going on, or that the active part of the storm has passed you by. The lightning may be many miles to your northeast when the tornado is in the vicinity!

Long flashes with long rolling thunder are a sign of an aging storm because they occur in a large, spread-out anvil. The shorter quick flashes and bolts indicate new updrafts. If you can't tell where a storm's core is because of low clouds or rain, listen for the booms. If they come regularly from the same direction, that is where the centre of that storm is.

A lively electrical storm can be a frightening experience. The heavens crackle, the ground shakes– it seems as if everything will melt or explode any minute! But luckily the

Storms at night

A combination of bolts and internal flashes, accumulated on film, lights this storm up from top to bottom. Closer scraps of scud are backlit and dark. The lowest, thickest clouds (new updrafts) block the light and show up as a dark shadow at lower right.

The good news about storms at night is that, for most regions, they rarely bring tornadoes. This means that you don't have to worry or alter your habits just because a storm is raging outside. In those rare cases (usually in spring) when a tornado risk does exist, your best defense is a Weatheradio on tone alert and a keen ear. All the same trends and signs apply at night, so if you sense a worst-last situation you can use hail, the calm, and the rushing sound to warn you. But it's much more likely to be a worst-first event with all the strong winds coming in a brief burst near the beginning. The roar of the wind can be rattling– and can cause damage at times– but it doesn't have the same impact on your personal safety as a tornado would.

Lightning dominates the stormy night sky, so use it to advantage. The light from lightning is a great illuminator and you can see many cloud details with it. Ragged scraps below a gust front are often clearly backlit and you can watch their changes (rising, increasing, and moving forward) with repeated flashes. A large updraft base will show up as a dark region, and if a lowering is present it will be a bowl-shaped "dark hole" through which no light passes. If most of the sky is bright with lightning and it's raining out, then there is nothing around that matters.

bark is worse than the bite. You are safe in your cars and homes to watch the spectacle– the dance of a billion billion excited atoms tracing their collective energy across your view. And in the dark of night, lightning becomes your visual guide to the stormy sky.

Low ragged clouds

Most of the lowest clouds you see around a storm are being pushed here and there by outflow. They move quickly, but in a straight line with the local winds near the ground. These clouds appear any time a pocket of moist air (from nearby rain) is forced to rise and condense. The extra moisture in this air allows condensation to occur at a lower height than usual, giving us the foggy scraps and lumps of cloud below the other cloud layers.

If you see low cloud scraps forming in mid-air, check to see whether they are drifting along horizontally or are rising to meet an existing dark cloud base above them. When air is drawn into strong updrafts, the moisture in it condenses into these low fragments below the cloud base, so they are handy markers to the strongest developing

Irregular scraps of scud under a dark storm base will look light or dark depending on the background they are seen against.

clouds around us. Sometimes these rising fragments form brief pointed tufts that look like funnel clouds but aren't. (See False funnels, page 109.) You will see this most often on damp, unstable days and along the forward edge of a gust front, near the rain. The ragged cloud base tells us that the cold air surging forward is also rising into the updrafts along the gust front. In general, very low scud and persistent hunks of cloud below a strong gust front with a worst-first storm indicate an intense downburst or microburst. These irregular low clouds form as the outflow winds increase, and evaporate as they weaken again.

This gust front has just passed overhead and is plowing forward, forming very low scud that rises into the dark cloud base.

The wall cloud is a special example of air rising and condensing below a storm. In this case the updraft has a spiralling motion (rotation) and this forms a more complete, sometimes circular cloud structure. A solid, persistent lowering forms under the main updraft in many strong storms. But when there is enough moisture and some rotation, the more pronounced and circular wall cloud that often precedes a tornado can form. (See **Chapter three** for more details.) Even if you don't see a distinct wall cloud structure, watch the lowest scraps for signs of rotation and the formation of a true smooth-edged funnel cloud. With a backlit distant view these features look black, but when you are looking up close into the dark base of the storm these fragments appear as a relatively lighter grey.

What does it mean if you see...

A green sky

According to popular wisdom, a green sky is a guaranteed warning sign for severe weather. In the media it ranks right up there with "the roar" and "big hail" as a certain sign of trouble! But is it reliable? How likely or necessary is it and where does that strange colour come from?

The colour green comes from blue and yellow, so let's look around the stormy sky for examples of these. You will need radar vision (a good imagination) because you need to see beyond all the low clouds– high in the troposphere– where the storm cloud stands like a creamy-yellow mountain in a deep blue paradise. Light from various parts of this view filters down through the cracks and thinner parts of the storm and arrives at your eyes as a pale-green hue. The cloud screens out more of the red portion of the spectrum of skylight,

The most common "green sky" around storms is a pale greenish-yellow, most often seen with turbulent cloud features. These are on the storm's north or east side, where small downdrafts break up the usual dark base. How green it looks is quite subjective and is affected by the other light and colours in the sky. In this example, a weak gust front (distant left) has moved far from the rain (right of view), leaving a chaotic-looking but harmless cloud sheet in its wake.

resulting in a green-blue tint at the cloud base. The vertical structure of a thunderstorm works with the highly contrasty cloud features nearby to allow you to see this effect. The sky's darker cast probably helps to accentuate the green colour too.

There are three shades of green you can look for. The most common is a pale green-yellow that accompanies textured or turbulent-looking low anvils and regions of outflow around a storm. These are usually seen on the north side of the storm, with or near the precipitation. A darker pea-soup shade of green can sometimes be seen in the middle of a storm when low, dark clouds and heavy rain or hail are nearby. Both of these are relatively common. Once in a while you may catch sight of a rarer pale-green or bluish-green glow that has a phosphorescent quality. This time the colour is very pure– beautiful but strange! It can occur whenever there is a small hole in the updraft base (caused by a narrow downdraft) or when there is a slit or thin clear layer between separate sections of cloud. (See photo at left.)

Is a green sky a sign of stormy weather? Yes– because it can only happen with dense, dark clouds. Only a large three-dimensional storm cloud is thick enough to filter the light coming down through it in this way. Is the green a necessary precursor to a severe storm or tornado? No. These green effects are mostly on the north half of a storm and the tornado is on the south side– so you can easily get the one without seeing the other, even though both may be present in the area. The green colour tells us that a storm cloud is here, but not how intense it is. Some severe storms– especially in heavily overcast situations with many cloud layers about– will not show any green at all. You are better off not to generalize or assume that there is a connection. Rely instead on the other features we have discussed.

Weird clouds

Many people said that it was the "weird clouds" that tipped them off on April 20th. So what makes clouds look different enough to make us take notice? Rarity is certainly one aspect that piques our interest– if we rarely see certain shapes or colours, they seem abnormal and out of place against an ordinary day's weather. In the storm environment the clouds spread themselves out in layers, as well as growing upward. The air is going up and down everywhere; and this creates a broken sky of varying element sizes, and light

A stormy sky with backlit parts, front-lit low clouds (reflected light) and an uneven baseline with many holes will look weird because of all the strange colours in it.

coming through between dark patches. The sky is full of chaos and contrast under a storm because the turbulent winds jostle cloud elements around. Some people also associate a pink-black combination with storms. This is because it is sometimes possible to see up through the cracks in a storm's dark base to the pinks and oranges above.

Another "weird" thing about storms is the way they can control the air flow and shape clouds on a small scale. The air around them not only rises and sinks– it twists and spirals to form tubes and tufts of cloud, and converges and diverges to create bands or slivers of cloud and clear sky. What could be weirder than the "spaceship" storm (next page)? When you see these strange, discrete formations you know that something up there has taken control. And in most cases, the stronger the storm, the more obvious its control over the air flow pattern. The results are fascinating to watch– but before you jump to conclusions, test what you see against what you know of a storm's structure and features.

The base of this unusual storm is sculpted into a compact structure by the tightly-wound updraft. Inflow air spirals as it rises and forms a banded lowered base. Higher up, successive updraft bursts emerge as towers which rise rapidly to form distinct steps in the flared-out anvil above them.

Swirling motion

Small swirls happen all the time around clouds and are almost always harmless. Many are caused by downdrafts and appear to swirl counter-clockwise as you look up at them. Many others are near the ground during windy conditions and you can only see them when the clouds are very low. There is also a bit of spin associated with many updrafts, and dark cloud bases often have tufts extending from them. These move clockwise but are always brief, scrappy, and small enough not to be mistaken for the rotation that precedes tornadoes.

How can you figure out what kind of swirling motion matters? First, look for the true base of the storm, so that you can rule out any loose low clouds that aren't connected with it. Then, if you see scraps of cloud attached to or just below this base, check to see if they are moving clockwise (as you look up). If they are significant you will see, not only the circular motion, but fragments of cloud forming in mid-air and rising to join in. If it is true storm rotation, this swirl will not be confined to a single spot but will look more like a circle around which the fragments move slowly. When you see an increase in this motion and/or expanding of the cloud fragments into a fully-formed wall cloud, you are already too close to danger and should take action. Don't let the apparent slow motion fool you– at cloud base the speed can easily be over 100kmh (60mph). Wall clouds are, on average, 1-2km in diameter (up to a mile), so a complete revolution at this speed can take from two to three minutes.

You can't easily see rotation at a distance. You will need to infer it from the cloud features. When you do see it, watch carefully to determine whether there is clockwise motion accompanied by rising cloud fragments. And if the whole cloud seems to be rotating– especially if it is a low hunk– beware! Steady rotation in a wide circle is the most reliable indicator of a potential tornado.

Clockwise swirling motion under a lowering beside the rain core is worth watching. Note the eerie green hole.

The severe weather threat

When it comes right down to it, most people would consider the tornado to be the biggest threat in a storm. Tornadoes are violent, destructive, costly and completely out of our control. The tornado is no accident, though. It is part of a highly organized storm with visible features that we can all learn to recognize. Tornadoes are rare and very unlikely compared with other storm damage effects. Don't be paranoid about every storm. Most of the people who have spent their whole lives in the American "tornado alley" haven't even seen one themselves. The most probable experience any of us will have is a few minutes of intense wind in a downburst.

Storms hold two other dangers that are easy to overlook– flooding and lightning. Flooding is the number one weather-related killer each year in North America. Flash floods form and move very rapidly. Water on the move has incredible force and no person or vehicle can stand firm against it. It only takes a few feet of fast-moving water to carry a car off a road and downstream. Never take the chance of driving through what may well be deep and fast-moving water across a roadway.

Lightning is also very costly each year– in deaths from strikes and in house fires. Bolts can occur "out of the blue" miles from the storm, catching people by surprise. Lightning travels great distances through water, and a far-off strike can paralyze swimmers before they have time to return to safety. Almost all lightning strike victims can be completely revived with prompt CPR. At home, the risk is not so much from the strike itself as from the fires that might follow. You are most vulnerable while asleep, but storms usually announce themselves with enough thunder to bring any problems to your attention.

Your risks from weather hazards depend on where you are, and are discussed in detail in **Chapter eight**. Each region has its own story to tell. Spring tornadoes are generally more intense than summer ones, but regions near the Canada-U.S. border are more likely to experience tornadoes in the summer. Storm types also vary from one region to the next. Mid-western storms are more frequently severe and are easier to see and study, but the drier air makes certain low cloud features less likely.

In this chapter we have given you a whirlwind tour of the stormy sky. There's lots to see and know but for the most part it comes down to a few simple things. Follow the progression of changes in approaching clouds and watch for the key signs. Take note of the easiest things– what the winds are doing, which direction the clouds are moving from and where the storm is likely to move. Always ask yourself where the storm's main inflow base is and whether the sky looks organized. Chances are, if it looks like an ordinary mess with no real design or purpose, it probably is.

We have all grown used to the idea that weather is unpredictable and our guess is as good as anyone else's. Although many of our assumptions are rooted in fact, they have long been removed from their original context and now reside largely in our fantasies. It is easy, for instance, to take our experience of the last bad storm and build an expectation of danger from the wrong parts of it. Bits and pieces of that previous experience are lifted from their true context and now float around in our memories, waiting to affirm the things we see on the next big storm day. The shadowy impressions of our previous fears become the facts in our present understanding. After the April 20th tornadoes we saw many examples of this– dark clouds, high winds, etc.– where people lived in fear because they could not distinguish between ordinary non-threatening situations and the genuinely risky ones.

Nobody wants to live with a fear of the unknown. Thanks to Doppler radar there are more warnings than ever before these days, but many of them don't result in a confirmed event. If we had to spend an hour in the basement for every warning we heard, our lives would be disrupted so often that we might start ignoring them. With a little knowledge and attention to the changes in the sky, we can learn to interpret weather forecasts and warnings in the light of the local conditions we are experiencing. Before we reach the point where we respond with indifference to weather warnings, let's reduce our dependency on them and temper our fears and uncertainties– by learning to read the stormy sky.

THE JOYS OF SKYWATCHING

Let's put aside our weather dislikes and fears for a moment. Let's forget all those dreary rains, snowstorms, and dull cloudy skies. Let's skip the analysis and the knowledge too— and just indulge in a purely pleasurable fantasy about clouds.

Remember those childhood dreams? Clouds were the playthings of our innocent minds. Our searching thoughts made them come alive. Our eyes roamed the sky, drawing in the light energy to feed a hungry imagination. The world was our oyster, and— whether we knew it or not— the sky was its pearl of dreams for us.

Like clouds on a windy day, the years passed before our eyes. Memories have come and gone, leaving traces behind to brighten another day. Each of us has that favourite sunset with a crimson charisma that holds us in awe at the sensual delights of sky. That's where it all begins— with simple appreciation, with the free-dom to feel it in our bones. Those feelings open the door to another world, to a place inside where clouds bring smiles and smiles bring peace.

Let's add a little spice to season our simple pleasures with a richer, heightened vision of the world of weather. A sharper mind's-eye view of sky yields a higher level of appreciation. When we learn to read the clouds we begin to see with dis-cerning eyes— see cause and effect, see motion, evolution, growth, transformation— see the meaning of things, the bigger picture.

After a while the wisdom of experience settles in. We gain perspective, balance. It fine-tunes our senses. It provides both pleasure and knowledge with every glance, any time, any place. The sky becomes a boundless source of inspiration— instant images for our emotions to indulge in, our minds to explore. That's the reason to be a skywatcher. And in the process, we renew our connection to nature and open our spirits to the splendours of our planet.

The practical value of skywatching becomes no longer our motive but our reward— the natural result of many hours spent enjoying our pursuit of the sky's mysteries. Getting into the habit for pleasure means that we will be watching when it counts for our safety, too. Knowledge engenders confidence and confidence brings us security. What we know can protect us, but it also lessens the burden of uncertainty. There will always be questions and surprises in store for us. But the surprises will please, will tickle our curiosity, instead of victimizing us. We will be able to view even the worst weather as part of a greater good. We 'll look past a grey overcast to the sunshine beyond. Our imaginations will sail like birds among the clouds and their secrets will be exposed by our renewed respect and appreciation for their pleasures.

The weather is not a forecast or an inconvenience to grumble at. It is molecules dancing, winds painting pictures with light, air building mountains. It's the Earth breathing— and God speaking. Clouds are a mere fog of vapours and crystals— yet they become patterns of precision and order. They are the illusion of simplicity— fan-tastic forces cloaked in the familiarity of an everyday sight!

3
The anatomy of a tornado

What do you think of when you hear the word "tornado"? Is it a distant memory from *The Wizard of Oz* or an action clip from *Twister*? Is it a news account of an unlucky town far away or the vivid recollection of your own personal encounter? We all have a ready supply of images and emotions when we hear that word.

A tornado is an unusual sight– a strange phenomenon that seems out of place among the other clouds in the sky. Across the spectrum of weather events, it is the most intense, most focused force on Earth. But it isn't something abnormal or bizarre. It's simply the extreme endpoint of a process in the atmosphere that serves us well in every other respect– the balancing act we know as weather.

Tornadoes are still largely a mystery to meteorologists. They know what they can do and when they are most likely, but not that much about **how** and **why**. Much of what is known has come from observing them. More than any other weather phenomenon, a tornado demands our watchful attention, because it is truly beyond detection by other means.

Our impressions and assumptions about tornadoes can easily be distorted by media accounts or our own particular memories. What we have seen or heard about may be true– but it may be only one of many truths. Tornadoes come in many shapes and sizes and can change quickly from one to the next.

Over their lifetimes, the April 20th tornadoes displayed many of the variations in how tornadoes look and behave– more than are commonly available in a single outbreak. Coupled with that, many of the victims had also experienced a very different tornado outbreak in 1985. In the sections to follow we explore what is known about tornadoes, separating myth from fact and emphasizing what you can learn from watching them.

Naming the beast

What shall we call it– tornado, twister, or just plain trouble!? As far back as the 14th Century, the term "whirlwind" was used to describe all rotating wind structures. A few centuries later the Spanish word for thunderstorm, *"tronada"*, became the basis for several variations on "tornado" which were used for a long time to describe the vicious, but not necessarily rotating, storms that sailors encountered while traversing the oceans. Eventually, our word "tornado" took on its current, more specific meaning, starting in North America. "Twister" is a colloquialism for tornado that originated in Mississippi and is used widely today. Some people think that a twister looks different and is worse than a tornado, but there is no difference between the two. One is simply a popular expression for the other. And only the word "whirlwind" has had a long association with **rotating** storms.

A few other words have been used incorrectly in place of tornado, most commonly "cyclone" and "hurricane". Both of these refer to a large circulation (hundreds of kilometres across) and not to the small vortex of a tornado. "Cyclone" is a descriptive term which has been widely used for any large, rotating weather system and was quoted frequently in media accounts of any damaging windstorm until a few decades ago. A "hurricane" is a large, destructive, but compact weather system originating in the sub-tropical ocean. Public familiarity with this term instead of "tornado" has allowed its incorrect use to continue even today.

Getting to know tornadoes

What is it?

A tornado is defined as a violently rotating column of air that is in contact with the ground and extends from a convective cloud, usually a thunderstorm. If it is not in contact with the ground it is called a funnel cloud. Most tornadoes have a visible funnel-shaped cloud with them but there is some confusion about the use of the term "funnel". Some people use it interchangeably with "tornado"; others call any tapered, pointed cloud a funnel. It is important to distinguish between a true funnel cloud, which is a precursor to a tornado (See also *False funnels*, page 109.) and the funnel-shaped cloud (the condensation funnel) which is the visible part of an existing tornado.

Spinning air creates smooth, simple shapes. But this "simple" appearance betrays a very complex structure and air motion within it. The moving air in a tornado is not always visible, however. What we see as the tornado is cloudy air that has condensed in this spinning column. Sometimes you can see the entire tornado but often it is only partially visible, even though its influence is present all the way to the ground. You don't have to see it for it to be there, but usually there will be a visible funnel shape and/or a dusty debris cloud on the ground with it.

Myth

Tornadoes won't strike twice— Along with "they won't follow the same path" and "they will follow the same path", this is an assumption we want to make to give a sense of order to this phenomenon. Tornadoes are no more inclined to avoid anything than to accidentally or deliberately select a path or location to strike. If a place is hit twice it's pure coincidence. A one-in-a-million chance will happen somewhere, sometime for one in every million opportunities— and that one becomes the one we have a hard time believing!

Characteristics in brief

The table below gives rough figures for tornado characteristics so that you will have a better sense of how variable their appearance and impact can be. Size and strength can change from one minute to the next. A tornado's shape ranges from a slender tube to a tapered cigar to a wide trunk or wedge, and what you see will depend on how much condensation and debris is present. For a detailed look at all the possibilities, see Rogues Gallery, page 120-121. Size and duration are loosely linked to strength– strong tornadoes are more likely to be large and long-lived– but there are exceptions which may fool you. The notion that a sleek, slender tornado is not worth worrying about could be a serious miscalculation!

Tornado characteristics

	weak (F0-F2)	typical (F1)	strong (F3-F5)
size (diameter/path width)	16-91m (17-99yd)	44m (48yd)	165-454m (180-496yd)
duration (path length)	0.48-3.5km (0.3-2.2miles)	1.57km (1.0miles)	10.82-37.50km (6.8-23.4miles)
strength (wind speed)	64-251kmh (40-157mph)	147kmh (92mph)	252-509kmh (158-318mph)

Adapted from Grazulis

Effects

When you think of strong wind you probably imagine air moving with force against an object. The variety of damage effects with a tornado suggests something much more complex. If you could slice horizontally through a tornadic vortex you would see a hollow structure– a ring of very strong winds surrounding a relatively calm region in the centre. What happens in the dead centre depends on the size and strength of the tornado but can vary from descending air, to a calm, to rising air. In most cases, though, the strongest effects are around the outside edge.

Within this ring of winds are smaller ribbons (jets) or spirals (vortices) which are very intense. They form and vanish regularly in response to rapid changes in the pressure field, which is the originating force of the air motion. The suction, pressure effects, and rhythmic pulsing all result from this very tightly-wound pressure gradient. Although some of the principles behind this process are known, we can't analyze what's going on inside a tornado because it is too difficult to get in there to take measurements!

Close to the tornado, near the ground, the air is drawn toward the vortex. It rises in a spiral motion and its abrupt ascent causes the pulling or suction we associate with tornadoes. When you watch the debris stirred up at the ground you can see the material rising and rotating– but in a very controlled way. There is a distinct outer edge to what is swirling around, because the ring of winds holds everything together as it draws the material skyward.

Can tornadoes be predicted?

The short answer is no. Using past records we can say that certain regions and times of year have a higher probability of a tornado occurrence. This means that a given area's chances of having one are known, but it says nothing about exactly when or where. We also know that certain weather conditions favour severe storms which can occasionally produce a tornado. This means that we can forecast the possibility a day or two in advance, with an even clearer estimate of the likelihood of an occurrence a few hours ahead, as the supporting atmospheric conditions become more apparent. But even the best forecast cannot tell us exactly where storms will form or which storm will spawn a tornado. All the prediction tools we have– including longe-range forecasts and the Farmer's Almanac– only give us a general idea of what is to come. We have to wait until a storm forms and becomes severe before we can begin to assume that it has tornadic potential.

It isn't true, however, that tornadoes are unpredictable. Tornadoes only strike without warning if we are inattentive to changes in the weather. The warning signs will be there for anyone who knows what to look for and stays alert. The maximum warning time we can expect is about a half-hour. The tornado circulation is a very small feature and progresses quickly from inception to maturity. Fortunately, it is preceded by certain storm characteristics, and in this sense a tornado can be predicted to occur just before it appears. The tornado is the culmination of an ordered sequence of changes that we can watch for and recognize in the sky. In observing a storm, your perceptive eyes will be the most reliable predictor you can count on.

The F-scale to measure damage

In North America, the degree and type of damage that a tornado inflicts on buildings is used as a measure of its strength. This "F-scale" (developed by Dr. T. Fujita, a renowned meteorologist) is now used widely because it is simple and catchy. It allows us to put a decisive label on an otherwise complex, elusive event. In a way, once we have rated a tornado, we derive a sense of certainty from doing so which helps to contain the many uncertainties that a closer look would inevitably reveal.

The F-scale has a few disadvantages too. Since it depends on man-made structures it can't be used unless buildings are affected; and judging the extent of structural damage and the sturdiness of a building's construction is a very subjective procedure that only provides a rough measure of impact. Some attempts have been made to develop an alternative rating system, with more emphasis on tree damage, but they all failed because trees are even less predictable than buildings. For a system to work with the fewest ambiguities, it has to be as inclusive of all events as possible.

The F-scale

	% of all	desc.	mph	kmh	damage
F0	29	weak	40 to 72	64 to 115	LIGHT: light damage to chimneys, tree branches broken, weak-rooted trees pushed over
F1	40	weak	73 to 112	116 to 179	MODERATE: barns & garages heavily damaged, roof surfaces peeled, mobile homes overturned, telephone poles snapped, moving cars blown off road
F2	24	strong	113 to 157	180 to 251	CONSIDERABLE: large trees snapped or uprooted, roofs torn off frame homes, barns swept away, mobile homes demolished, small flying objects
F3	6	strong	158 to 206	252 to 330	EXTREME: roofs & some walls off well-built homes, most trees uprooted, cars thrown, trains flipped
F4	~1	violent	207 to 260	331 to 416	DEVASTATING: well-built homes levelled, desbris carried some distance, large flying objects
F5	~0	violent	261 to 318	417 to 509	INCREDIBLE: steel-reinforced concrete structures badly damaged; everything else destroyed and/or carried away
F6	0	violent	319 to 379	510 to 606	INCONCEIVABLE: complete destruction: unlikely to be descernable from F4-F5 damage nearby

Note: The damage descriptions are adapted from the original Fujita scal and include modifications suggested in Significant Tornadoes Vol. 1 (Grazulis).

The "F6" tornado (510-606kmh/319-379mph) probably exists only in the imagination, because to date no winds have been measured this high (the maximum was 459kmh/287mph). And since F-scale winds are estimates based on observed damage, it is unlikely that the F6 rating could ever be verified. It's doubtful that we could distinguish F6 damage in a given location from nearby F4-F5 damage. Winds over 440kmh (275mph) are likely to cause complete destruction anyway.

There's another, more important concern about this system. The rating applies to the maximum damage anywhere along a tornado's path. If one house is deemed to have sustained F3 damage, then the tornado becomes an F3 even if it spent most of its time as a much weaker F1. This, in turn, tends to over-rate the damaging effect of tornadoes and it encourages a higher damage mindset in the public. Tornadoes are trouble enough without overrating their impact! If we see them all as violent or deadly (and most aren't) then we may feel a sense of despair or concern which robs us of our ability to take control of our own destiny in a weather crisis.

Using the F-scale is convenient and simple– maybe a little too simple. We have reduced the tornado to a rating which does no justice to its complexity and uniqueness. Instead, it puts all the emphasis on a tornado's destructive impact. What begins as a true marvel of nature can become just another disaster-reporting obsession for the media to feast upon.

Myth

Everything about a tornado is unpredictable— Many people believe this. "It kind of went helter-skelter just about any-where it wanted to go. Plus it didn't have a distinct path– it rose up and then it dropped down again. And there didn't seem to be any rhyme or reason as to why it came down where it did, or went through where it did." This is what it feels like as we are watching– but it doesn't hold up under scrutiny. Most of it is a projection of our own uncertainty. We tend to magnify (out of proportion) the small exceptions and deviations we notice in a tornado's shape and movement. If we strip out our personal reactions, most of a tornado's behaviour is surprisingly orderly and predictable.

Vacuum cleaner or blender?

Searching for an analogy that does justice to a tornado's unusual force is no easy task. The most obvious impacts– spinning and suction– may lead you to think of a tornado as a giant blender or vacuum cleaner. Is this comparison realistic or absurd– and can it help us understand the risks involved?

A vacuum cleaner draws air in at one end by first pushing the air out the other end. In a way, that is what seems to be going on in a tornado too– the air is drawn in and is channelled up the column into the storm. When the suction force on an object is too great it gives way and sails off. This might suggest that all we need to do is get a sturdy grip on a solidly anchored object and hold on– but it is not as straightforward as that. The wind force that tugs at you is more like fingers than a fist. It can grab hold of an object by seek-ing out its handles– any small variation in shape, any loose part that gives it some-thing to grip. At high speed, air can behave like a solid in strength and like fine thread in its dexterity.

When you see a building taken apart by a tornado and all the pieces scattered around, you might think that a blender analogy is appropriate. The debris left behind is shredded and strewn about as if it had been scrambled to pieces. Video images of a barn being hit reveal a different process. The building appears to explode, but a closer look shows that the pieces are separated or broken apart in rapid succession. Neither the suction nor the scrambling are obvious here– the whole thing has a neater, more controlled appearance.

Even though these analogies are not scientifically accurate, they may help you wrap your mind around the degree of force and destruction tornadoes can bring. If you can imagine being a speck of dust inside a blender or vacuum cleaner, you can begin to appreciate the powers at work. A tornado is an incredibly potent phenomenon, and it shouldn't be compared with ordinary strong winds.

Origin and life cycle

Before a tornado can occur, the atmospheric conditions must be right for it. (See **Chapter two.**) The updrafts and downdrafts that accompany convective clouds can interact to form brief, weak tornadoes in isolated storms in a variety of situations. If the instability is very great– as when heat and moisture build up under an inversion– all the pent-up energy can be released in an explosive outburst. This forms a near-perfect severe storm (a **supercell** thunderstorm) which has the potential to produce long-lived, damaging tornadoes. When this condition affects

A supercell storm is very powerful and efficient. This is evident here by the high anvil (note fine detail) and short updraft base– both indicating that air drawn into the storm rises abruptly and rapidly to great heights. Notice, too, that there are no lower clouds outside of the storm due to sinking air surrounding the storm's big updraft core. A tornado had been seen about a half-hour earlier.

a large area, bringing an active weather system and warm, humid air together, we may experience a tornado outbreak from numerous supercell storms along a potent squall-line.

Tornado types

The definition of a tornado has come out of what it does and, consequently, what it looks like and what its impact is on us. If we knew more about how and why they formed we could probably redefine tornadoes into several classes to account for different circumstances

 ## Other kinds of whirls

Since air is a fluid (does that surprise you?), it responds readily to the forces in nature. It is easily moved about, and changes in its density by warming or cooling set it into motion. Where there are air currents there are also boundaries between them and the airstreams (usually of different densities) exert a force on each other. The laws of physics come into play and a circulation forms. These vortices are an efficient way of handling the forces present, and whirls of varying sizes– from microscopic to continental in scale– exist in our atmosphere.

On the grand scale there are large swirls– low pressure areas, cyclones, hurricanes– while on the small scale there are dust whirls on the ground or tiny "vortlets" in clouds. Most are not visible, but when they happen in something that we can see, these vortices reveal themselves. Uneven heating of the ground can initiate a dust devil, which looks a lot like a gustnado except that it only happens in sunny weather. Fire whirls over forest fires, steam devils over warm water in winter, and snow devils are only a few of the many other vortices we might encounter. Many of the same principles that operate in these harmless rotating structures also contribute to a tornado's circulation. Just as there are scales of size, there are scales of strength and the tornado is certainly the most concentrated whirl imaginable!

A dust devil

and degrees of impact (risk). This would help to separate the relatively rare but very important strong tornadoes that truly threaten life and property from the more common weaker ones. Until then, "tornado" is a general term and the only way we can tell if we should be concerned is by knowing all the likely situations and which ones to watch out for.

There are three tornado variations which have been named and defined as separate entities because they are weaker and do not behave like most serious tornadoes. They are described here, but in the rest of the chapter we will concentrate on "strong" tornadoes–those which have the greatest impact.

The waterspout

Any tornado over water is currently considered a waterspout, and this poses a problem. How can we tell if what we see over the water is a "typical" waterspout– a weak, thin vortex under a large cumulus cloud or small thunderstorm– or a regular tornado that happens to be over water? The only way is to look at the situation. If it is a relatively thick, large funnel and/or is attached to a well-developed severe storm, then it is a tornado in every sense and would be just as dangerous as if it were over land. More probably, though, the waterspout will occur over warm water in summer or fall and live out its life there.

Most waterspouts are weak tornadoes that rarely come onshore and do not persist over land. They can most often be seen in cool spells over the Great Lakes in late-summer and fall, and off the southeast coast of the U.S. during fair days with strong vertical cloud development. In extreme cases, winds can exceed 160kmh (100mph), causing damage, but most waterspouts are more a marine nuisance than a serious threat.

The landspout

The same situation that causes waterspouts can result in cold air funnels over land. These rarely touch down, but if they do they are very weak and brief. This landspout tornado type is like a waterspout over land but it also forms during the summer half of the year in warm, unstable weather under very strong updrafts. They most often occur along and just east of the Rockies, under large cumulus clouds or the rain-free updraft base of a thunderstorm. They are rare in eastern regions. Landspouts don't always have a full condensation funnel and they are sometimes only made visible by the dust they stir up.

A landspout tornado under a relatively small updraft base. The vortex is visible as a diffuse column of dust.

The gustnado

The most common weak tornado type is the gustnado. It forms along the gust front in the transition from warm to cool air, as a thin vortex which can do brief damage to trees or roofs, but dissipates quickly. The only indicators you can spot beforehand are the dust they stir up and, sometimes, a ruffled, lowered part of the cloud base that shows some swirling. The best hint is the gust front itself. If it is a strong one, there will probably also be microbursts and lifting dust. Within this forward-moving dust and wind, a gustnado will stand out as a distinct vertical column. But if the vortex is over

A gustnado, mostly hidden within a wall of dust along an intense gust front. The only visible evidence of the column is a rough funnel cloud on the cloud base.

The Doggie Early Warning System (DEW)

Animal sense

"One of the things that we watch here are the horses. They were just going wild–just running from one field to the next. The horses are one of our best early warning signs around here."

"The horses were running the fields just flipping right out, racing– totally out of character. And the chickens were squawking and carrying on louder than I've ever heard them!"

"Everybody said if they had listened to their animals they would have known."

Most animals are sensitive to their environment, including sudden or exceptional weather changes. Their awareness and reactions are not necessarily consistent or foolproof, but when they do sense a storm coming they may give us early warning. They may become restless or edgy, seek comfort and safety, or behave strangely. Horses and dogs may hear things well beyond our hearing range, even before there is any visible sign of danger, so your dog may truly be your best friend in the event of a tornado. But don't count on it. Some animals respond only to more immediate and apparent dangers. (Cows, for instance, often remain placid even as a tornado swings into view.)

It is possible that some tales of "doggie early warning" are exaggerated by hindsight. Behaviour that we would normally have forgotten may assume undue significance after a tornado occurs. Even so, there is much to gain (and nothing to lose) by being attentive to an animal's behaviour. It may provide a handy early-warning system, and it will certainly bring us closer to the pets that bring so much pleasure to our lives.

wet ground or forest, you may not see anything at all. As it comes closer you will hear the wind rush, too, but this wind is unlikely to be accompanied by any signs of a funnel.

Gustnadoes occur everywhere and account for a large number of the weakest tornado reports each year. Their localized impact and damaging effects have allowed them to be counted as tornadoes (although many also go unreported each year) but most are probably not true tornadoes. The vortex forms along the boundary of two air masses, near the ground, and most of the time it doesn't reach to a convective cloud base. But because they happen with a nearby storm they are easily mistaken for and labelled as regular tornadoes. The strongest gustnadoes are more likely to be connected with new updrafts (wide black bases), along a gust front that is close to the storm it precedes.

A dusty whirl and column mark this gustnado which is on the boundary between hot air and the cooler outflow from a nearby storm.

Weak vs strong tornadoes: two ways to make air spin

Our interest in tornadoes is guided, at least in part, by how likely they are to threaten us. From this point of view it is reasonable to divide tornadoes into two groups: weak and strong. The weak ones include those mentioned above and most often are brief, short-lived and not too serious. The strong ones include most of the long-lived, larger damaging tornadoes that form with supercell severe storms. They may not be that common in many areas, but when they do occur we are forced to pay attention when their disrupting effects capture the headlines.

The two groups can also be distinguished by cause, but it's worth keeping in mind that few processes in nature are exclusive to a given phenomenon. All causes play some part in all results and the distinctions we make here are chosen mostly to contrast the two groups and help us recognize those tornadoes that matter most for our safety. There are always exceptions, and there is probably a continuum of tornado strengths and forms. In the end, they are all vortices– each with a slightly different set of influences leading to an infinite number of manifestations. What permits us to group them is the recurrence of predictable influences, like a storm which behaves a certain way and can be observed by us.

Weak tornadoes: simple rotation

The spin of a weak tornado is usually initiated by a boundary between two kinds of airstreams– either warm-cool or dry-moist. At the meeting point, the uneven forces cause small circulations to begin. This meeting point is also a place where the airstreams converge and if it is unstable, cumulus clouds will grow there. If an updraft has some circular motion, the air moving toward the centre of it begins to move faster and faster. Like ice-skaters pulling in their arms, the energy of the motion is concentrated inward, and the spin increases to adjust for it. This is one of the principles that contributes to many weaker vortices. It is still not clear exactly how or why it occurs in some situations and not others, but most weaker tornadoes derive their spin this way to some extent.

The spin starts near the ground (below cloud base) and is enhanced as the vortex is stretched upward in the rising updraft air. But it is a tricky balance that can't be maintained for very long– changes in the strength of the updraft, the arrival of outflow, or dominance of one airstream over the other can quickly disrupt the rotation. These kinds of vortices are usually too weak to condense water vapour, so you are not likely to see a funnel. At cloud base, the spinning updraft sometimes reveals itself in the cloud fragments just below a bulge or rough spot on the base. At the ground (where it makes contact) swirling dust and debris are all that you are likely to see. Weak tornadoes with this kind of simple rotation do not have wall clouds.

Inside a tornado

Air drawn toward a tornado speeds up and spirals into a ring of maximum winds around a quieter core within it. The strongest winds occur about 50-100m (150-300 feet) above the ground. The air motion is a combination of three directions– rotating around the outside, moving inward, and rising upward. All three are present everywhere within the vortex, but in different amounts. Toward the outside, the winds circle horizontally for the most part, while nearer the centre they mostly rise. Right at the centre they may rise or be calm; or the air may descend as part of a multiple–vortex pattern. This simplified cross-section diagram compares these two examples of the upward air motion.

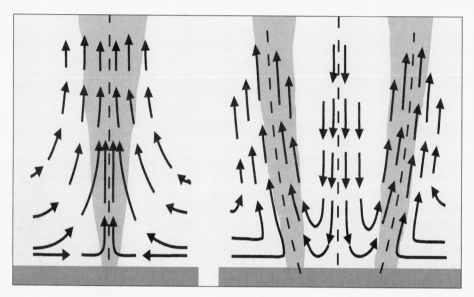

Adapted from Davies-Jones, 1983

There is nothing simple about the wind pattern inside a strong tornado. Instead of a perfect circle with symmetry and uniform winds, there are many irregularities and small-scale wind features embedded inside. Two important features are jets and vortices. Jets are smaller streaks of very high wind within the vortex, along the side of it, or entering the base near the ground. Vortices come in various sizes, from small tight whirls, only a few metres in diameter, to major sub-vortices, which are large parts of the original tornado, and can be 10-50m (30-150 feet) wide.

A tornado's impact is further complicated by the motion of sub-vortices and by its forward motion. To give you a taste of how different the conditions can be from one place to the next inside a tornado, we have created a top-down view of the total wind experience (see opposite). Shades equate with wind strength, taken from the net effect of adding the contributions from the main vortex, the two sub-vortices, and the forward motion. We assumed arbitrary maximum rotating winds of 100kmh (63mph) for both the main vortex and the smaller ones, plus a forward speed of 50kmh (31mph). The arrows show wind direction. We chose to "freeze" the positions of the two smaller vortices at right angles to the motion to show the maximum internal contrast. The whole thing becomes a single picture of the total wind impact at every point within a tornado at an instant in time.

You will notice two "eyes"– calm spots with no wind– and a "hot spot" where the maximum winds occur. This representation is based on the **most simple**, generalized, horizontal–only depiction of the flow pattern– yet it is still complex! Nobody knows for sure what is going on in there. Everything is constantly shifting in position and strength, all the parts are intertwined and interdependent, and every split second presents a new configuration.

Other considerations

What happens when these smaller features encounter a rough surface? Instead of blocking the flow, buildings or other obstructions make the winds increase in unpredictable ways. The wind is trying to achieve balance. If the air in one area is slowed down briefly, the air nearby speeds up to compensate. As a result, a tornado passing through a city or very rough landforms may become more unpredictable and destructive for short stretches.

What happens at the ground when a tornado lifts slightly? It may surprise you, but the wind pattern remains nearly identical, but weaker. The wind doesn't suddenly vanish– it just decreases as the strongest parts lift farther away from the ground.

How does the wind pattern relate to the pressure effects with a tornado? In the centre there may be a pressure drop of up to 10% (~10kPa or ~100mb). This can plug your ears but it can't do most of the things we attribute to it– explode buildings, intense ear pain, etc. When the strong wind begins, one part of the house is under a different force than another. This will either decrease or increase the pressure inside, depending on whether there's a temporary surplus or shortage of air there. For instance, in a well-sealed house you may lose air up the chimney which can't quickly be replaced inside. Or, an open window on the south side will let the air pile up inside the house initially. For that short period, a large pressure deficit or surplus can induce great pain or discomfort. It isn't from the actual air pressure in the tornado but from a brief pressure anomaly induced by the wind interacting with an enclosure.

About 1% of all tornadoes spin anti-cyclonically (counterclockwise, looking up). Anticyclonic tornadoes are usually weaker, short-lived, and unlikely to have wall clouds. Many of them may be gustnadoes that form on the backside of storms in association with downdrafts. In rare cases, a tornado couplet forms with a mesocyclone and consists of two vortices rotating in opposite directions.

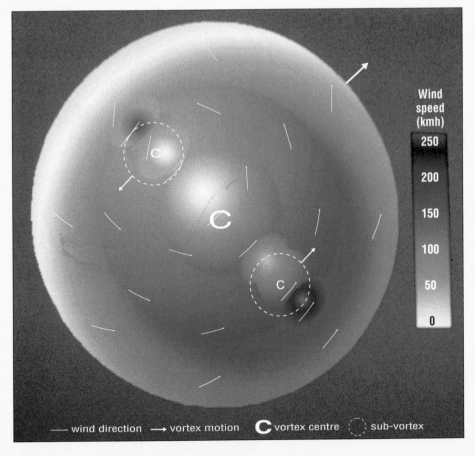

— wind direction   → vortex motion   **C** vortex centre   ⟨ ⟩ sub-vortex

Strong tornadoes: complex rotation

The rotation that eventually leads to a strong tornado begins with the air that enters a severe storm's powerful updraft. These storms form when there is strong wind shear— when winds both turn in direction and increase in strength with height. Imagine a stream of air moving toward the updraft of such a storm. The upper portions move faster and at a slightly different angle than the lower portions for any sample that you consider. This exerts a force on that stream of air which makes it start spinning about its axis of motion. This happens for all of the air entering the storm— it develops a component of spin (vorticity) as part of its energy of motion. When this air turns to rise into the vertical updraft, the spin translates into rotation about a vertical axis and the entire cloud starts to slowly rotate. This feature is called a mesocyclone and extends throughout the height of the cloud, averaging 5km (3 miles) in diameter.

A complex set of interacting influences work together to tighten up the mesocyclone. Upwardly accelerating air stretches forward, narrowing the air stream and enhancing the spin with the help of the "ice-skater effect". This also decreases the pressure under the storm, which draws more air in. The rotating cylinder becomes narrower and begins to build downward too. The air moving around the mesocyclone makes it more difficult for air moving toward the storm to enter the updraft, forcing most of the updraft air to enter near the bottom. Everything comes together to create a tight, persistent, self-sustaining structure that directs air efficiently into the storm. It's hard to believe, but updrafts in such a supercell storm can reach 240kmh (150mph)!

The next step is still mostly a mystery. We do know that downdrafts play a part. Descending air beside the updraft also acquires spin, which finds its way into the updraft. The cooler downdrafts also wrap around the mesocyclone, focusing the inflow and spin even more tightly. A much narrower vortex then forms at mid-levels and descends toward the ground. You can't see the initial storm rotation (which started 10-30 minutes earlier) but as the mesocyclone tightens and descends it can be seen as a wall cloud. This circular lowering under the storm's updraft base is visible because moisture from nearby

The smaller circulation of a tornado is part of the larger mesocyclone inside the storm. Here, the rain-free base and gust front extend away from a wall cloud and tornado, faintly visible as lighter parts just above the horizon.

rain is drawn into the updraft and condenses sooner than in the surrounding air. Its presence tells us that the updraft is wound tightly and could progress to a tornado within minutes.

The tornado derives partly from the vortex structure up inside the storm and partly from a counterpart of the spin close to the ground. Exactly which part comes first, which is more important or predominant, what their relationship is, and what causes them are not yet known. Their relative influence or importance is different for every storm.

Touchdown!

To spot a tornado's first touchdown we need to watch the wall cloud part of a storm carefully as rotation increases. This requires locating the rain-free base (usually to the left of the heavy precipitation) and a true wall cloud lowering on it. (See the diagram on page 71.) If these are all in view, you will want to look closely at the wall cloud itself, check for a funnel or other rotating structure in or near it, and then check the ground below it for signs of a debris cloud (rising dust).

The wall cloud

The transition from a flat cloud base to a wall cloud can happen in minutes. Cloud fragments form in the air under the base and rise to join it. Although this can also occur along a surging gust front, here it will persist in one isolated spot. As this lowering takes shape, it will become more solid, blocky, or rounded. It will look dark against a lighter sky, but if the background is dark it will be a lighter grey or even have tinges of yellow. Since it is the lowest part of a storm, it reflects light from outside of the storm cloud. At a distance it looks like a downward extension of the base, with vertical sides. You may see cloud scraps or a roll of low cloud extending toward the rain from it. Wall clouds in humid weather can be large, foggy or brushy masses hanging close to the ground, but in dry weather they may only look like a small step down from the base.

The wall cloud is roughly circular and symmetrical, which is hard to visualize when you are looking into the distance. As it nears, you will begin to see both sides (the forward edge and a back edge) as well as a three-dimensional shape. By watching the edge closest to you, you can see slow rotation from left to right. A full revolution takes from a half a minute to two minutes, so don't expect a spinning top! The motion is sometimes hard to see clearly because new cloud is being constantly formed along the edges and bottom of it. If you don't see any circular motion it may just be an ordinary non-rotating lowering (an updraft) and not a wall cloud– but just in case, watch for a funnel cloud within it.

More than half of all wall clouds do not lead to a tornado. They can exist for hours or last only a few minutes. They can change shape continuously, fall apart and rebuild;

Wall cloud formation series— The first photo shows the heavy rain core and rain-free base of a young storm. After 15 minutes (second photo), the base has become lower as the updraft concentrates in one location. A lowering forms in the next 15 minutes and evolves into a circular, rotating wall cloud (photos 3 and 4) which had a brief funnel under it. The storm's tightened-up mesocyclone is visible as the dark cylinder. After ten minutes (next photo), the wall cloud has weakened and has lost its compact shape. This was caused by a surge of outflow which later pushed into the updraft, elongating the lowering and bowing it forward (sixth photo). However, in less than ten more minutes, a new, larger wall cloud has formed (last photo). This one could lead to a tornado soon (there are already hints of a circulation on the ground from the dust underneath it).

Lowerings and wall clouds

If you master lowerings, you master the most reliable warning signs of a developing tornado. The top row of photos shows non-tornadic lowerings– either because they are not connected with an organized storm (often along a gust front) or because they are merely brief manifestations of a locally strong updraft (not persistent, not symmetrically round). The rest of the page gives a variety of wall clouds showing varying degrees of formation, rotation, size and height (dry vs moist). In every case of a true wall cloud, the storm's main updraft base (often also lower and dark) has a small extension under it that is the lowest cloud you see and is integrally connected to the base.

All the wall clouds in the smaller photos above were followed by a tornado within ten minutes. Notice how different they can look from each other! The two larger photos show funnel clouds in contrasting situations: a worst-last storm in a dry, western airmass and a hybrid eastern storm in which the wall cloud is forward of the heaviest rain. Below, a large tiered updraft base has a fluffy wall cloud under it that looks white from the reflected skylight. The vertical and circular shape of this storm's base is quite obvious. The wall cloud is not as obvious because it is not present as a completely visible structure– but its location and other storm characteristics would leave us with no other conclusion.

and they come in endless shapes and sizes. (See wall cloud photos, page 106-107.) When you watch this part of a storm it is like taking the storm's pulse to see how healthy and vigorous it is. If the wall cloud is, indeed, going to evolve into a tornado, this can occur from 15-30 minutes after it begins to form. The rotation may speed up just before the tornado comes. The wall cloud, when properly identified, is your proof of storm rotation and tornado potential.

In tornado-prone areas, the term "wall cloud" has become widely accepted for describing a lowering under a potentially tornadic storm. Many people loosely apply this term to every lowering they see, even if there are no signs of rotation. We, the authors, prefer to define a wall cloud as a **rotating** lowering rather than any ordinary lowering which weaker storms often have too.

The funnel cloud

In the perfect scenario, a funnel cloud appears under the wall cloud and lazily descends. If that happens, you won't need any of this information! Many funnels are hard to spot, though. Initially, you might see a brief point form, then vanish again. Or you might see a small spot within the wall cloud that seems to be twirling faster, with a few cloud fragments in it. The funnel cloud will appear somewhere within the wall cloud– on the edge, in the middle, or, most often, on the side away from the heart of the storm. In rarer cases it can form just outside the wall cloud edge, but close to it. With a small, high-based wall cloud it appears as a discrete appendage with smooth sides and a tapered shape. With a large, low wall cloud, the funnel may be a bulge or lump under it– or the entire cloud mass may descend toward the ground. If you aren't sure, look at its edges. A true funnel cloud will have rapidly rising air along its edges and maintain a compact shape. But if a wall cloud is rotating, seems to have some of these features, and hangs close to the ground, consider that

it may already be a tornado, even without the usual structure. Large messy tornadoes often form with large messy wall clouds.

The funnel may make several attempts to descend and may dart down, elongate, or widen with time. In all these cases you should assume that it could already be touching down as a tornado, even though it looks incomplete or disconnected from the ground. To be sure whether a funnel cloud is likely to become a tornado, the context is as important as the shape you see. A true pre-tornadic funnel cloud will only show up in or close to the dark, lowered cloud on the storm's rain-free base, to the side of the main area of rain and lightning. When you are near this part of the storm, there may be nothing going on outside but a dark quiet.

The photo above shows a true tornadic funnel– the shape, location and surrounding cloud features are all as expected. There are also non-tornadic funnels (right) which will not be connected with a dark base or lowering. These are usually thin and brief whirls that are not part of the updraft region under a storm.

108

False funnels

Stormy weather brings with it a flood of funnel cloud reports from the public. Most of these are not true funnels. They are usually funnel-shaped pieces of cloud hanging from a dark cloud base. Such "false" funnels are most often seen along the gust front where cool moist air is rising abruptly. They form in the updraft below the main base, as strands of scud in mid-air or as tufts joining it. The situation (usually dark, windy and turbulent-looking) is enough to convince many that the clouds are up to no good!

A true funnel cloud will be solidly connected to the cloud base, tapered, and have smooth sides. If you are close enough to it you will see a spinning motion too. But many funnel clouds are also harmless, being small vortices in a non-threatening sky (see bottom photo, opposite). The real concern is with tornadic funnel clouds, which only occur in particular places within the storm. Context is at least as important as appearance. Before you panic at the sight of every momentary wisp of pointed cloud, check that it persists and accompanies a circular lowering. There are many false funnel possibilities– rain shafts, virga, scud, irregular updrafts– waiting to bring us unwanted and unnecessary worry that we can avoid with a little patience.

Three false funnels– a distant rainshaft (top photo) mimics the funnel shape but on closer inspection is too diffuse while a tapered lowering from a sudden updraft (middle photo) is not smooth enough or sufficiently anchored to the base. Both are not in the right location and will lose whatever resemblance they may have to a funnel within a short period. The last photo is also a tapered lowering under a strong updraft which has some rotation with it (symmetrical shape) but is not a tornadic funnel because there is no storm or proper lowering with it. It, too, will change shape and/or evaporate in a minute.

You may see other kinds of funnels with other clouds or situations, but they are not tornadic or may even be **false funnels**. (See box, above.)

The debris cloud

As soon as the vortex in a rotating storm touches the ground it is a tornado, regardless of how it looks. You will most likely **not** see a full funnel with it initially. There may be no funnel at all, but most of the time there will be a partial one. First contact is often marked by a cloud of swirling dust and debris at the ground.

Myth
You'll always see a funnel— No! Some tornadoes have no funnel at all and are completely invisible, except for any debris present. In addition, if a tornado is close, the funnel will be overhead and harder to see.

With no funnel visible, the debris cloud is your next best indicator of a tornado touchdown. Moments after first contact (left), a tornado has stirred up a perfectly symmetrical bowl-shaped spray of dirt at the ground. The debris cloud isn't always so perfect and compact (right) but will always have a gathered-together look which will soon progress to a column shape.

This usually happens several minutes **before** the visible funnel is completely formed, so don't use the obvious funnel cloud as your only basis for determining what is happening. The density and size of this debris could indicate strength, but it might also be influenced by what the tornado is passing over. A weak tornado over loose, dry dirt can stir up quite a cloud of fine smoky material. A strong tornado can do the same even over wet earth, trees or buildings, but the debris will look coarser. Your perception of the texture and motion will depend on its distance from you.

At a distance, the debris cloud looks contained– it won't just be a mass of dust floating aimlessly. The debris rises and circles within discrete boundaries, with the occasional piece or bulge poking outward. It will look symmetrical and rise in a column. If the visible funnel is small or thin, the debris can extend well out from it. Right at the ground, the debris will be compact and narrow but just above this it often flares out and becomes more diffuse. With large tornadoes, the debris cloud and condensation funnel may be mixed together as one dark shape.

Within about 2-3km (1-2 miles), debris with a tornado starts to take on a textured appearance. Objects become discernible, and instead of looking like a dusty cloud, they will look like separate particles. Many people first think that they are looking at a flock of birds. This not only hints at the controlled movement of this debris, but also points out how tough it is to recognize its distance from us. We are not accustomed to seeing a tornado– a large three-dimensional object towering for a thousand metres or more– moving through the sky. Everything it carries along is miniaturized by the sheer scale of the spectacle!

Imagine that the sky is dark, and when you look outside you notice with alarm that smoke seems to be rising in the distance. How can you tell if it is a fire or a tornado? Rising smoke will billow upward and outward, then trail away in one direction. With a tornado debris cloud, the motion will twist upward along a straight axis (which is sometimes slightly tilted). Debris also appears to be held together more, and shows signs of bubbling, as if something were blowing it outward in tiny puffs before it spirals upward.

Peak intensity

A tornado can reach full strength within minutes of first contact. It usually widens and darkens, and a large amount of debris will rise to meet or encircle the visible funnel. The funnel is often visible to the ground but can also remain part way up, or close to the cloud base. Wider tornadoes can have a blunted funnel that doesn't look like what you would expect, but will show the same characteristics– rapidly rising air, smooth or gently-rolling sides,

111

The life cycle of a tornado

This sequence began with the first photo on page 110. The vortex was already a tornado in contact with the ground for several minutes by the time the debris column began to take shape (top left). The dry dirt being stirred up by the tornado is held tightly together and rises mostly up the outside of the vortex column. In the wider view (top right), a short funnel is elongating slowly downward while the debris is rising to meet it. The mature stage (at right; see also photo on page 111) shows the tornado at peak strength and size. The black column stands in sharp contrast to the tranquil sunshafts behind it.

The view is to the west here. The tornado was moving slowly to the left and was about 4km (2mi) away. The motion would have been east (with the storm) but was briefly altered by a large pool of outflow that pushed out of the storm toward the south. The tornado was connected to a thunderstorm to the northeast, which began to drop golfball-size hailstones by the end of the series.

After a few minutes
full strength, the tor-
do began to weaken.
e column narrowed
d the debris cloud
gan spreading out
p). The condensation
nel was then visible
st of the way to the
und, but had shrunk
a thin and wobbly
e-like shape. There
s a crink about half-
y up where the ouflow
ming from the right)
d distorted it. After
other minute, the rope
d evaporated, leaving
ly a sprawling dust
me to disperse slowly
e a fading memory.

and a ragged bottom edge where the rising air condenses– as would be seen with thinner ones. Some wide tornadoes also have separate visible vortices within their main circulation (see *One tornado, many funnels?*, page 122).

Some wall cloud features may shrink or vanish during the tornado's mature stage. You may also see rain moving behind and around the tornado, partly obscuring your view. The tornado will be mostly vertically oriented, but lower down it might be tilted away from the storm. It may remain in a similar state for a long damage path or vary in intensity and appearance along the way. Periods of pronounced shrinking of the funnel or debris cloud indicate a weakening phase, but if the upper parts of the funnel remain solid and wide, a reintensification is quite possible. The vortex is constantly changing and pulsing, and will remain strong until the mesocyclone weakens.

Two examples of the rope stage. This indicates rapid weakening and is usually seen after the tornado has already lifted.

Winding down

The vortex begins to weaken when the storm's updraft weakens. This can happen when too much cool air descending at the back of the storm moves around the inflow region, cutting it off. The storm may also gradually diminish in intensity for other reasons. The tornado will begin shrinking, reversing some of the formation steps. It may weaken but stay on the ground, or be quite strong even as it appears to shrink in size. It can also lift off the ground, then come down again briefly.

When the funnel begins to look thin and snaky, the end is near. At this time, it often looks quite lively and threatening, but is about to dwindle away. The funnel may become disjointed, kinked, or wobbly in shape. You may see the top of the tornado at a different location than its touchdown point as the vortex stretches out more horizontally. After writhing in the air like this for a short time, this last "rope stage" will suddenly vanish. The wall cloud might remain for awhile but unless the storm rebuilds, it, too, will probably shrink and lift, or elongate away from the rain area.

There are always exceptions. Large tornadoes may not have the usual clearly-defined features and stages and can form or die as wide, messy structures. With some storms, as one tornado dies the original wall cloud re-forms or shifts over to spawn a new tornado a short while later. Some tornadoes go through the life cycle and then come back to life, repeating previous stages. In most cases, though, you will see a progression from small to large (maximum size and strength) to small again in a smooth, continuous transition. Some stages may be very brief, but this progression is a natural outcome of the way all the forces within the cloud come together and crest as a tight vortex.

Myth
It can move with the speed of lightning— This notion comes from confusing a tornado's travelling speed with the much higher speed of its winds. Tornadoes can travel at most about 100kmh (60mph) but often go at about half that speed.

A closer look

Common features

Many people believe that tornadoes are all erratic and unpredictable and that each one is unique, behaving with a mind of its own. At the same time, they hold onto fixed, singular impressions of what a tornado looks or sounds like. We all have a tendency to take our experiences and build our facts from them. The experience may be a dramatic personal encounter with a tornado or a television account– either way, it is not the whole picture. Even if we have only seen one tornado, it is such an unusual, memorable sight that we can't help holding on to that image and drawing conclusions from it.

Our impression of a typical tornado was probably shaped by *The Wizard of Oz*, and then later by video clips on the news. We imagine a tornado as a sleek, slender shape dancing its way across the open fields. This is the west Kansas impression, where high cloud bases and dry air make this shape more common. But many tornadoes are much wider, messier, and not quite so perfect! We also share the assumption that we will hear the familiar "freight train" sound, and this does often occur. By contrast, most people are less sure about a tornado's size or the way it moves. Every tornado is unique, but they also have many features in common– a few will probably surprise you.

Appearance

What we see depends on all these things: cloud base height, the tornado's size and type, how close it is to the rain area, how dense the visible funnel is, how close it is to us, and where it is in our view.

Cloud bases— Humid weather gives us low cloud bases, which dramatically alter our view. The storm base is darker, the wall cloud is larger and very low, and haze may limit visibility. Being low, these features are hidden until they are close to us, so we might not have time to observe advance warning signs clearly. Tornadoes will also be less obvious because they are less-shapely and come out of the murky darkness at the last minute. These conditions are most common in regions farther east and south, and in mid-summer. If cloud bases are high, as they would be in a dry atmosphere (farther west or early in the season), our view will be clearer and we will see a tornado much farther away.

A comparison of high cloud bases (dry air) with low cloud bases (moist air) under a storm with a tornado present. The tornado in the second photo is vaguely visible at lower left and is enlarged below.

Tornado size/type— When watching for a tornado, remember to put aside your expectations. Take a look at the variety of shapes and sizes possible (see *Rogues Gallery*, page 120-121) and focus on storm features. If and when a tornado does form, it could be anything from a thin rope to a wide dust-swirl. The range of shapes and sizes is so great that if you have only one possibility in mind, others may fool you completely.

Distance from rain— In the classic situation, the tornado forms under a part of the storm where no rain is falling, usually with lighter sky beyond.

The main part of the storm is then a few kilometres to the north or northeast. In some cases, however, some of the falling rain is wrapped around the updraft, partly or even completely surrounding the tornado. What's worse is that this is more likely to occur with large, low-based storms and some of the larger, stronger tornadoes. The tornado could be fully obscured until close to the last minute or two and you would need to rely on other evidence (like wall cloud rotation, winds, your location) to determine what was going on.

The visible funnel— Besides debris, the visible funnel of a tornado is what identifies it to most people. If the funnel is dense, it will stand out against most other backgrounds. But if it isn't, you may only see a faint outline or wispy shape— nothing distinct enough to be sure of. A tornado's cloudy funnel can vary from moment to moment and can become thin or faint enough to "vanish", especially when it is close to us. The funnel can also become so filled with rain or debris that it loses its familiar shape.

When a tornado gets close, it may be hard to identify because the funnel is above you. In this photo, the debris plume is a giveaway but without it, you might not have seen the funnel which is high up against the cloud base.

How close it is— As a tornado gets closer, we lose perspective on it. The upper portions are nearly overhead but the base may still seem a long way off. This may be partly from a tilt in the vortex, but it is mostly because of the way we judge distance. The closer a tornado is to us, the more we focus on and see only the very bottom of it. If the visible funnel doesn't quite reach the ground we might think it has lifted because it is all overhead. We would then be looking up at it– down its length– so the size and shape look small and unfamiliar. The bottom of the funnel may also be less opaque and narrower than parts higher up.

These two photos show the same tornado from different angles. The first one, viewed to the southeast, shows it as dark against the brighter background while the second shows it as lighter against the dark storm to the northeast. What you see depends on what's behind the tornado.

Where it is— As with every other cloud in the sky, a tornado condensation funnel's colour and brightness depend on its density and where the light comes from. A dense, solid funnel is both darker (backlit) and lighter (front-lit, reflected light) than a thinner, more wispy one. If you look at it with a brighter sky behind, it will look black. This is often the case looking west or southwest, as it approaches, or if it passes to the south. But as a tornado moves by to the north, it moves in front of the darkest part of the storm and will look lighter. If it is very dark everywhere, the tornado looks a lighter shade of grey because, like lower clouds, it reflects some of the light getting in underneath the storm from the sides. In a brighter, high-based storm the tornado will look white to the north or east because the bright sky from the opposite direction reflects back to your eyes. Many witnesses of the April 20th tornado thought that it had weakened or disappeared as it passed to their northeast because it was no longer dramatically backlit. What you see at any moment is governed by what is in the background and where the light source is– and both will change continuously as the tornado traverses your view.

Size

Tornadoes can be as wide as 2km (one mile) in diameter or as little as a few tens of metres (yards) across. On average, a width of about 200m (650 feet) is more typical of a strong, persistent tornado. The tornado's influence (its true size) extends out two or three times the visible diameter. One way to estimate the position of the outer edge of damaging winds is to look up at the widest part of the funnel and then extend that width down to the ground as an imaginary cylinder.

Our estimates of size are affected by distance and perception. For instance, a thin tornado from a high cloud base will look smaller than it really is because our mind looks at the context to size up an object. We see a longer than usual funnel and assume it starts from a typical cloud base. Our interpretation of a cloud base's position in the sky comes from experience, and when it is higher than usual we can be fooled. We assume the shape is closer and therefore smaller than it truly is. Tornado size is relative anyway, and a smaller size doesn't diminish the risk.

Movement

When it comes to a tornado's forward motion, many people are convinced that it can go anywhere, move erratically, go where it wants, or come back without warning. Sometimes people confuse the speed a tornado travels with its much higher wind speed, too.

Can tornadoes seek out a path of their own choosing? Can they make sudden, seemingly unpredictable turns? Or, can they skip here and there like a whip flicking about? On the larger scale none of these is possible, because the tornado is part of the wind field of the thunderstorm. Where the storm goes, it follows. Storms move in straight lines with an occasional deviation as weaker or stronger phases shift the position of the main updraft slightly. These changes are gradual, smooth, and not very large. A tornado moves forward at the same speed as the storm does and along the same path— with no big surprises along the way.

 Is it coming for me?

When you see a tornado, how can you tell if it's moving your way? First, verify that it is in the western half of the sky— otherwise it is moving away from you. Next, quickly note its position relative to a distant tree, chimney, or similar object, and watch to see if the tornado is moving left or right in your view. If it is, it will most likely pass by— but it may still be close enough to throw debris your way. If it appears to be standing still and/or getting larger, you are right in the path and should take cover! It is easy to be deceived into thinking that it is stationary, because we expect to see lateral motion as the proof of actual motion. But consider how a distant car or airplane coming your way looks, for a long time, as if it is not moving much. By the time you realize that the tornado is becoming clearly larger, it may already be closing in. Tornadoes travel at 30-80kmh (20-50mph). Remember, too, that a tornado's influence may extend beyond the edge of what you see.

There can be smaller deviations along the path. Certain tornadoes have a secondary motion within them that will look to us like a swinging or shifting motion. Small changes in the direction of movement (for less than a few blocks) are possible if the lower section of the vortex is stretched slightly out of position by downdrafts from behind the storm. After all, it's only a column of air and can be pushed around a bit by other air currents nearby. These fluctuations are all small and do not merit the degree of uncertainty attributed to tornadoes by many of us.

How loud is it really?

"But this one was so quiet. Some people talk about this noise that sounds like a combine going or a washer going really frantically– there was nothing. We could have been sitting in here and never known anything had happened!"

"You wouldn't believe how loud it was. I'd never heard anything as loud as that! This noise was so loud, the best simile I can think of is– stand behind a 747 winding his engines up ready to take off– I can't think of anything louder!"

Two neighbours share their memories of the sounds from the tornado. One was overwhelmed by the noise, while the other couldn't believe the silence! Admittedly, they were about 3km (2miles) apart, but both had vivid experiences and a close encounter with the tornado. Can these differences be reconciled?

People have described the sound of a tornado as "eerie", "loud hissing", "grinding", "bad whistling", "humming", "deep grumbling roar", "thunder that won't quit", "rustling", "it screamed", "squealing", "whine", "voom-voom-voom", "raw wind" and "the worst sound I ever heard". Colourful analogies abounded too.

But others heard nothing. How can we explain the differences? Up close, sounds are loud and may completely dominate our experience. But as we move farther away, sound levels drop off quickly, and what's left may easily sound more like an ordinary wind than the expected roar. A tornado looks close and ominous, even at 1 to 2 miles' distance, so people who see it from that distance would be primed to hear the roaring winds. If they expected a freight train and heard only a wind, they might discount what they heard and downplay its significance; or they might do the opposite– hear a wind noise, see the tornado, and interpret the sound as the familiar, expected roar or train. Both can be simultaneously true. One person's roar is another person's rush of wind. In the excitement of the moment and against our expectations of something louder, a tornadic wind may be overlooked as just another big wind. Distance is still the biggest factor in what people hear, but what they think it means or sounds like is a very personal matter.

Sound

If there is one thing that everyone is certain about, it's that a tornado will sound like a freight train. So when a tornado passes within a mile of your house and you don't hear a thing (as some April 20th observers said), what's going on? Many tornadoes are silent until they are very close by. And the sound– which has many causes– is a complex "wind" sound far more unique and unforgettable than the simple analogy we are told to expect.

Air in motion makes no sound until it touches something. Tornado winds come in contact with two main sources of sound– debris in the air, and the surface of the ground. Thousands of debris fragments create a whistling sound or roar and it is probably the loudest part of what you hear. When the debris is breaking up or vibrating, as with larger pieces of sheet metal, the noise can be deafening. A very loud noise can be heard as far as several kilometres away, but more often it will only become audible in the last half-minute, or well within one kilometre of you. If the tornado moves over fields and has no suspended debris it will create a variety of softer, swishing sounds. The predominant sound is a rushing wind effect that grows steadily louder, sometimes with a pulsing character to it.

It is not inconceivable that other inaudible sounds and vibrations are being created by a tornado. Animals certainly seem to respond to something– even when there is nothing to see, hear or feel nearby. Just as thunder comes from the pressure wave of rapidly-moving atoms, smaller pressure effects within the tornado might well put out a low buzz that is lost to our senses.

Infinite variety

When you have seen one tornado you haven't seen them all– not by a long shot. No two are alike, but each one can also look completely different from one minute to the next. What is the reason for this tremendous variety? It's a combination of two simple consequences of the vortex– its shape (structure) and the pressure drop it creates. These are very fluid, mutually dependent characteristics. The slightest change in either can cause a major change in what we see.

Leaving out variations in lighting and debris and changes over time, let's look at why this is so. The vortex structure is not well understood. All we know for sure is what we can see from moving bits of debris. Since little is known about how and why vortices form, we have confined our explanations to simple representations of the most likely wind patterns that make up a vortex. This simplified viewpoint is only a start. The finer details, complexities and instantaneous changes can only be speculated upon. Vortices come in many different sizes and strengths. Each one is a consequence of its unique environment under the influence of similar forces dictated by the laws of nature.

The lower pressure within a vortex (which is as much as 10% lower than the pressure in the surrounding area) condenses moisture, forming the cloudy air in the visible funnel. An identical vortex forms a larger visible funnel on a humid day than on a dry day. But there are also variations in the moistness of the air entering the vortex. They can be subtle, as with a slight increase over a forest or river, or widespread, as with a large influx of moist air from nearby rain. A patchwork of moisture sources surrounds us, each contributing its small part to the changing funnel we see. Surges of outflow, alternating with drier downdrafts, are also drawn like wet and dry ribbons into the spiralling vortex. Each moment has its own blend of invisible water vapour molecules coming to life as they materialize at the edge of the tornado.

On the inside of a tornado the pressure is constantly fluctuating, and so does the moisture on the outside, so it's no wonder that we see so many shape changes. And this picture is only the **simplest** one– the deeper we delve into the actual structure of a tornado, the more complex and detailed it becomes. What we see as a tornado is largely an illusion– only a fog of tiny water droplets captures the certainty of the moment.

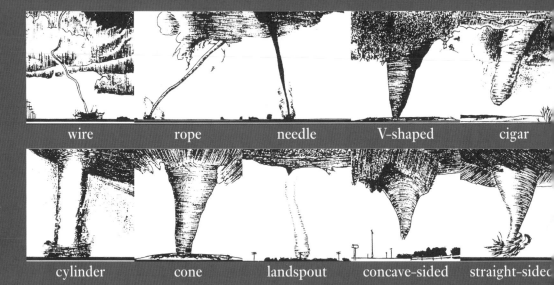

| wire | rope | needle | V-shaped | cigar |
| cylinder | cone | landspout | concave-sided | straight-sided |

A rogues gallery of tornadoes

No two tornadoes look alike. People who watch only for the classic tapered funnel, extending the full distance from the cloud to ground, may be taken by surprise by one of the many other faces a tornado may show. They all contain dangerous rotating winds deserve our attention and respect. The sketches above run through some of the variations you might encounter, and the photos be give a taste of the real thing. (See also the Life cycle photo spread, pages 112–113, and the photo spreads for the 1996 tornad pages 130–133.)

convex-sided   segmented   truncated cone   bulb-shaped   bowl-shaped

wedge   flared base   hourglass   sheathed   loop/ring/knot

One tornado, many funnels?

When we look more closely at many tornadoes we begin to see that our simple single-vortex model has a few unexplained loose ends in it. Besides a main vortex, we might also see small funnel-like appendages, tubes or snakes in mid-air, or even a split vortex structure. These things look strange and out of place, but we shouldn't be surprised by them. A tornado may **look** like a solid object but it is only air, and air can be easily distorted and twisted into all kinds of smaller whirls. Most of these side-funnels are brief and don't come near the ground. They appear and disappear within seconds, as small vortices briefly spin and condense into smoky fingers.

Adapted from Fujita, 1971b

Many of the largest, most intense tornadoes are multiple-vortex for much or all of their existence. The vortex begins as a column of rising air but the low pressure within it helps to break down this flow by drawing air down from above. Where this descending air meets the rising air, the vortex becomes unstable and may separate into smaller, distinct vortices (see diagram, above). Three seems to be the preferred number, but from two to seven have been observed at once. Each of these sub-vortices can be very intense and contributes to a more complex damage pattern. They spin separately but rotate around the larger circulation.

How many tornadoes can you get at once? Only one from one mesocyclone, even though it may look like there are several. The closer you are to a multiple-vortex tornado the more distinct and separated sub-vortices will look to you. In rare cases, a second tornado forms independently nearby while the first is still present, but this only happens with storms that create a new rotation adjacent to an older circulation that is waning. Every other sighting of more than one tornado at a time is probably due to a multiple-vortex tornado. A tornado is a single event with a single cause, even if we see more than one funnel-shape with it.

A multiple-vortex tornado with three sub-vortices. A very tight vortex has formed a condensation tube at left. The other two are less distinct but one is in contact with the ground at right.

Examples of multiple-vortex tornadoes with separate vortices close to the main one. In all cases, these are confined to an area under the wall cloud containing the larger rotating structure.

When you watch a multiple-vortex tornado move along, you are looking at the positions of its separate vortices. At a given moment only one may be visible or prominent. Since it is moving forward while also moving around in a circle, the total motion appears to swing in a rhythmic manner. If you are watching it pass by, this gives the effect of uneven forward motion and brief pausing. If it is moving toward or away from you, it will look like a sideways shifting, as if the sides of the tornado were breathing in and out. The change to a multiple-vortex structure can happen repeatedly and can revert to a single vortex during the tornado's life.

Adapted from Fujita et al., 1967

Solid air– twister tricks

A tornado is like a floating physics laboratory. The winds are created by the low pressure within the vortex and the air accelerates by conserving its angular momentum (the ice-skater effect that we mentioned earlier). Put simply, momentum is the energy any object has when in motion. As you bring a circling object closer to its centre of rotation it has a shorter circle to travel on, so it speeds up to adjust for its inherent momentum. This energy of motion increases exponentially with speed and high winds can cause even small objects to have an incredible impact. The difference between an object moving at 10kmh (6mph) and 200kmh (120mph) is 4000 times! This is like the weight difference between a book and a two-ton truck in impact. Air moving at high speeds acts more like a solid than a gas and that's why it can do such incredible damage.

If you know the basic principles at work in a tornado you can unravel some of its secrets. You probably thought that you would never make use of that obscure science from high school days, right? A tornado certainly does! The complex interplay of wind and pressure effects is responsible for all the strange things we discover afterward. Our mobile laboratory employs acceleration, friction, momentum, the Bernoulli effect and many other principles as it tests the objects it encounters.

The shape of an object affects the force exerted on it. An airplane wing creates a flow that puts more pressure on the bottom than the top, giving enough lift to hold a 400-ton jumbo jet aloft. In a tornado, some objects are lifted, others left. Some become airfoils and travel great distances, while others become missiles along the ground. Friction, which normally holds most objects in place, is easily overcome by a tornado's sudden acceleration and wind force. Momentum can add so much energy to small, flimsy objects such as straws that they behave like spikes as they hit other things, rather than buckling. The Bernoulli effect (which tells us that the pressure in a moving fluid decreases with its speed) accounts for many odd things, as well as many that we take for granted– like a pump-spray bottle. The air, blowing across an opening, reduces the pressure there and draws the liquid up to the nozzle. Similarly, tornadic winds blowing across an opening (for instance, in a roof) cause a pressure drop that draws air out of the attic, along with the insulation.

Myth

The pressure change will blow your house up— This is one of the most entrenched myths. Only a very well-sealed building (and none are) will have any difficulty venting the pressure change— and that's after it has endured the ferocious winds which are on the outside edge of the low pressure core. All damage to buildings comes from wind force and flying debris, both of which are much greater stresses than a minor air pressure change. Also, empty buildings are no more likely to be demolished than full ones— whatever the result is, it's for a reason other than the pressure or the contents.

☞ Where does debris go?

Many people were surprised by how far objects were flung and how some buildings were swept away completely, without a trace, by the tornado. They were baffled when heavy things, like tool chests, vanished without leaving a single piece behind– seemingly into oblivion. They wondered, "Where does it all go?" Do things disappear– like dust to the wind– or are they all hiding in the neighbour's swamp or forest?

Although some things (like old barn boards) are pulverized by the winds of a tornado, most solid objects do not disintegrate, but break into smaller pieces which are then flung back down. They land elsewhere– and when we don't find them again it is mostly because there are so many places they could be. (It's like looking for a needle in a hay **field**!) Many objects are no longer recognizable after their far-flung adventures. Others are buried in the ground. But all of them are hiding somewhere– we just haven't discovered them. They may well turn up in the years to come as out-of-place curiosities from another time.

The way that debris is moved and deposited by a tornado is complex and variable, but it follows a few basic principles. Almost all of it falls out in bands within several kilometres of the tornado, to the north of its path. A tornado's vortex is usually tilted toward the north, so that debris drawn up into it falls mostly in that direction. How far an object is flung is largely determined by its density and shape. Debris that is light or shaped like an airfoil is carried along by the storm cloud, falling out farther north or northeast (down the path). Some very light items, like paper, may be drawn into the storm's main updraft and circle around for hours before they finally descend with downdrafts hundreds of kilometres away.

Heavy or hard to grab objects are moved, rolled, or lifted briefly close to the ground. But if a tornado succeeds in lifting very large objects well above the ground, they may revolve around the outermost part of its circulation (because of the higher centrifugal force on them) and be flung out farther from the path than other debris,

Did you wonder...?

What causes the bouncing?

In most cases when we see a tornado bouncing up and down it is only the visible condensation funnel position moving, and not the tornado winds. The illusion, induced by our orientation to the ground below us, is that something that goes down and retreats is being c ontrolled (like a yo-yo) from above. But the visible part is a stream of condensed air moving up, even as the funnel descends. This is a lot like the illusion that lightning comes down, even though the visible stroke travels upward. In both cases the facts defy our sense of normality.

If you are close enough to clearly see the tip of the funnel, it may resemble an upside-down waterfall or tap. Like a stream of flames in reverse, the cloudy parts materialize in mid-air and quickly rise to form the solid funnel. The airstream extends invisibly below the tip to the ground. When the base of the funnel lifts, you are watching a slight decrease in the moistness of the air entering it. This drying delays condensation until the air has ascended just a little farther up the column. Variations in the pressure field within the tornado are also possible, but their effect is longer (minutes rather than seconds) and is accompanied by other changes in the structure or intensity of the tornado. Most of the small-scale bouncing is from changes in water vapour entering the vortex.

Why is the contact sporadic?

Long stretches without much damage (more than a kilometre, or half a mile) can occur when a tornado lifts briefly. A weaker phase within the storm may cause this, but it is not too common. The tornado is usually on the ground more or less continuously while it is fully

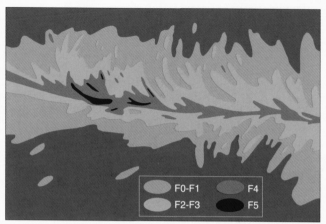

Example of an F5 tornado damage pattern. Even an intense F5 tornado with a continuous swath of destruction has over 50% of the affected area in F0 damage and only about 1% in F5 damage. This 2km (1.2 miles) damage swath is not uniform but has many patches and streaks in it corresponding to intense smaller-scale features or overlapping wind effects adding to the general tornadic winds.

F0-F1		F4
F2-F3		F5

Adapted from Fujita, 1974

which has been carried away. Things that are lighter or easier to lift will rise, circle, and proceed forward before falling out. Most of the debris will be carried up hundreds of metres, then billow outward (mostly on the north side) and descend in a more scattered pattern.

There are other factors that complicate the debris pattern: the existence of sub-vortices; the relative influence of horizontal and lifting winds; where objects are relative to the tornado's centre (see the box, *Inside a tornado*, on page 102-103); and how long it takes for an object or structure to be dismantled. To further complicate the picture, the relative strength of the wind when and where it hits an object varies greatly; and different objects are more or less resistant to the wind's force. It's no wonder that so many people marvel at where things end up after a tornado passes through!

formed and it will lift or rope out only if a weakening sets in. If you see sporadic damage, it is at least partly from a lack of debris or evidence of damage, rather than an absence of strong winds. For example, a tornado passing over damp grasslands may appear to lift because there is nothing for it to pick up, but it is still making ground contact. A multiple-vortex tornado will have an irregular, spotty damage swath too, because the worst damage is confined to the localized vortices which oscillate forward along a helical path (see sub-vortex paths, page 123). Some spots are destroyed while others are skipped, giving the swath a hit-and-miss appearance.

Why doesn't it just destroy everything in its path?

There are two ways to view this perfectly reasonable question. The first is to look at a tornado, not as a single, solid mass of whirling destructive power, but as a collection of stronger and weaker pockets of wind– including larger structures like sub-vortices– all operating within the overall framework of a vortex column. The extent of damage depends on which of these pockets make direct contact with an object, and for how long. (See tornado winds diagram, page 103.)

The second way is to consider what a tornado strikes. Not all strucures or objects are alike. They differ in stress tolerance and shape, and parts of any one structure may have different capacities to resist the wind force. When you add wind shadow effects, flying debris, and access– the ease with which the wind can get at things– it is easier to see why the end result is not simply a complete obliteration or clean sweep, but a complex pattern of effects. In the few seconds it takes a tornado to pass over a house, some parts break away sooner than others, allowing the wind to selectively reach into some places more than others. Combining wind strength, time, opportunity, and relative position yields a different degree of damage tolerance for every object and every step of the way along the path.

Why did it turn suddenly?

A true turn along the path (verified by damage) is actually hard to explain. If we think of the vortex as a long hose hanging in the air, we can imagine that changes in the air currents can distort the bottom of it slightly. Small displacements are not uncommon, but the tornado will readjust because it is connected to the storm moving on a straight course. The most common reason for a brief position change is the emergence of a new or renewed sub-vortex which repositions the point of maximum impact.

A more prevalent perception of sudden shifts comes from the interpretation of distance and motion. When a tornado is far away, its lateral motion is minimal and it will look like it is heading right for you. When it comes near, the lateral motion (previously not very obvious) is magnified in your view and becomes increasingly apparent. To your senses, it looks like the tornado is turning more and more off the earlier path, or is suddenly shifting to the side. This is only an illusion, heightened by the small fluctuations in the tornado's nearly straight path. Unless you experience a direct hit, the tornado will always look like it veered at some point and missed you, as if it had changed direction.

Why are some things put down gently?

Have you ever vacuumed up a large stone that went part way up the hose and then hung there, suspended in the airflow? It is suspended in a balance between air pushing up on it and gravity pushing down, but a slight decrease in suction and it descends back toward the opening. In a tornado, the stream of air rising in the vortex will only change slowly and smoothly from one moment to the next. If an object survives the initial wind force around the outer edge of the vortex, it may be lifted by the winds nearer the centre, which are mostly going up rather than in a circle. This lifting force can offset gravity and elevate very heavy objects, which then reach a point of balance while suspended. The object may then come under a slightly weaker upward wind force, allowing gravity to re-establish a slight edge. The object will then sink slowly back to the ground and may be put down as gently as a feather. All this, of course, happens in an instant or two. It's a tricky balance to maintain, and can only happen if the object is in exactly the right position inside the tornado and is not flung outward.

"What say we go back?"

The April 20th, 1996 tornadoes

The northern tornado

On the afternoon of April 20th, 1996, a strong cold front was sweeping across eastern Michigan. The first storms raced northeast across Lake Huron and arrived at Kincardine with high winds and moderate hail. They carried on to Owen Sound where an ominous greenish sky preceded golfball-size hail. In the meantime, a separate cell formed to the south and matured very rapidly into a compact thunderstorm southwest of Williamsford. This new storm may have been triggered by the cool outflow from the now aging storm complex to its north. At about 5:50pm a thin funnel cloud was sighted. It darted briefly to the ground, lifted again, then went down to stay, about 5km (3 miles) southwest of Williamsford, in the Krug bush. Early damage was sporadic and the young tornado seemed to skim the tree tops at times. But within a minute or so, it grew steadily stronger and widened as it approached town.

This storm was relatively high-based and very stretched-out by the greater than 150kmh (80mph) winds aloft. The storm's anvil streamed far ahead (and away) from the intense updraft base. People watching the storm approach saw clear sky ahead and behind a narrow black line of clouds, with a greyish area (precipitation) passing well to their north. The gap between the tornado and the nearest rain or hail was several kilometres and stayed that wide all the way along. The wall cloud was fluffy and round, and showed clear signs of turning. The tornado formed in the middle of it and became almost as wide as the whole wall cloud as it crossed Highway 6, just south of Williamsford.

The tornado was large and dusty at Highway 6. It seemed to turn briefly north– or linger there– because the initial single vortex had already separated into at least two sub-

Why were there only two tornadoes?

Let's take a big step back and look at the larger picture. The weather system responsible for these two tornadoes stretched from the Great Lakes down to the Gulf of Mexico. Conditions favourable for tornadoes existed along the entire length. Thunderstorm cells did form all the way down and many went severe.

The gap between these two tornadoes is typical of supercell tornadic storms, which need to be far enough apart not to compete or influence each other. There may be weaker cells between the stronger ones, but a healthy distance– usually more than 50km (30 miles)– almost always separates them. There is no room for two tough guys in the same neighbourhood! And continuing the analogy, there was only room for two such neighbourhoods within the favourable region.

A number of other destructive tornadoes did occur farther south that night (in the U.S.). Southern Ontario is surrounded by lakes full of cold water in the spring. It is not the best place to trigger a severe storm. The area least affected by the cold lakes is a belt running midway between the Lake Erie-Ontario region and the Lake Huron-Georgian Bay region– a narrow axis along which storms can flourish with a minimum of interference (see **Chapter eight**). The northern tornado seems to have been an exception– it was just so unstable there that nothing could stop it. But south of the southern storm there were two other weaker thunderstorms on the same line. One moved along the north shore of Lake Ontario and another crossed the Niagara Peninsula. Neither produced a tornado because they were too far south to benefit from the exceptional winds and instability aloft to their north, yet too far north to draw on much warmer, more humid air as an alternative. They might still have become tornadic if the air crossing those lakes and entering them had not been so much colder.

vortices which rotated around the wall cloud. One crossed the highway, damaged a house and destroyed a barn on the east side, while the other took down forest and several poles on the west side. The damage path here was 400m wide (1,300 feet) as a result. Extensive debris filled the air. It looked like black smoke from the northeast side (backlit) but others saw a brown-rust colour from the opposite side. Good lighting on the tornado's backside made it look white, and for a brief time it was visible almost to the ground. After Highway 6, the visible funnel only made it as far as about halfway down, but was often shorter too.

At Williamsford the tornado turned to the east and did extensive F2-F3 damage to a strip of homes along County Road 24. It was becoming a blunted cone, but continued with signs of separate (but invisible) vortices. As the tornado crossed Williams Lake, some of these vortices became clearer as they stirred up columns of spray over the water. From farther away this divided structure was apparent in the way the tornado moved from side-to-side like a waddling duck. By this time it was maintaining F2 strength, but became a little more compact in size and appearance. Moving east-northeast, it skimmed the south side of the lake, did extensive tree damage, then emerged at Highway 10.

Myth

There may be more coming— Except for the very rare case of a second tornadic storm arriving later at the same general location, this cannot happen. Some people interpret the separate sub-vortices as different tornadoes, though, but they would all occur within the minute or so it takes the entire structure to pass by.

Back at Williamsford, a cold wind (outflow) had briefly surged in behind the tornado. Then it cleared abruptly, only to cloud over again and darken. Several smaller cells had formed along the same axis and one of them brought brief, heavy showers of rain and hail which were unrelated to the tornado's storm. The strongest one of these passed over Durham with quarter-size hailstones. After that it became quiet again, cleared completely, then grew windy and drier into the evening.

Over at Highway 10 the tornado strengthened, knocking down large poles and hurling a 2,000 gallon gasoline storage tank (estimated at 2 tons) for more than a mile. It also broke more distinctly into several vortices. One became completely detached and wandered like a thin hose around the south side of the main vortex. Some places along the path were straddled by the separate parts of the tornado.

As the tornado moved on toward Walters Falls it became very compact, but didn't weaken. A long swath through trees showed that the damage was continuous, but sometimes less than 100m (300 feet) wide. As the tornado, moving mostly northeast now, came out at County Road 4, it seemed to pause again. It turned briefly north and widened, then turned right and followed the road for another stretch of farm damage. The vortex became more separated again and began to form into two distinct funnels with distinct damage effects. It then turned back onto its original east-northeast path. The air was very calm and quiet near the tornado and the sky was bright all around it. Many people wondered where the storm was!

As the tornado passed south of Walters Falls it weakened and narrowed. The visible funnel– which had been bobbing up and down, but always reached at least halfway down, retreated to near the cloud base. The wall cloud had shrunk a bit and there were signs that a large outflow phase to the north was beginning to stretch the updraft farther and farther from the core of the storm. The dark cloud bank was becoming more and more like a gust front with a ragged base. The tornado damage became intermittent but still reached F1-F2 in spots. The two funnels seemed to operate almost completely independently, with separated damage swaths through trees and an unaffected gap between them.

From Walters Falls east, the tornado looked its strangest. Two parallel funnels hung in the sky. At first they looked like two hooks on a claw but later the one on the left dominated while the other one rode along as its companion. They took turns darting down to inflict small stretches of damage. The damage swath widened and increased from F1 to F2 again and the tornado rolled into Blantyre under full steam. But just east of there it lifted briefly, then came down again, but it didn't stay down consistently any more.

The storm moved out over Georgian Bay. The last clear tornado touchdown was just southwest of Griersville around 6:30pm. For this last stretch the funnel remained mostly aloft. After it vanished the mesocyclone and rotating updraft still held together for a long time. Although outflow and another storm to the south were putting pressure on this storm, it is probable that the cold waters of Georgian Bay provided just enough cooling of the inflow air to rob the storm of its tornadic potential.

Most people who came into close contact with the tornado saw only a swirling mass of debris. It almost never thundered and the sky remained relatively bright. It was like a brief interruption to a fine day– and the tornado was far enough south of the precipitation to completely surprise many people. Winds, which had been breezy south ahead of the storm, became light near the tornado. The stillness was unnerving. A few kilometres to the north, a swath of large hail and rain raked the countryside. The day was warm for April but nothing extraordinary. Snow and ice from the weeks before were still lying around in patches. A few days after the tornado, snows returned. The tornado came like a burst of spring in the midst of a very cold, wintry month.

 ## Our take on *Twister*

Turning nature into an evil, out-of-control menace is a Hollywood specialty. The message is clear: tame the beast, be a conquering hero– life's a bore unless we bury ourselves in conflict and drama! Tornadoes were cast as the villains in the movie *Twister*. With the help of amazing special effects we were yanked to the edge of our seats and taken for an up-close-and-personal ride to the edge of a Hell from Heaven. And we ate it up!

It's fun to be entertained– but don't hold your breath for a science lesson here! Reality is far too slow, too complex, and too unco-operative to be of much use in a Tinseltown twist on tornadoes. The movie had many flaws and technical gaffs in it, but also gave a truly distorted picture of what a tornado situation is like. If you have seen it or plan to, enjoy it but don't take it too seriously.

The only actual sky scenes in it were at the beginning and end. Everything in between, including all the skies around the tornadoes, were either faked or inappropriate. We have never seen so many stable stratocumulus skies posture as portenders of power! The tornadoes themselves were lively– or was that alive? They writhed and groaned, always holding tightly together like solid objects. It gave the impression that a tornado has a discernible outer edge to its influence– and it doesn't. The movie also presented a direct correlation between size and intensity, and generally implied that tornadoes can come anytime, anywhere– from just over a rise or behind the trees– and move, vanish, or re-form at will. The uglier it looked, the worse it became– a nice, convenient, uncomplicated scenario.

Don't get us wrong– we enjoyed it. You can't help being gripped by the sound effects. And as veteran chasers, we found that the challenge and sense of respect for nature somehow survived Hollywood's heavy-handed offering. Many people said, "Great!", "Loved it!", "...a real thrill". Others were a little more reticent. As one put it, "I've seen the real thing and those tornadoes on TV don't do nothin' for me!" Go ahead and call us old-fashioned, but we'll take the real thing too. Everything is so natural, so original– so perfect there. The beauty is in the mystery– in what you don't see or know. Tornadoes don't need digital enhancement or a troubling facade– they simply demand our respect and admiration– exactly as they are.

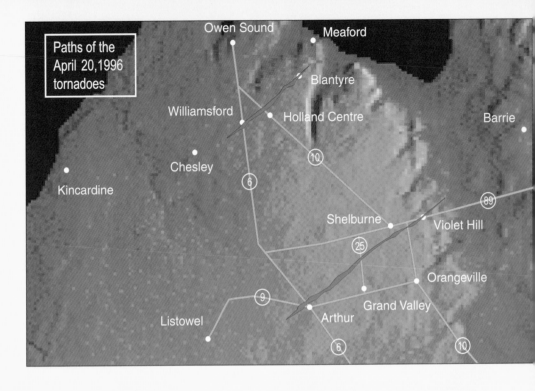

Paths of the
April 20,1996
tornadoes

Owen Sound   Meaford

Blantyre

Williamsford   Holland Centre

Barrie

Chesley   ⑩

⑥

Kincardine   ⑧⑨

Shelburne   Violet Hill

㉕

Orangeville

⑨   Grand Valley

Listowel   Arthur

⑥   ⑩

The northern tornado

"I saw two funnels– switching. It was just bouncing. It looked like a great big jackrabbit."

"I saw clouds moving so low and so fast that I thought it was smoke from the neighbour's house. A half a roof went tumbling right up to the top of the funnel cloud, end-over-end. It went very quickly black, got a little bit noisy, and got real wide."

"It didn't even look like a tornado. It just looked like there was a dip in the cloud. You could see the tornado but the clouds were separate and they were still pulling in together. ... You could tell each one was coming from a different way."

"I couldn't tell in which direction it was moving. It appeared to be dancing on the spot. There was this lowering black cloud that just hung over us. You felt as if you could reach out the window and it was a few feet above you. You could almost touch it. It seemed to separate as if the top were separating from the bottom and the two bits were spinning separately, and then it reformed again– and all in the space of a few seconds, I guess."

"When it touched down it just looked like a big humongous barnfire– black billows of smoke."

"It didn't look like a tornado like you see on TV at all. It just looked like this big huge cloud."

"The funnel– the top of it– would go back and forth like a weed caught in water."

"The sky went very dark, then quiet and calm, like out of the twilight zone, like watching a horror movie build up the suspense."

"It just looked like it would pull the cloud up and down like an elastic. It was coming back down and back up and then little ones would develop beside the major one."

"There was the main funnel and these little streamers off to the side, and they seemed to be around it all the time and they were just like little whirlpools."

"The sky was all blue, all around it, but there was a huge black cloud all enclosed (like the kind we have in Broom Hilda in the funny papers– just over her head), pitch black. On the left-hand side of it, coming toward me very, very slowly there was a little trail. Sometimes it would come down and wibble-wobble right to the ground, and then it would go back up."

"The funnel of the actual tornado when it come down was buried in bluey-grey clouds, all the way down. It was just like the sky fell. It was just like a wall of clouds– a wall of swirling smoke. But inside you could see the funnel."

"It was like 12 different layers of clouds, all going in different directions and on different levels, and then it started to boil. It came together and started to roll and bubble."

"One was a big grey mass. Then we saw another one. It looked like a long black dirty piece of rope. That was the small one. It was discernible, it was very skinny and very long and very black. The grey one didn't have a bottom but the black one, you could see a bottom to it. It was just snaking around– it would be crooked. They looked to be about 200 yards (metres) from each other."

"When I first saw the second one– because it was behind the big fat grey one– they kind of looked like they collided at the corner, and then split apart. It just seemed like they were going together and separating. I saw it do that probably twice."

"It was the cyclone shape, black as the ace of spades. I've seen them on TV here and there– but no, I mean, this thing was big and it was rippin'!"

"Instead of just coming at you it was just swinging kind of like a pendulum, you'd swear. If you were looking at it, it was like a thing that couldn't make up its mind which way to go. It was just weaving."

"I saw what looked like heavy black smoke, but not like you would see smoke behave. It kind of feathered and went over and would stop, and feather out again."

"At one point it went up and two funnels came down. They looked like they were twins. My son said they looked like fangs."

"I kinda remember it spinning around like whipped cream or something. It was very, very pretty. It wasn't scary– you were amazed that these clouds were just swirling."

"It came in with its tail behind it and it was on an angle."

"It was a disturbing type of sky. It was like you see in the pictures except it was white instead of black– like a big white plume."

The April 20th, 1996 tornadoes summary of key features

	Northern	Southern
Time (E.S.T.)	5:50-6:30pm	6:10-7:05pm
Path length	37km/23mi	63km/39mi
Forward motion	55kmh/35mph	70kmh/43mph
Path width (approx.) max/avg/min	450/200/100m 1400/600/300ft	500/150/50m 1600/500/150ft
Intensity	F3/average F2	F3/average F2
Injuries	1 (+5 minor)	0 (+3 minor)
Damage*	est. $1.5 million	est. $6.5 million

*Conservative early estimation by insurance, for insured losses only

131

The southern tornado

"The clouds looked unlike anything we'd ever seen before. They were moving very, very quickly and then going right up, straight up into the sky."

"It was like a dark cloud come out with the tail on the ground. As it come up the field it just looked like a black wall coming. It looked like it was just sitting still and it was just getting bigger and bigger and bigger."

"It just looked like a gigantic donut spinning around. It looked like a snowcone."

"You could see stuff– whole pieces of buildings or barns– huge pieces of stuff, and they were just flipping, just whirling. It was really amazing. The other thing I noticed would be– I don't know what you call it– like a spur would go off the side of it."

"It was like the sky was being sucked into the ground. That's the way it appeared– like the whole sky, all those black clouds were being sucked towards the ground opposite of what it shoulda looked like."

"Both times– in 1985 and this last one– I've noticed the sky has changed a really weird colour. It's kind of a peach and a purple mixed together– black clouds with a peach and a purple over top of them, and it's visible over top of them. It's very pretty, but now whenever I see that colour of sky I get a little panicky."

"It was like this funnel thing goin' across and every once in a while it changed colours– it would just be black. As soon as it hit something it seemed to billow and change colour. We were describing it afterward like the Peanuts cartoon and Linus with that cloud of dust that goes with him– it was almost like that. There was more dust than there was tornado. It seemed like it moved so slowly across the horizon."

"You could actually see a finger coming out of the big spout."

"The funnel was still black, and I just couldn't believe the thinness of it."

"These two columns or pillars appeared to come out equally on each side and just stay there for a couple of seconds and then go back into the middle."

"Have you ever watched on a beach when somebody has a metal detector and they're walking along and they're just swaying it back and forth, and they're very deliberate in their movements? That's what it reminded me of. It snaked down and just sorta swept across the ground. The clouds were tumbling over each other. It's like they were angrily gobbling each other up."

"When the funnel was down you could see– that was very distinct and fairly narrow– because that was like a surgical knife that went through the Kottelenberg farm And then when it went back up it widened. But it stayed fairly wide– it didn't seem to oscillate wide and then narrow and wide."

"From a distance you can't tell how big these things really are. When I was getting closer to it and seeing the base of it, it was only about 100ft (30m) when it was touching down. It was lifting up and setting back down. That was kind of neat to watch. It did it a couple of times. I thought it was just dissipated and was gone, but after a couple of seconds you could see it gaining power again and then coming back down again."

(Photos are numbered in order along the path.)

7

8

9

"It seemed to be that it started to descend from the sky in a triangular shape and then elongated and the part touching the ground would almost stay in one area for a moment while the storm moved away; and then the funnel itself would either pick up and catch up with the storm or else it would break off and disappear, and descend again further along."

"It kinda danced across our horizon. And at times you could see it was much more severe than others."

"There was a funny thing. Once that thing went past you, you couldn't see it. You couldn't see it! As it was coming toward us it was as black as coal– and it was daylight, eh? But once it went past you, you couldn't even see it. I thought the thing had disappeared!"

"You could see the way the clouds were so high that day too– it just stuck out like a sore thumb. It was like snake things comin' off the side– at one time there was a bunch of them."

"But the other thing that totally amazed me was the tail that ran along behind it. It would just be like somebody had a rope and holding on to the end of the rope and twistin it, flipping it. And that was dragging along maybe 100 yards (metres) behind, and it just literally had a life of its own. It was just bouncin along the ground."

"That was the most frightening thing to see– this funnel and then it becomes almost like a bolt of lightning, the way it hits."

"The visual impression of the slowness of the debris flying was something. It was deceiving, like birds flying in slow-motion."

"The cloud itself never came and touched the ground. All the wind around at the ground was doing all the damage. And then when I went over and I saw the damage done to the other houses, I was amazed! This thing didn't look that strong at all! Only a few times does it ever even look like a tornado looked to me. It just sorta looked like a bulb."

12

13

15

16

17

18

11

14

The southern tornado

At about the time as the northern tornado first touched down, another thunderstorm cell formed rapidly near Listowel. It was a very compact storm and also had an anvil that streamed well ahead of the updraft base. The transition from a flat black base to one with a wall cloud occurred in only minutes. Some people saw this as vertical fingers of cloud hanging from the base. The lowering became large and solid and it took only about ten minutes in all for it to form completely and begin rotating.

The first touchdown was 8km (5 miles) west-southwest of Arthur at 6:10pm. From a distance, a funnel peeked out, vanished, then re-emerged and went right down. Up close the touchdown was first seen as a plume of debris, but shortly after that the visible funnel came to the ground as a narrow tube. Within even the first minute, the vortex began showing signs of dividing into separate vortices. In the section before Highway 9 as many as four distinct damage paths were seen and the collective swath width was almost 500m (1500 feet). The tornado went quickly from F1 to F2, widened steadily, and became an F3 as it came up to the highway from the southwest.

The tornado in this storm was initially much closer to the precipitation, which was mainly golfball-size hail. People under the hail noticed a series of hail showers, each with larger stones. Initially there was also regular thunder with it, but no wind at all. The sky was bright ahead of and behind a single black cloud bank, which extended south from the precipitation

A large, dark, dangerous tornado greeted the farms and homes at Highway 9 and extensive damage began on the west side of Arthur. The condensation funnel was a wide wedge, right to the ground and mixed with debris. Several large appendages, including a

✍ The 1985 "Barrie" tornado– the other end of the spectrum

The May 31st tornado outbreak in 1985 included two F4 tornadoes and several weaker ones in Southern Ontario, plus many others in the U.S. The two F4 tornadoes had a combined damage path length of 275km (172 miles)– yet **not a single person** saw a tornado! (We have since discovered a few who saw the initial funnel.) How is this possible? What kind of tornado could be so different from the 1996 experience?

Let's put aside the element of surprise, which was significant back then because there hadn't been such a severe event in that area for a generation. The main difference comes down to moisture. Although the weather system, winds and conditions aloft were similar in both cases, the 1985 event was much later in the season and the air feeding those storms was hot and choked with moisture. When storms formed, they went severe right away, just as they did in 1996. But the very high dew points caused huge amounts of rain and hail to form. This deluge forced a typical worst-last storm to evolve into a special kind of supercell, in which the wall cloud sits out ahead of the rain and is often enveloped by it. The humid air caused cloud bases to be very low, and added widespread lower cloud layers as well. It all added up to a storm that was black, messy, hard to see, and very dangerous. These kinds of storms are more frequent in regions farther south– not a comforting thought for the people of tornado alley.

Fortunately, the 1985 tornadoes were as far to one end of the spectrum as the 1996 event was to the other. When the next tornado outbreak comes in this part of Ontario, it is more likely to be neither, but rather a blend or midpoint between them. We will probably see it, but we won't be sitting on the deck or in our car, waiting 20 minutes for it to arrive! The 1985 event put everyone on alert, as if an enemy had crept into town unseen. The 1996 event may have encouraged some people to be less concerned– thinking that the next one will also show itself clearly. We have to develop a more realistic perspective on what may happen in the future.

black lobe, formed in mid-air ahead of the main vortex, which also had sub-vortices embedded in it. These features came and went repeatedly while the main vortex churned forward. As the tornado came to Highway 6 it was at peak F3 strength and at its largest, averaging 300-400m (1000-1300 feet) across. The main vortex had a companion for a brief time– a thin, black rope-like vortex that swung around the southeast side of the larger circulation and was quite separate from it. As the main vortex crossed the highway, it destroyed a barn full of hay and wrapped itself in a camouflaging dusty yellow haze for a short time.

The storm itself became larger too. A torrent of rain and hail preceded the tornado just on the north side of the path. The mesocyclone was large and pulled some of the precipitation right around itself. Even as the tornado was moving away, partly obscured by precipitation, rain and small hail continued behind it. But a transition was already under way that would soon change the tornado's appearance. As outflow increased in the Arthur area, the updraft began shifting more to the right and the tornado turned onto an east-northeast path. Many farms and homes were heavily damaged before it moved into the sparser territory of the Luther Marsh.

East of the marsh, the storm began to stretch out and the tornado narrowed to a fat, tapered cone and weakened a bit to F2. Strengthening winds aloft were pulling the anvil and precipitation farther away and a gap between the tornado and the nearest rain or hail opened up gradually. On the north side of the path, there was a mixture of golfball hail,

black sky, and a cold wind. Along the path it was quiet– until the tornado arrived! To the south, a steadier south-southeast breeze lightened, then turned to the southwest and increased. It remained fair and bright on this side of the storm. All the air in the region seemed to point right at the tornado. It damaged more homes, swept through a power corridor– taking down three giant towers with a huge electric flash– and then headed across Highway 25.

The tornado was now a "classic" shape– but had many small snake-like appendages. The condensation funnel remained on the ground and its base was narrow and focused. From ahead it looked black, but from the southwest side it was like a graceful, haunting white column, gliding silently across the open countryside. It was a magnificent sight– nothing like what the people at Arthur saw and nothing like what it would become later. The tornado funnel lifted a little as it came closer to Shelburne, but F1-F2 damage continued.

Shelburne was a town of weather contrasts. A dense curtain of rain and large hail skirted the centre of town but hit with full force a few blocks to the north. At the same time, chunks of metal from barn roofs littered a wide area 2-4km (1-3 miles) north of the path. Some large crumpled pieces landed silently, as if by magic, in the yards of astonished onlookers. South of town, good visibility and the prominent backlit tornado allowed people to see it coming well ahead. Except for the hail, though, there weren't too many other clues about. There was only the occasional flash of lightning, and the clouds weren't as dark or weird as on many other occasions. The high bases, good light and open view provided the best warning of all– for those who looked out. The tornado passed several kilometres south of the town centre and chewed up more homes and businesses. Although the visible funnel was off the ground (up about one-third) the damage path was continuous and contained pockets of intense F2-F3 destruction. Oddly, the tornado looked less convincing here than earlier, yet was just as dangerous.

As the tornado neared Highway 10 it weakened briefly and crossed without doing much damage for more than a kilometre. The visible funnel had lifted over halfway back up and had shrunk to a V-shape at the top with a thin spear extending down below it. But in about a minute, another short stretch of heavy F2 damage ensued. As the slender tornado moved toward Violet Hill it marked its path with occasional bursts of debris and a continuous swath of damage. The path had narrowed to 100-200m (3-600 feet) but was very concentrated. For a few seconds the visible funnel darted elegantly all the way to the ground, then quickly retreated. It oscillated up and down in rhythm with the stronger stretches of ground contact. The tornado was now several kilometres away from the nearest rain and the drier air around it kept the visible funnel closer to the cloud base.

Another large outflow phase began just east of Shelburne. This pulsing character– with regular, approximately 20-minute cycles of weaker-stronger activity– was like a tug-of-war between the powerful updraft and tenacious downdrafts trying to displace it. North of Violet Hill, the hail and rain were accompanied by strong northerly winds. The tornado, which had moved slightly more northeast during its recent weaker phase, now turned back to the east-northeast as it came to Highway 89. After damaging many homes in Violet Hill (F1-F2) it began to enter the final stages of its life. The vortex, mostly invisible except for a dusty debris cloud at the ground, was only about 50m (160 feet) wide but still quite potent. The wall cloud was compact and round. A large sunlit rain curtain to its north contrasted sharply with the bluish-black cloud bank containing the protruding visible funnel and tornado.

Outflow surged forward, undercutting the lowering and stretching the vortex toward the south. It lifted, briefly hung like a thick, curvy sausage, horizontally in the air, then evaporated around 7:05pm. The wall cloud and rotation continued for awhile as the storm headed northeast toward Barrie. There were hints of brief damage near Angus but it wasn't clear that another touchdown was responsible.

Many people saw this tornado coming, but many others were surprised by it. Most thought that it looked relatively small and innocent in the later period. When they checked out the damage they were shocked by what they discovered. The storm had a little more cloud around it (especially ahead) but none of it looked too threatening. Fair weather persisted to the south of the tornado. From farther south, a mammoth thunderhead filled the sky, trailed by a long gust front "tail". Right after the tornado the weather became unrealistically sunny and placid. A short time later, another line of towering clouds swept through with the cold front. In eastern parts of the region at sunset, this dramatic wall of orange-pink clouds put the finishing touch on a remarkable day. The front was followed by very strong west-southwest winds and clear skies, as the cooler air swept in.

Myth

Tornadoes won't cross water— "It didn't want to come across the lake. They never cross water; they'll jump around it." There is no effect whatsoever by water in any form on a tornado's strength or movement. (Cold air over very large lakes can weaken a tornado.) This impression comes from selectively interpreting what a tornado does while near or over water and then associating that information with the presence of water. Any nonstandard feature along a tornado's path is vulnerable to this kind of a "coincidence of convenience."

MAGNIFICENT OR MONSTROUS?

Tornadoes present us with a philosophical dilemma: do we view them as destructive, unwanted threats or as rare, beautiful treasures of nature? Put another way, can we accept and respect nature for what it is without automatically imposing our wants and likes as the basis for our attitudes? Is it reasonable to interpret everything we experience in the light of our own preferences and pleasures? Can nature be properly appreciated if we interpret its effects as bad or unwanted? Tornadoes, like other natural phenomena, are out of our control— but they are ultimately a testament to forces greater than ourselves, to the presence of God in the world around us. It's almost like the clash between good and evil. Both are present together and we need to accommodate both in a positive way to make the most of our lives.

It is tempting to villify tornadoes as unwelcome intruders. Their threat is clear and straightforward— an easy target for our frustrations with a force that is not under our control. Tornadoes can easily become an evil entity, a potential enemy of our stable, self-directed existence. In reality, of course, the tornado is far from being a pervasive threat or daily concern. There are tougher issues, bigger problems, much better examples of evils that require our attention. If the tornado is our enemy, it is one we can live with and learn from. It is a mirror to our own limitations and vulnerability, a lesson in humility and the grander principles in nature. In one sense, the tornado should be deemed a priority. It gives us all a chance to rekindle our interest in science, in natural phenomena— in what's happening outside our daily grind. It's an opportunity to be intrigued and inspired by one of life's mysteries, a formidable force in the mere whirling of air.

In its threat, in its way of personifying our own fears and perceptions of evil, it is a monster— but only in our minds, and only if we let it be. As a rare, complex concoction of fascinating manifestations, it is a magnificent creation, a sight we are privileged to behold. A tornado, representing the very limit of nature's fury, can be the beginning of our enlightenment.

How they compared to each other

These two tornadic storms were more alike than different because they both formed in similar conditions. Each began as an isolated cloud, exploded to severe levels quickly, was preceded by golfball hail but not too much rain, and had little thunder and lightning. In each, the anvil and core of the storm were stretched out far ahead and to the north of the updraft and tornado. Although the cloud and precipitation with the storms travelled at 80-85kmh (50-53mph), the tornadoes themselves moved more slowly under the regenerating updrafts. Both storms were near-perfect examples of the worst-last type, mainly due to the very strong winds aloft and dry early-spring air. Both came and went as brief events in an otherwise fair day.

Another similarity was the way they both began with an intense burst, settled into a steady state, then slowly diminished in strength. This was mainly the result of conditions around the storm being compromised by the ever-present outflow. The ingredients were already skimpy (after all, this was very early in the season!) and the maximum instability aloft raced across at just the right time to keep a delicate but fragile balance in place for a few hours.

The two tornadoes evolved similarly too. Each began small, widened and strengthened to a maximum within minutes, then slowly shrank in steps until they withered. This trend even continued after the tornadoes had lifted, since both storms carried on as well-built hailstorms with a lowering and signs of rotation. Each tornado exhibited many variations during its life and produced persistent F2 damage with a few weaker or stronger pockets along the way.

So what wasn't the same? It is interesting to look at differences and try to search out the causes. And differences under a similar set of conditions must arise from changes in specific ingredients. The visible funnel in the northern tornado was much shorter because the air was less moist (lower dew point). You might expect that to render it weaker too, but it is possible that slightly stronger winds aloft and a better inflow direction (more southeast than south) helped that storm offset the disadvantage. By comparison, the southern storm had a little more trouble with outflow because of the moister air (more precipitation), but a better "fuel mixture" gave its updraft that little boost it needed too. The northern storm died prematurely thanks to frigid Georgian Bay, which still had some ice in it. (You could say it threw cold air on the party!). The southern tornado travelled a little faster than the northern one on average, but also sped up gradually as it moved along.

The biggest difference between the two was probably in our reactions. The northern one was a total surprise. Nobody expected such a thing to happen, especially so early. The storm looked innocuous. The tornado wasn't that obvious and was often hidden by trees. There were few hints on the radio yet, as the weather office scrambled in its attempts to verify what was going on. When the southern tornado got under way, it hit a larger town and immediately triggered a media and communications alert for those farther east. Memories of 1985 were still fresh in people's minds and many were waiting for it. The view helped too. With fewer trees and excellent visibility– and a larger population base– this second tornado could not sneak up and surprise as many people.

Myth

Tornadoes are affected by what they hit or lift up— "It took so much dirt when it hit that hill that it slowed down." We all want to believe this because it feels so reasonable– but it's false. A tornado can't get "heavy" because it's not carrying anything. All the debris is in suspension under wind force and the only thing that determines how much stuff is being held is the balance between what is being added and what is being thrown back out. The winds respond to a pressure field, independent of the volume or weight of debris involved.

How they compared to the norm

How do these tornadoes stack up to the hundreds of other strong tornadoes we have had in North America? If you consider the norm to be an average over all similar tornadoes (excluding the weaker gustnadoes, landspouts, etc.), they looked and behaved more or less normally. They were more like the tornadoes that you would encounter on the Prairies or in the U.S. upper Midwest than those that occur in more humid regions. But they were more potent than most tornadoes out west. The large-scale weather system, with its sweeping cold front and racing storms, is more of an eastern phenomenon.

Myth

The winds are hundreds of kilometres an hour in a tornado— Peak winds in a tornado occur for short times and in small pockets within the wind pattern. They are not sustained at very high speeds over the entire circulation or for an extended time period, even in a large, intense tornado.

For this part of Southern Ontario they were much more exceptional. We rarely get such a taste of western Kansas– high cloud bases, dry air, and a tornado you can **see**! They were also very early in the season, more persistently intense, faster-moving, and longer-lived than average. The southern tornado took the same track as others in recent years, so we could presume that it was less uncommon there. But the northern one was a true rarity– a once-in-a-century event. It may be the earliest long-track F2-F3 tornado we will ever see that far north and that close to the cold waters of Lake Huron.

Most people who saw one of these tornadoes only saw one particular sight– one moment out of a long sequence of continuous evolution. It's easy to take that single, memorable moment and imagine just one tornado image. But these tornadoes ranged through a gamut of shapes, sizes and behaviour. At one time or another they showed us almost every variation imaginable and in one event we witnessed a very thorough exposé of all the tornadic effects seen in dozens of other situations.

Discoveries and mysteries

Every tornado leaves us with more than debris, disruption, and vivid memories– it raises many unanswered questions and offers only a complex trail of evidence to sort out the answers. These two tornadoes had their fair share of mysteries. Exploring them reveals that the mystery lies both in how they behaved and how we reacted to or perceived them. They also gave us confirmation of many poorly-understood traits or hard-to-prove effects, and threw in a few new discoveries to ponder in future research.

The mystery of the sudden silence

"And then all of a sudden it stopped– very quickly."

"I'll tell you, when it passed– at our place I'll bet you could hear people whispering ten miles away!. There wasn't a bird– you **couldn't hear anything**! Oh, God, it was quiet– and like, just all the animals or whatever– birds, everything– were just petrified, standing in awe!"

"Dead silence! There wasn't a bird– nothing! You could have heard a pin drop in Chatsworth, I swear! There wasn't a noise– there was nothing! It's the quietest I've ever ever heard it!"

These sentiments were echoed over and over by people right on the path. Not only was the silence after the tornado absolute, it seemed to come on very abruptly. With few exceptions, people heard the noise increase gradually, yet end suddenly. Is there something about the winds in a tornado or the air around it which could cause this? It's not likely. Whatever causes the roaring should be just as apparent at the same distance either side of it.

But consider the psychological impact of impending danger. A strange noise arrives, peaks, then fades. Your ears tune in and a heightened sensitivity kicks in as you realize the danger that is present. The approaching noise is the focus of your attention and every second is stretched out in your mind. Then, as the tornado passes over, an altered reality sets in– a mixture of disbelief and relief– and your mind goes into a brief period of suspended reality. At the same time, every other usual sound outside has fallen silent in the wake of the whirlwind. Going from one extreme to the other, the mind is tricked– preoccupied by a silence which discounts, even denies, the sound of a tornado in retreat. A skewed sense of time coupled with the contrast of going from noisy to nothing would seem to be the most likely answer. There is no doubt it was abnormally quiet afterward, but people also had other things to dwell on once the tornado was safely past them.

The mystery of the silent destruction

"That awful roar was gone, which we didn't hear obviously when it was hitting the house– which is strange because there was no background noise that could have drowned that out. So I can't explain that– why coming toward us there was this incredibly loud roar and it seemed that when it was visiting us there was no sound to be heard."

"We were in the centre of it and I think it was just so quiet."

This mystery has led to a few really wild conclusions about what is going on inside the tornado– everything from the absence of noise in a vacuum to something akin to a black hole in there. Since the noise originates in the contact of wind with objects, we can reasonably assume that it cannot be silent when the tornado's winds are blowing over a house. It is quite likely, though, that the sound will change character from a uniform roar to a less blended, more erratic series of separate noises. But that wouldn't account for hearing nothing at all. A tornado may be powerful, but it can't suck the noise out with the rest of the stuff!

Could a fear-stricken victim cowering in the basement be overtaken by a panic that blocks out sound? Possibly. Was the basement or other place of shelter too well insulated? In a few cases, it is possible that the tornado brought along its own "insulation"– a mass of mud and water that may have dampened sounds. But the most probable cause is the physical changes imposed on our hearing by a sudden pressure change. As the pressure changes our ears close up quickly and we may not even realize that the outside sounds have been blocked out. Pressure changes can also induce a distracting pain in the ears. These temporary changes, when combined with contradicted expectations and some of the effects of the trauma, may impair normal hearing for those critical few seconds of noisy rampaging above us.

Myth

Tornadoes will follow ...— This idea can be completed by many examples: rivers, ridges, valleys, underwater tributaries, sources of ground heat, etc. In fact, a tornado doesn't follow anything but the laws of nature— and the storm it is attached to. Everything else is folklore, wishful thinking or selective interpretation of the evidence.

What's that smell?

"It smelled of dirt– like, not the dirt on the ground but dust, you know– like the vacuum cleaner has– that smell."

"That is one thing I did notice, that it was the strangest smell I ever smelled– a smell I never smelled before, after the tornado. I think it was a mixture of broken trees, and– I don't know what it was. And it was in the clothes, it was in the air– everything."

If you think the dog smells funny after sniffing around in who knows how many different places, then imagine the possibilities with a tornado! We don't usually think about what a tornado **smells** like, but after it churns through houses, forests, swamps, fields (some with manure on them) and everything else, it is going to smell a little peculiar. That was especially true for those people who were directly downwind of a marsh or swamp. A patch of stagnant water filled with roots and mud just after spring thaw is not going to come up smelling of roses. After a tornado mud-slinging session in which this foul odour has been spread around onto everything, the smell can be hard to live with or eradicate. We can only wonder what it would be like to have a tornado sweep across a meadow of wildflowers instead!

Deflected danger

Imagine having a house surrounded by large trees and receiving a direct hit by a tornado. You come out to discover that all the trees were taken down, but none of them landed on the house. Coincidence? After hearing several reports like this we began to wonder what was going on. Could the tree roots be uneven– stronger or larger in one direction underground so as to influence how they fell? Some people suggested that the winds deflected off the house and blew the trees away from it. But tornado winds don't work that way. They turn as the tornado's position moves by, so things can fall in every direction. For everything to fall **away** from a central point would be quite an accomplishment!

Here is another idea. Is there anything about a large obstruction that can affect a tornado? Not in the usual sense– the wind strength and source are not affected much by what is on the ground. But if we think of the house as a barrier in the flow, it is possible that the wind strength is increased in a ring outside of this to compensate for the slight slowdown at the obstruction. It's a momentary effect and may only have a small impact, but it doesn't take much to alter the end result. A combination of coincidence and probable distribution is still more likely. With a fast-moving tornado the preferred direction for things to fall is forward, even though the winds blow in every direction around it (because of the forward motion carrying stuff along). So the trees will have a tendency to fall to the northeast and it is only a tree directly on the west side of a house that would need a sizable portion of coincidence not to fall on the house. But of course, there will always be a few exceptions among the many occurrences of any expected result. We only need a few of these exceptions to make us wonder if there's another, more mysterious cause afoot.

The mystery of the birds

"All the birds came out of the trees and laid on the ground just before it hit. ... Every kind of bird– there were hundreds or thousands and you could hear it all throughout this area. They were down on the ground making all this noise– and then all of a sudden it was silent."

If birds react to a tornado's noise and vibrations by hiding or going quiet, that is to be expected. But what strange vibes were they picking up when they vacated the trees for the ground? Whatever the message was, it must have accompanied the tornado, because this behaviour hadn't ever been seen before. All the usual factors like wind, temperature and humidity change would have happened many times before. Noise doesn't usually cause birds to all behave one way either. Maybe small electromagnetic or pressure waves that we can't sense were responsible. If we could only figure this one out, we might be able to use it to create an unconventional detection device.

A peek at multiple-vortex behaviour

At the beginning of the southern tornado, the vortex began narrow but almost immediately showed signs of a multiple-vortex structure. Within minutes the entire structure widened greatly but the separate vortices remained, oscillating from a spaced-out arrangement to a compact one at the ground. A look at one stretch of the damage showed some signs of four separate damage paths, with unaffected areas between them. There were signs of an abrupt widening followed by a gradual narrowing. This suggests that the separate vortices began far apart but converged soon afterward and it holds out at least a hint of what was going on inside the tornado.

The multiple-vortex structure begins when a single vortex is disturbed by a descending airstream. It is fairly certain that the change begins aloft and comes down to the ground. The vortex spreads out away from the centre and divides up into separate whirls. That would account for separated damage swaths starting abruptly. But ,when they come together again, it suggests that there is an opposing force countering this separation process. This change seems to originate at the ground and tries to force the separate vortices together again. It's almost as if the bottom of the tornado has a life of its own and can recreate a single, concentrated vortex from the convergence of air at the base near the ground. This holds until the next bubble from above repeats the cycle. There is not a lot to go on here, but so little is known about the details of tornado evolution that it is worth speculating and wondering about every tracer a tornado leaves behind.

Why is the water waving?

"Instead of lapping ... the water was going straight up and down when the hail was hitting it. And even after the hail was done, with the wind it seemed to be just going straight up and down! That was the most unusual thing I had ever seen. I had never seen water waving a foot up and down out of the pond."

"It was almost like if you had held the vacuum cleaner above it and it was sucking the water– like, the water was in suspension in the pond. It was really neat– like, it was very fascinating. The water was still but the sucked up part was hanging there in suspension."

These two stories imply that there is something about the air or wind which could cause the water to jump up. In both cases, it was confirmed that this oddity persisted even without anything falling from the sky and with relatively weak winds. Can air pressure play a role? If you could drop the pressure enough (much more than would happen with a tornado) you could affect the pond– it would boil away! To make water jump up as freely as a moon-walker, you would need a drastic drop in gravity, instead. What about opposing air currents or gustiness? These could cause the water surface to become choppy, but wouldn't explain large, separated jumps in the water level. Nor would it arouse the kind of fascination we see here.

An intense storm holds a lot of rain and hail within the cloud. Where updrafts are strong enough, only very large water drops or hailstones are heavy enough to fall through to the ground. Some places under such a cloud may only see a sparse few of these land– so few that it could look like nothing was going on outside. There could be just one here, one there, and none over this way. The distance from a house to a pond is enough to separate a small shower of these drops or stones from completely dry conditions. This is the most logical answer– a smattering of fat raindrops or hailstones plopping into the pond like stones, throwing up small bursts of water while an adjacent spot has none. The surprised onlooker would not be able to tell what was causing this because there would be too few to see them falling. This stage in a developing shower is rare and brief and would not be familiar to most people.

The underground connection

One person noted that they had clay in their well water after the tornado. At first that didn't seem to be more than an unrelated matter– until he discovered someone else who had the same experience in the 1985 tornado. Clay was mixed with the water that time too. It began with the tornado and took two years to clear up. Could there be a connection?

We may need to look at another odd thing during the tornado– flushing toilets. Just as the tornado can draw air through a house, it can draw water through pipes as long as it can exert an uneven pressure at an opening in the network. This caused some toilets to flush or "glug" as the water shifted around. A drilled well is like a window to an underground water world. Change the pressure at the opening and you could expect a chain reaction farther down, in which water channels move or slosh back and forth in quick response. It is all connected and it is all easily moved around. This sudden sloshing could have loosened the clay layers and filled the water with clay particles. Add to this the earth-shaking vibrations of a pounding wind force and it's not too far-fetched to imagine the underground world being as much in shambles as the above-ground one!

The mystery of the tinted twister

"It was just like a reddish paint or something, like a real funny colour. Well, I figured now it had to be all the dust and the dirt that it was picking up in the bush and blew on the way through."

"It looked like kind of a burnt reddish swirl and I realized it was the bricks swirling in the wind."

The colour of a tornado will come from what it has in it. If we leave out the larger debris, then most of the time that is simply cloudy air– the condensed water vapour in the condensation funnel which has a neutral colour. If this funnel is absent near the ground you will only see what the tornado is picking up. Usually it is finely-distributed dirt, which has a dark brownish colour (unless the earth is red in the area, as it is in much of Oklahoma). The farther we get from these typical greys and browns, the more unusual and surprising a tornado will look.

The northern tornado had a decidedly pinkish or reddish hue at times. Some of it was from pink insulation which had been used extensively in the area. As a house was hit, the debris cloud became tinted pink for a short time, until the next batch of dirt blotted out the colour. Another tornado years ago acquired a reddish glow, as if it had a fire within it, when it hit a greenhouse full of red flowers. In the '96 case, insulation couldn't account for it all, because the colour also appeared after long stretches of forest. For those times, a mixture of rotting leaves and other organic material from the previous fall (not yet decayed) may have given the tornado its mysterious crimson garb.

Myth
Mobile homes attract tornadoes— It may seem that way, but the reason we might think this is because it takes little force (F0-F1) to do enough damage to a trailor or mobile home for it to become important— either to the occupants or the news. They sustain damage easily and are inhabited, which are two reasons why we get to hear about them so readily.

Far-fetched fury

"And in one room– we couldn't figure out how this happened. There was glass on the floor, but in that room all the windows were still intact! And we don't know how in the heck it got there because in the next room, there was only one window broken and it was at the far end of the room."

There is one thing about tornadoes that is just beyond understanding– how they can reach into places far from any opening or air passageway. The wind seems to have the ability to open drawers or closets and remove the contents or impregnate them with debris particles– even when there is little serious destruction around. One person not only found the clothes gone from the line outside (to be expected) but found all the clothes had been taken out of the dryer too. Many people opened closed drawers and were surprised by the mess inside them. It's as if the wind could reach inside the house, feel around with debris-laden fingers, then retreat. Getting into enclosed spaces wasn't that unusual– it was only when they were discovered re-closed that it looked like a mystery. The real question is how the air can be made to move with such precision and power so far from the source!

We will have to leave this one for future study– perhaps after an immersion in the fascinating world of fluid dynamics. From observations like the example quoted above, the air behaved like a tentacle which maintained its cohesive force far from the outside window. Vortex structure on the larger scale has some of the same properties but these smaller whirls have characteristics that are beyond comprehension. They do suggest one thing, though: The fewer openings in a building the less likely the wind will be to reach far inside. We want to keep windows and doors shut and force the tornado to open them if it wants to snoop around!

Mysterious manifestations

"After it was all over I had blood underneath the skin of my legs and my arms, the same as the grandchildren. It just looked like someone came along and gave you little pinches– you know how they draw the blood."

"We could not brush his hair down. You could wash his hair but it would not stay down. We had to give him a brush cut– that's the only way we could do anything with that hair!"

Some of the strange afflictions people get after a tornado can leave us scratching our heads. Was it the debris, the pressure or the stress– or was there something else in the air? Since only a few people are affected by any single condition, the cause is probably specific to a person, family, or moment in the tornado's trek. High winds and dusty air may have created a "charged" environment that could have induced a physical reaction. A whirl of small debris bits could have left their marks without being noticed at the time. Or, the tornado may have carried along a fine dust of insulation or plant matter that triggered an allergic reaction. We will never know for sure, but these stories will live on as legends of a tornado's ever-widening sphere of influence.

Dreamy debris

You can learn a lot about the winds and pressure field in a tornado by observing small changes along the outer edge of the condensation funnel. But if this funnel is absent, only clouds of debris can show you what the wind is doing– and debris is often sporadic and hard to see. When a tornado passes over water you have a rare opportunity to see the tornado's winds in exquisite detail, as water is transformed into a special form of debris. The water is thrashed into a fine spray, which rises like a dreamy fog in the vortex. Every irregularity in the flow is made visible and the very detailed plume reveals subtle variations in the winds which are not normally visible.

Both tornadoes passed over several water bodies and rivers. Each time, the debris cloud became dense and lively as the water was carried up, then dispersed as it evaporated. The water didn't recondense– it was blown into a spray that looked just like a cloud. With regular debris, the particles are dispersed by mixing with clean air. The same thing happened with the water, but evaporation probably outpaced dispersion– the upper parts vanished like flames above a fire. These bursts of water were very visible from behind the tornado, where they appeared suddenly as brilliant white blobs near the ground.

Order and chaos

Despite the overwhelming power and potential destructiveness of a tornado, small things create large differences in the outcome. We could look at these as minor disadvantages that alter the wind strength or direction slightly. Some examples are large or heavy objects beside a wall that remained standing, two buildings with only their adjacent walls left standing, or less damage to buildings that were full rather than empty. Tornadic winds are easily strong enough to overcome these minor factors, but there was still a difference. This tells us that many things may have exceeded their tolerance threshold for being ripped apart by only a tiny amount. A little less wind power, or a little more structural strength or reinforcement– and those objects might have survived. One sturdily built barn was tugged and yanked until it almost came apart. It held together. While most of the beams were loose or shifted, it was possible to correct and secure it without an expensive rebuild.

The fact that a small change can effect a large consequence is a mysterious aspect of tornadoes. The tornado's power works against us. Time works in our favour. Combining the two gives every object a survival limit. An object's shape and position relative to other nearby things determine a third component of its survival. We could picture this as a "chaos factor" which rearranges the wind profile just enough to decrease its maximum destructive potential. Of course, the opposite can be true too. Some pockets of extreme damage may result from amplified power, when one object inadvertently contributes to the annihilation of another. With a regular wind, other factors such as frictional resistance counteract the wind force and greatly dominate over minor chaos effects. But with a violent tornadic circulation, small disturbances, surprisingly, are not wiped out– and may even be magnified– as they propagate through the air.

Power failure

And finally, here is the wackiest, most extreme example of coincidence you can imagine– or was it? One person (who was not directly affected) exclaimed that just about every electronic device in his house went on the fritz after the tornado– the stereo, TV, VCR, computer, even the satellite dish! Can we blame the tornado for this one too, or should we accept the fact that someone, somewhere is bound to have a string of unlucky events that coincides with it?

The biggest mystery of them all is the one that you can't get out of your mind. It's like the unfortunate marriage of an unforgettable event with a memorable moment– two strangers thrown together by circumstance. The perfect, undeniable coincidence! It is such a temptation to do this, and we all do. Our minds love to put things in their proper place and we sometimes create a reality where there isn't one. The tornado leaves a crisp imprint on our minds. Other thoughts, opinions and experiences jostle for their place, too, and some find themselves woven around our tornado memories. The coincidence is too great. Unrelated facts join hands to become a new kind of truth– the certainty of a coincidental association.

Weather radar and the shift to Doppler

Conventional weather radar gives us a picture of precipitation patterns in storms. Since the heaviest rain and hail fall close to a storm's core, we can use a radar image to interpret what kind of storm is coming. Weak ones show up blotchy and without sharply defined centres. A strong storm has a distinct cell shape and tightly-wound contours, such that the heaviest precipitation is close to its edge, usually on the south side. You can imagine the storm's entire structure– from anvil to core– if you compare the radar image with your knowledge of thunderstorm types from the previous chapter.

A few years ago, Doppler radar became popular because it could also show whether the air was moving toward or away from the radar source. This was a breakthrough for severe storm detection because the rotation in these storms was now made visible. Previously the best we could expect to see was an occasional hook echo, a curved finger on radar which showed that some of the rain had curled around the mesocyclone. Doppler could not detect the actual tornado, though, only the larger rotating circulation within the storm.

Since rotation usually precedes tornado formation, Doppler led to improved warning times (from three to eight minutes, on average) but also to greatly increased numbers of warnings. Recently it has become apparent that a simple relationship between rotation and a subsequent tornado doesn't exist for many storms. The "technological fix" for tornado detection has slipped out of reach and we now realize that there is still no substitute for being there and seeing the tornado form first-hand. Lead times have improved. Warnings are pointing people's attention in the right direction– but they can't beat the trained, watchful eye.

Odd twists— By the time the northern tornado made it to the Phillips property it had at least two distinct funnels much of the time. Scott Phillips said, "I saw two of them, side by side. One was a little bigger. It came right over. The other one went right alongside." The damage path the two vortices left was erratic– like a limping giant dragging his feet as he ran. Mike Phillips said, "It was like he was running and then skidded about an eighth of a mile, and then both of them just flattened everything. And then they started this silly 2-300 yard (metre) difference [alternating steps]."

Trees were affected differently along its path. Mike said, "The tamaracks were "just twisted out of the ground. ... Tamarack is green and springy and it's real tough. None of the tamaracks were snapped off. They were either torn right out of the ground or just partially twisted and then fell over." On top of a hill the trees were all blown over. "All of the trees up there are just bent over permanently. ... And then it didn't go 100 feet (30 metres) and everything was just being ripped up again. ... Some of them looked like you just put a bomb in the middle of the tree and blew it off."

So did one of the Phillips hay bales. Mike told us, "[The tornado] just took the thing and gave it a perm, like you put it in a blender. And it was all nice new hay sticking out. Just like you gave it a haircut and got rid of all the old hair. It looked like a porcupine."

I'm having a bad hair day!!

Tornado research has progressed greatly over the past few decades but the answers to many questions remain elusive. The study of thunderstorm structure led to several theories of tornado formation which held out the hope for a simple answer– a clearly defined storm type or situation which could be counted on to produce a tornado. The supercell severe storm seemed to fit the bill, and Doppler radar made it possible to detect its defining feature, the mesocyclone. But it wasn't long before scientists realized that there were too many variations and exceptions to the rule. Many mesocyclones didn't result in tornadoes and many tornadoes didn't have a detectable mesocyclone beforehand. The characteristics which had been cited as reliable advance indicators were only a part of the picture. There would be no single answer, no simple cure.

Research in the past few years has uncovered more questions than answers. Scientists thought (and hoped) that there would eventually be a theory of tornado formation which was simple and elegant, but this no longer seems possible. This is partly because the definition of "tornado" is too wide-ranging and independent of the cause or situation. It is beginning to look like there are many kinds of tornadoes, each with its own pattern of causation. When all tornadoes are grouped under one umbrella, researchers are forced to generalize

Looking forward

We sometimes think of a tornado as a living thing with a mind of its own– erratic, changeable, willful– but most of this feeling is a projection of our own fears and fantasies. It is a fluid in motion, constrained by all the laws of physics. The mystery is not in the forces that shape this fluid flow, but in their infinitely varied manifestations, most of which we would never come across in any other way.

Despite popular myths, a tornado has a remarkable degree of certainty to it. The uncertainty is in the details– like a chaos of details within an orderly structure. In a tornado, everything we see as chaotic or orderly coexists in harmony. In the end, they are the same thing– the main difference is in our interpretation. Many of life's great truths contain both, simultaneously. One depends on and sustains the other. The coexistence of chaos and order is part of the paradoxical nature of truth and it applies to natural processes as well as ourselves.

Tornadoes are rare events with complex, hard to measure forces within them. They are beyond conventional study and thus out of reach of extensive scientific analysis. This means that they are available equally to us all– to discover, observe, study, and ponder. It allows a rich folklore about them to survive scientific scrutiny, because proof (or disproof) is difficult. We could say that the tornado is a cultural blessing. In our lifetime, few events can have such impact, be so memorable, and still remain so unexplored.

There has been a century of tornado observations but we still don't know some of the answers to our most basic questions. What exactly goes on inside a tornado? Why do some storms have them while other similar ones don't? Why are certain locations favoured or avoided regularly by tornadoes, even though there are no apparent local causes for the discrepancy? What is the true trend in tornado activity? Even a question as simple as "How many are there each year?" comes up against a mountain of problems– detection, definition, subjective observations, and so on. So far, scientists have just scratched the surface. The tornado is like a very large puzzle. There are only a few pieces on the table and each occurrence adds another. In the next hundred years we might see enough of the picture to stop guessing at the answers.

too much to accommodate all the possibilities. It now seems that many factors co-operate to varying degrees to form a tornado and there is no single combination which exclusively leads to the end result.

Recently, thinking on how tornadoes form (and what research needs to be done) has changed in two important ways. It is now recognized that some tornadoes form very quickly and simultaneously both aloft and at the ground. (Previously it was thought that tornadoes formed only aloft– in the cloud.) And, if scientists are to fine-tune tornado prediction, research must be done to accumulate much more detail about the low-level environment in storms (near the ground, where only on-site measurements are useful). The real question now is, "How much do we need to know about what's happening near and under a severe storm?" It may take many more field studies and the use of new methods of measurement and analysis to build up enough information to make the next stab at explaining how tornadoes happen. They are too violent, too brief, and too rare to let us probe their secrets easily. When it comes to why and how, anything is possible and nearly nothing is absolutely provable. Tornado research is an exciting and challenging pursuit– but for now most of what we know comes from the shadowy truths of our clouded weather crystal ball.

Lessons from Oklahoma City

On May 3rd, 1999, many people in Oklahoma and Kansas endured an experience they won't soon forget. Across the two states there were more than 70 tornadoes, and 46 people were killed, 36 of them by a single, F-5 tornado that was on the ground for 87 minutes and 68 miles.

But, deadly as it was, this event couldn't have happened in a location better prepared to deal with it. Oklahoma City is "Severe Storms Central." The National Severe Storms Lab is located just outside town; there are probably more storm chasers, spotters and researchers per square mile than anywhere else in the world; the local media pride themselves for on-the-spot, minute-by-minute reporting of tornadoes in the region, and the public are much more tuned into weather warnings and safety procedures than they would be in areas less central to "tornado alley". Had the same event occurred in another metropolitan area there would have been more fatalities. There are a few lessons we can all learn from the experience.

Fleeing in cars

Since a 1979 Wichita Falls, Texas, tornado in which there were 25 fatalities in vehicles, people have been advised not to take to their cars during a tornado. Properly-anchored, permanent homes can provide sufficient refuge from all but F-4 and F-5 tornadoes (which are rare). However, many of the people whose homes were devastated in Oklahoma chose to flee by car, and none of them were injured. This was an unusual situation: the tornado was on the ground for a long time, with street-by-street media coverage of its progress, and ample warning for all but those early on its path. People had enough time to leave their homes, and enough information to judge where they would be safe. Unless you can be sure you have the time and knowledge to reach safety away from a tornado's path, you are better off going to an interior room or closet, away from windows, on the lowest level of your home.

Hiding under overpasses

People who fled to sturdy shelters by car may have made the right decision, given the unusual circumstances, but those who chose to leave their cars to seek shelter under overpasses soon found out how dangerous a choice they had made. "The myth that an overpass is safe shelter was dispelled as people were swept out, dismembered, and thrown to their deaths. The last mutilated body was found a week after the tornado. It was that of a young woman who was thrown from an I-35 underpass, carried to a flooded ditch, and covered with debris." (Grazulis, page 29) Storm chasers and researchers have been warning that seeking shelter under overpasses is dangerous ever since the notion became popular several years ago. Oklahoma City provided grim confirmation of their worst fears.

Mobile homes

Of the 46 people who died in the 1999 tornado outbreak, 18 were in mobile homes. For about 70 years, U.S. death rates from tornadoes have been declining, but in the last 25 years the proportion of Americans living in mobile homes has been increasing. As a result, the decline in tornado death rates is slowing down. Mobile home residents are 20 times more likely to die in a tornado than are people in permanent homes, and in the southeastern U.S. the increase in people living in mobile homes has been particularly large - this in an area that gets many tornadoes, often at night, when it is difficult to warn people of the danger. **If you live in a mobile home you must be especially weather-savvy.** Buy yourself a weather radio with tone alert, stay tuned for weather watches and warnings, make sure that there is a safe shelter (below ground) available nearby, and have an emergency plan for your family.

House construction standards

Researchers studying the damage at Oklahoma City wrote, "It is hard to understand how and why construction practice is so marginal in a part of the nation that shows the highest likelihood of violent tornadoes." (Doswell and Brooks, 2001)

A house is as strong as its weakest component. If the roof or foundation is poorly anchored, it doesn't take a devastating tornado to open it up to further damage from wind and flying debris. (Hurricane clips and anchor bolts are inexpensive if included at the time of construction.) But even if your home has been well-constructed, it is vulnerable to being opened up to destruction by flying pieces of other homes in your neighbourhood - you might say that a subdivision is as strong as its weakest house!

4
Don't just stand there!

In the best of all possible worlds ...

In the best of all possible worlds we would all receive ample warning that a tornado was forming or approaching. We would be able to expect at least 20 minutes warning in classically structured weather systems.

Forecasters would have all the tools they need to see the first signs of rotation on their radar screens and there would be no holes or weak spots in the network of radar coverage. There would be trained severe weather watchers positioned across the countryside, calling into the weather office as soon as they saw severe weather developing. The forecasters would be able to call around to observers in key locations to verify that the weather is unfolding as they expect from their analyses and radar imagery.

"The only thing you can do when you see something like that is get human beings somewhere where they are not going to get injured."

☞ Don't be lulled ...

The astonishing absence of serious injuries or deaths in the April 20th tornadoes should not tempt us into believing that F2 and F3 tornadoes pose little risk. They are classified as dangerous tornadoes and could easily have resulted in fatalities. It is also possible that the greater number of brick, log, timber frame and stone houses, built for Canada's snowloads, gave an added measure of protection to the victims of these tornadoes. And despite the folk wisdom that tornadoes take aim at trailer parks, there were no mobile home communities on that day's tornado tracks. (Two of the victims lived in mobile homes, but not in trailer parks. Significantly, one of them was the only person who required hospitalization for his injuries.) We can only give thanks that those few who were caught unprotected managed to survive.

There would be an active network of ham radio operators with severe weather training (CANWARN in Canada and SKYWARN in the U.S.) reporting to the weather office and ready to provide emergency communication if it is needed.

There would be enough staff and weather offices to ensure that watches and warnings are issued and updated promptly on Weatheradio, radio and television, as well as to schools, municipalities and emergency personnel.

Many people would have Weatheradios with tone alert and others would monitor weather updates on radio and television whenever the day's forecast indicated a potential for the development of severe thunderstorms. They would also understand what watches and warnings mean and keep an eye on the sky when a watch is issued.

Radio and television stations would be quick to broadcast and update watches and warnings. They would not confuse their listeners with commentary which downplays the weather's significance; and they would take any reports of tornado or funnel sightings they receive from their listeners seriously, immediately relaying them to the weather office.

And everyone would have planned and practiced what they would do in the event of a tornado.

But in real life ...

The technology and severe weather watchers' programs for this "best of all possible worlds" exist, both in Canada and the U.S., and they often succeed in providing twenty minutes warning of tornadoes. But sometimes, as on April 20th, 1996, in Southern Ontario, the warning system does not play out so smoothly.

The weather picture isn't a "classic" scenario for tornado development. (There is still snow on the ground, the weather system which might produce tornadoes– it did in the U.S. the day before– is likely to be weakened by passage over frigid Lake Huron, and the various models and indicators of severe potential are contradictory or inconsistent over time.)

The only warning Lee Swallow had was from a friend, who called her on his cellular phone as he raced from the far side of town.

The radar network is only partially operational, and there is not enough coverage to take accurate readings as the storm system makes landfall in Ontario. There are very few severe weather watchers located along the storm's path, and they are out with their friends and families because it is the first warm Saturday of the spring.

The forecasters have issued thunderstorm watches, but they cannot issue warnings (of thunderstorms or tornadoes) unless they receive some verification, so the weather office strains its meagre manpower resources (government cutbacks) calling around to observers and radio stations in an attempt to verify that the storms are at least producing damaging winds or large hail, two indicators of tornadic potential. But nobody is home and the radio stations are manned by weekend staff with little interest or experience in watching the weather. To their extreme frustration, the overworked staff at the weather office can find no confirmation of their forecast.

Even CANWARN is inactive. They are holding a training session in an area remote from the storm's track and have advised the weather office that their network is down for the day.

Very few people have Weatheradios, and those who do aren't listening to them. And although watches and warnings are sent out to the media as soon as they are issued, many

"I've gotta get this on video!"

radio and television stations do not bother to broadcast them. But very few people have their radios or televisions on anyway ... it's such a nice day! Who wants to be inside? And those who hear the thunderstorm watches and warnings assume there is nothing to worry about because nobody mentioned tornadoes.

When the first funnel sightings are called in to radio stations by the public they are dismissed as unimportant, ("Ah, those things just form and dissipate. There's nothing to worry about.") and the stations make no attempt to relay the reports to their listeners or the weather office.

And when people start calling ahead to friends and relatives, telling them that a tornado is heading for them, what do their friends do? Many of them get out their video cameras rather than heading for safety.

Ay-ay-ay-ay-ay! What's a weatherman (or woman) to do?!

No amount of technology ...

After damaging tornadoes strike there are usually calls for better alert systems– more bells and whistles (sirens, public address systems, better technology). But the best warning you can have comes from keeping your eye on the sky. What matters most is whether people, the media included, take weather watches seriously enough to be watching the skies and listening for warnings when they occur.

Even if there were Doppler radar on every corner, the weather office could not alert people to dangerous weather without much better communication (a responsive media) and public awareness about severe weather (those weather smarts you learned in **Chapter two**!).

Even if every town had a tornado siren (and many do in parts of the U.S. where damaging tornadoes occur much more frequently than in Canada) the best warning you could expect is 20 minutes. Even that depends on **someone** watching the sky and alerting

Should you hide in the southwest corner?

Where have you been told to take shelter in the event of a tornado? Many people still believe that they should go to the southwest end of the basement (because this is often the direction the tornado is coming from, and they assume that debris will be blown away from them). They favour the southwest even when it is not the corner with the most protection from flying glass and debris.

Even if you could be sure that the southwest was the windward end of your home (and you can't– the rotating wind patterns in a tornado are complex and the wind direction as it hits your house will vary with your position on the track), you would be huddled at the end of the house where you are most likely to end up under a fallen wall. Years of research on damage patterns has established that the windward wall of a building that fails in a windstorm (and that includes tornadoes) nearly always falls inward. The other walls fall outward.

The first priority in deciding where to go is to **find the place with the least potential for flying debris** (away from windows and dangerous objects) **and the most structural reinforcement** (on the lowest level, under a stairway, or in an interior closet or reinforced room such as a furnace room, cold cellar or washroom). If the only location that meets these requirements is at the southwest end, by all means take shelter there. The extra shell you have gained by being in a structurally reinforced area will provide protection from both falling walls and flying debris. If you were in another area with more windows and fewer protective walls you would be at greater risk.

the authorities. Why not watch it yourself? Is it realistic to have someone manning a siren throughout severe weather season in an area that only experiences dangerous tornadoes every three to five years (as in Southern Ontario)?

But were people watching on April 20th? And did they know what to watch for?

Many were taken completely by surprise, and many more saw the tornado coming but stood transfixed, watching in wonder until they barely had time to dive for cover.

"This thing just snuck right up on us ..."

Sherry Henry thought the storm was over. The hail had stopped, the sun was shining. But then she saw it.

"It was just lucky I looked out the window and saw a black wall. There was still no wind at the house, and the sun was still shining– like cloudy-sunny. There was debris in it, and I think the debris was the other side of the barn ... just a black wall. I yelled 'Get to the basement,' and grabbed the kids. They knew I meant business. ... It just hit so fast. When I saw it at the barn there was still no noise and still no wind at the house."

Should I open the windows?

Don't waste precious time opening windows when you should be running for cover. You are putting yourself at risk and you may actually make things worse.

Years ago people were advised to open windows, especially on the side of the house away from the tornado. It was thought that pressure drops caused much of the damage during tornadoes and that this would help equalize the pressure. But we know better now.

Extensive studies of damage effects have made it clear that most tornado damage is caused by wind and structural features (see *How buildings fail*, **Chapter eight**), rather than from pressure differentials. Besides, houses have enough other openings to equalize pressure differentials as they occur.

As Tom Grazulis, author of *Significant tornadoes, 1680-1991*, has said: "The idea that moving one thin pane of glass is going to protect a roof or a home from one of the most violent natural forces on the planet has a certain absurdity about it."

The tornado will open them for you.

Now, researchers believe that opening windows may actually decrease the ability of a structure to withstand tornadic winds. But, more to the point, **windows are normally the first part of a building to go, even in weak tornadoes. So it is downright dangerous to be near them as the tornado approaches.**

Remember– the greatest risk you face is from flying debris, and that includes spears of glass. Don't open your windows– the tornado will do it for you.

"I always thought there would be a warning for a tornado, and wind, but this thing just snuck right up on us. ... I guess now you take hail as a warning. Now I really understand 'calm before the storm.'"

"Wow, was that ever close ..."

The Gratton family turned on the news just as it was announced that there was a tornado near Shelburne.

Russell Gratton knew it would be coming toward him, but his immediate response was to get the video camera and run outside. "I thought we'd see something coming over the horizon, but we couldn't ... and fairly quickly the wind started to pick up ... and then I started seeing little chunks of stuff up in the air. The cloud was up there [almost overhead] and for some reason I was thinking of seeing a funnel cloud going [all the way] down.

Sherry Henry barely made it to the basement with her friends and children before her home was demolished by the tornado.

That wasn't there, so I was thinking, 'I gotta see something farther out,' [but the cloud above me] turned out to be the tornado."

He backed up and ran into his house, just in time to see the barn outside his window whisked into thousands of fragments.

"Part of me thinks I'm really lucky to have [had] the opportunity to see a tornado so close. The other part says, 'Mmmm– could have been killed!' I'm more and more respectful of nature in a way. I wouldn't want to be scared of nature ... but I [find myself thinking] hey, I'm nothing compared to that power! When it happens, we're ants."

Taking shelter

Whether taken by surprise or surprised by wonder, many people have little or no time to get to safety when a tornado strikes. Your life may depend on knowing where to go and what to do, and in no uncertain terms. Confusion can be a killer.

But how do you know who to believe when you receive conflicting advice? Do you open the windows, close the windows or forget the windows and run for safety? Do you run to the side of the basement toward or away from the tornado? Do you get under the stairway or into a closet? Do you run out into the open from a mobile home? Do you stay in your car or get into a ditch?

It seems that everyone is eager to tell you what to do, and it is easy to become confused. How can you penetrate the morass of conflicting advice you may have received?

Whatever you do, find shelter.

We offer you a very simple rule of thumb: **Do whatever gives you the best protection from the most likely risks.**

But what are the most likely risks?

How can a tornado hurt you?

The most likely cause of injury or death during a tornado is flying debris- missiles, as the scientists call them. That means glass, nails, pipes, wood, sheet metal, dishes, furniture, trees, cows, barns, you name it. It's amazing what a tornado lets fly.

On April 20th John Mackenzie found himself flying through the air, along with tires, barn boards and a tractor cab. Nine-year-old Dale Martin saw plates flying around "like flying saucers," and his mother watched his father "moon-walking" through the kitchen. Eleanor Saunders had a nail driven into the wall over her head by the winds. David Hill watched the bricks of his house whirl around like so much dust. Kelsey Butler was struck by a patio door as it blew into the basement. Time and time again we were told by awestruck people that they could not have survived without serious injury if they had been upstairs, where the house was a pincushion of glass shards, or peppered with objects from parts unknown.

There are so many dangers from flying objects during a tornado that the most astonishing aspect of the April 20th outbreak was that there were no life-threatening injuries. There were many cuts and bruises, and many people emerged praying with renewed vigour, but there were no deaths. However, we cannot allow this unusual good fortune to lull us into underestimating the risks. With the force of tornadic winds behind it, a piece of straw can become a lethal object.

The next greatest risk you face is from collapsing structures. The first part of a structure that is likely to go is the roof. This is especially true if it spans a wide area or is not properly anchored. Even strong winds of less than tornadic strength can take these roofs off, which is why you so often hear of roofs being damaged in arenas, malls and gymnasiums.

Even homes that survive the tornado can be dangerous, as glass and branches whirl through the rooms.

Once the roof goes the walls of a building are more likely to collapse (see *How buildings fail*, **Chapter eight**), and the outside walls pose the greatest risk to anyone huddled near them.

SAFETY QUICK REFERENCE

The following is a quick reference chart to help you determine where you and your family should take shelter during a tornado. We suggest that you photocopy it, and post it wherever you keep emergency instructions for your family (emergency numbers, fire and poison information).

Plan ahead for weather emergencies. Take the time now to choose the best shelter within your home or office. Try to choose a small interior room or stairwell, ideally with walls reinforced with pipes (e.g. bathroom) or concrete (e.g. basement), on the lowest floor of the building. Make sure that everyone concerned knows where to go and what precautions to take (below). Also, choose a meeting place where your family can gather after a severe storm, to ensure that you are all safe and accounted for.

Keep an emergency pack with a battery-powered flashlight, radio, tools for emergency repair, food supplies, first aid, blankets and extra clothing (especially shoes). Keep your car gas tank full in case gas stations are closed after the storm.

If a severe weather **watch** is issued, bring all your pets and livestock to shelter, secure or put away loose objects such as lawn furniture, listen for weather updates and watch the skies.

When a **warning** is issued for your area, keep calm, close windows and doors **if you have enough time,** bring children indoors and go to your shelter.

Special note: People who live in mobile homes are particularly vulnerable if a tornado hits. It is **especially important** that they learn how to be alert to changes in the weather and to **weather watches and warnings**. They should also buy a **Weatheradio with tone alert**, which will sound an alarm if there is a warning in the area.

In a building

Stay inside with the doors and windows shut.

Stay away from windows, doors and exterior walls.

Go to a small, interior room or stairwell on the lowest floor of the building. (Bathrooms are often the best choice.)

If the telephone rings upstairs, ignore it and stay where you are.

If possible, crouch under heavy furniture.

Protect your head with cushions, a mattress, or other thick padding.

In a vehicle

Run to a nearby solid structure (a building, or, if that is not available, a low bridge or dry culvert)

If, and only if, you have no time to get to a safer place, park the car, do up your seatbelt, and protect your head.

Do not try to outrun a tornado by driving, especially in populated areas.

Outside

Look for shelter in a building (not a car or a mobile home) immediately.

If, and only if, no shelter is available, lie flat in a low, dry spot (a ravine, a ditch or a culvert), or under a low bridge. Be on the alert for flash floods.

Protect your head.

As a last resort, that is, only if you have no other choice, hang on tightly to the base of a shrub or small tree.

In a mobile home

Do not stay in a mobile home.

If there is time, run to a nearby solid structure (a storm shelter or building).

If there is no solid structure nearby, lie flat in a dry ditch, ravine or culvert outside.

Protect your head.

The car or a ditch?

Neither, if you have any choice. If there is any solid structure nearby, take cover there. (Don't be afraid to knock on a stranger's door.)

Your first impulse when you see a tornado approaching may be to leave home and take to the road. This is not a good idea unless media coverage and warnings make it clear that you have plenty of time to get out of harm's way. In your home you have protection from strong winds and flying debris. In your car or in a ditch you are much more exposed. Neither is a great place to ride out a tornado.

If you are caught away from any solid structures and there is no nearby overpass to huddle beneath (see *Lessons from Oklahoma City*, page 148, for proof that an overpass is not the best place to seek shelter!), it might be better to lie down in a deep ditch. But even this advice has been questioned in recent studies.

Much of the research which led to past advice to leave your car and take shelter in a ditch was derived from statistics which may have been skewed by two factors:

- High injury and death figures in populated areas, where victims were trapped not only in their cars but by road obstructions (rush hour traffic, blocked roads)

- These deaths and injuries occurred in areas where few people wore seatbelts, so they suffered the additional risk of being thrown out of their cars or into their windshields

A study of deaths and injuries in the 1985 Barrie tornado (where seatbelt use is required by law) reported that "buildings and vehicles provided equal protection when compared with outdoor locations." A young boy making for home on his bicycle was found decapitated in a ditch.

It is arguable that if you have open road before you and you wear your seatbelt you are better off in your car than in a ditch. If you are outside you are exposed to lightning, flying debris, traffic, tipped cars, high winds and flash floods. Cars are padded and designed to protect you in a rollover. And if you are able to judge the angle of movement of the tornado you are much better off to drive away from it at right angles (preferably south), provided that you can truly judge the tornado's speed and distance well enough to make this decision. **Whenever possible, the best option is to take shelter below ground level in a solid structure.**

If the makers of *Twister* had concerned themselves with reality there would have been little left of the heroes. They and their cars would have been shredded and whipped by the debris and winds. Take a look at these tornado-scrunched cars (opposite page). Would you really have chosen to be in them?

Our answer to the question, "Am I safer in my car or a ditch?" has to be, "Try to make sure you have better options available!"

For those who may be tempted to leave their homes by car when they see a tornado, remember, there may not be enough time to reach safety, and you may be trapped out in the open. If your house has no basement and you have ample warning, it may make sense to drive away from a strong tornado (see *Lessons from Oklahoma City*, see page 148), but a house with a basement is a very good shelter– and a place where you can be found when concerned friends and relatives come looking.

Where are you safest?

The best place to take cover is below ground level, in a reinforced interior room (no windows) or stairwell. Bathrooms are often good choices because of the extra reinforcement plumbing adds to the walls. For additional protection you should be under a large piece of furniture and/or have heavy blankets, mattresses or cushions with you, to shield you from flying debris. (See *Safety quick reference*, page 155)

If a branch can impale the siding, imagine what it could do to you.

This ideal choice provides you with the greatest protection from flying debris and collapsing walls. You are away from the threat of flying glass or other objects crashing through windows or outside walls; you have put as many walls between you and the outside as possible; and you are not under a large expanse of unsupported roof that might collapse on you.

Schools without specially designed storm shelters usually send their students to interior hallways as far away from windows and doorways as possible. If there is no time to get to the hallways the students are told to huddle under heavy furniture such as the teacher's desk. They do not send children to the gymnasium, even if it is an interior room, unless it has been specifically designed as a storm shelter.

Family emergency plan

Now is the time to get together with your family and **agree on where you should go in the event of a tornado.** You will not have time to argue it out when your lives are at risk.

Not every home provides an "ideal" location, so you need to agree on what choices provide the best protection from debris and collapsing structures where **you** live. (If you live in a mobile home you should agree upon a safe shelter nearby, **not inside the mobile home**.)

Look at all the options, and put yourselves through the motions of getting there. You may have the perfect spot in your basement but, if you must run the length of the house or go outside to get to it, you should agree upon an alternative, in case you don't have time to reach the ideal location.

Discuss tornado safety in casual conversations with members of your family, so that you can discover misconceptions anyone may have and **develop their sense of how to make the right decision no matter where they are**. Let them imagine various scenarios— they might be riding their bikes, in the barn, at a supermarket, on their horse, at the ballpark. Wherever they are, they should be given the chance to think through what the safest course of action would be.

Having these conversations can alleviate a lot of their fears, because they become confident about how to react. Once they have this confidence they are less likely to fear the unknown and panic with every passing storm.

It is also important to encourage the whole family to become keen skywatchers. It will **develop their weather smarts** and give them hours of enjoyment for years to come.

Once you have all agreed upon where you should go during a tornado, take the time to decide on one last, but very important, detail. **Agree upon a place to call or go to if you are separated during a disaster**. You would not want a taste of the terror that grips families who don't know whether a loved one is lying under the rubble. (See *A teenager's tale*, page 198.)

Flying debris can pose risks far from the tornado track.

Is it safe to come out?

Our safety advice cannot end with the tornado's passage. When the roar subsides, when the debris stops flying, there are still risks to be confronted by tornado victims. Climbing out from under the rubble, they will have to be alert to all the dangers of a disaster scene, as will anyone who comes to their rescue.

There will be glass, nails and debris everywhere; sections of walls and ceiling may collapse with the slightest disturbance; there may be dangers from live wires, propane, gas and fire. And the victims may be inadequately clothed to protect themselves from these hazards. An elderly couple was found standing in front of their levelled home– in shock and in bare feet. The children in another family had to stay in the basement until help arrived– because no shoes could be found for them.

To complicate matters, tornado victims are usually in a state of shock, even if they have had no physical injuries; and they are unlikely to be alert to the dangers surrounding them. They may wander about aimlessly, possibly into the path of a car that is speeding to the rescue.

Everyone on the scene– victims, rescuers and sightseers– should stay clear of fallen wires. (See *On again, off again*, opposite.) The first people there should make sure that power, gas and propane are turned off, and immediate efforts should be made to keep people clear of areas where there are dangers from collapsing structures.

And then we are ready for the work to begin.

Far-flung debris sometimes combines with wires to present special dangers.

☞ On again, off again ...

Never assume that downed or severed power lines are safe to be near (or drive over). Even if the power has been turned off or the main line is disconnected, there is a distinct possibility that they could become live again, if only briefly. On April 20th, two women walked right by downed wires which had been dead, only to be startled when the lines sparked a fire seconds later. (See photo, page 18.) Wires set tree limbs on fire in several places, and the roadside power at another location sparked on into the night. There were large explosions in the power corridor on the track of the southern tornado, several minutes after the tornado had downed three towers.

There are a few possible explanations for this on again, off again power. Towers that are downed trip a safety switch when they topple, but this may not occur immediately. Dead lines can become live if lightning hits them up to three kilometres (two miles) away. After a power failure there may be a brief off-on cycling (three times, then they stay off). Or, power could come back on if a manual try is initiated by the power authority to see if the lines will hold power.

The best advice is, clearly and with no exceptions: "If a power line is lying on the ground you should never assume that it is dead."

The centre was chopped out of this pole, probably by a large flying object, yet the wires remained unbroken. (This picture is from the 1985 tornado outbreak.)

"But I've gotta get this on tape ..."

Before you decide to stay upstairs to videotape a tornado there are a few questions you should ask yourself:

"Can I do it safely?"

- Do you have a quick, clear path to safety should you need it?
- Have you learned enough about severe weather watching to know when you are in danger?
- Will you be able to judge accurately the distance, speed and direction of movement of the tornado?

"How will it affect the other people around me?"

- Are your kids huddling terrified and lonely in the basement because Daddy (or Mommy) is up where they have been told it is not safe?
- Have you been able to reassure them that you won't put yourself at risk?
- Do they need you more than you need the videotape?

If, after considering these questions, you still want to stay up there with your camera, here are some pointers to help you capture a video worth the effort:

- **Find a location with as clear a view as possible without compromising your safety.** If you can avoid nearby trees and wires, so much the better.
- **If you can use a tripod, do.** Otherwise, you are likely to end up with a very shaky end-product. You may be Mr. or Ms. Cool under normal circumastances, but watching your neighbour's barn blow up can set even the steeliest nerves on edge. Besides, a tripod allows you to keep your eye on the storm without disturbing the video camera.
- **Is your battery fully charged? How much film do you have?** If there is any risk of running out of power or tape too quickly, be discriminating in what you shoot.
- **If you are inside, turn off any lights that may reflect on the window through which you are filming.** Also make sure that the camera is not autofocusing on water or dirt on the window, or on nearby objects. (That branch may be lovely, but wouldn't you rather have a clear picture of the tornado?)
- **Look through the viewfinder as you film.** You'd be amazed at how much footage people take of fields and feet, with the tornado cut completely out of the picture.
- **Don't use the video camera as you would your eyes.** Your eyes can wander the sky without losing the larger context or continuity of the tornado's movement, but people watching your video footage want the camera to stay with what the tornado is doing.
- **Keep your attention on the videotaping.** If you are distracted by conversations around you, your filming is likely to be erratic.
- **Don't keep zooming in and out**, especially if you are on autofocus. Your video will be frustrating to watch because you are constantly fading in and out of focus.
- **Use your zoom lens with restraint.** Zooms are wonderful. They allow you to "get in close" without risking your life. But take the time to establish the storm context, and don't zoom in so close that you can't see the whole tornado. (Zooming in too close also increases shakiness.) Occasionally, a rare shot of a flying object or fascinating detail justifies a closer zoom, but do it sparingly.
- **Remember that no tornado video is worth as much as your life is.** It is easy to become mesmerized once you start watching a tornado, so be sure you are ready to pull up roots quickly and run for safety.

5
Coming to the rescue

The Williamsford community cleaned up in wintry conditions.

"Just a whirling, and noise, and everything's gone."

Victims and helpers alike confront the aftermath of a tornado with shock and disbelief. One of the first people to arrive on the scene of the tornado in Williamsford expressed it well: "You just wanted to cry. You couldn't believe that the houses– the brick houses that were sitting there– were gone. I said, 'Where's the bricks?' You couldn't believe that those places could be such a rubble ... just a whirling, and noise, and everything's gone."

The victims are emotionally devastated. One said, "When we came out we just stood there in shock," and another, "Your initial reaction is to dig a hole and cry. There's just so much damage you don't know where to start."

Not only are they confronted with overwhelming losses; they are faced with an endless procession of details and decisions, all of which cry out for immediate attention. As one victim told us, "You've got all this garbage to look after, you've got all these other things in your head. ... I was depressed for about a week and a half of just trying to organize, 'Okay. What's next, what's next? No, we gotta clean that up. What's there, what's getting rusty? What's getting ruined that could be salvaged?' So it takes a long while."

But help is on the way ...

Time after time people told us how astonished they were at the many people– friends, neighbours and strangers– who were there to help them almost immediately. Some of the victims on the track of the northern tornado lived down long forested laneways, but even they had rescuers at their doors in short order– rescuers who had to crawl under and over many downed trees to reach them.

The firefighters who were first on the scene at one home were astonished to find the victims eating dinner in the ruins. One member of the family had taken her insulin just before the tornado hit, but hadn't eaten yet; so when the firefighters came rushing in, having scrambled through the fields and climbed over trees to reach them, the family was sitting

"I couldn't get over how everybody was just there ... All the people that helped– that was really a surprise to me."

161

down to table. She had to eat to avoid diabetic problems. Even in the face of disaster it is important to attend to pre-existing medical conditions.

If you are first on the scene ...

If you are one of the first people on the scene of any emergency, give yourself a moment to assess any risks and take precautions against them. If it is not safe to enter the scene you should wait for emergency personnel to arrive (having made sure that they have been called and the road is clear for them to get through). Tornadoes present hazards from downed or broken power lines, fire and gas leaks, unstable structures, and a mess of sharp and broken debris. Having taken these hazards into account, you can go on to establish the whereabouts and safety of victims (especially those who may be unable to fend for themselves due to age or disability). Administer first aid and call in emergency assistance as necessary.

Comfort the victims. They may be too deep in shock to speak or take any action themselves. They need your help, even if they are unable to say so. Get families together and away from danger, and make sure that a route for emergency vehicles is kept clear of obstacles and traffic. (The sightseers are already starting to jam the roads.) With the parents' permission, get children to a safe quiet shelter away from the devastation.

You (and the many others who are on the scene by this time) can now begin the search for important items– essentials such as clothing and wallets and, just as important, personal comforts such as teddy bears, wedding rings and family photos. The victims have just had their lives torn apart. They are too numb and disoriented to be able to pick themselves up and start again. Anything you can do to reconnect them with their daily lives will help them face the daunting task of beginning again. They need others to start the process of cleaning up, piece by piece, the ruination spread out for miles around them.

 Tips from the twice hit

For most victims tornadoes are a once-in-a-lifetime ordeal. Few people have the opportunity (?) to learn from past experience. Here are a few tips from Judy Eden– one woman who did:

- Get things out of your home if you can't stay there, even if it's tarped (and it should be).

- Get volunteer work crews to help with the urgent needs of your barn/farm operation.

- Gather up everything outside that is salvageable (it will rust, rot, or seize up outside).

- Find storage space for salvaged items.

- Have people around to talk to you and bring coffee and sandwiches.

- Do whatever you can to restore some sense of normalcy as soon as possible (re-establish some of your family routines).

- Don't rush on long-term decisions. "I find that if you plan things out, get ideas from different people, get enough ideas, maybe you will come up with something that will work for you. Whatever you decide now, it's a lifetime decision. There won't be real big mistakes if things are planned out."

- "You've gotta have the spirit, the faith to keep on going. It's like any tragedy. You've gotta put one foot in front of the other– you can't just sit back, give up and say, 'That's it, I don't care what happens, I don't want to see anybody.' You have to go on. You have to be strong for yourself. No one can do that for you. They can be there to help you– a nice pat on the back or a hug means a lot– but you have to help yourself. And it really helps to get busy. The busier you are, the more you don't sit and dwell on it."

"People were very generous or super kind. Especially right at the start."

If you are in a position (as a friend, neighbour or family member) to take control of the initial cleanup and organization of volunteer help, this can be very helpful (but only if you can be sure the victim accepts your help). Victims are usually too overwhelmed by the devastation to take charge of what seems an impossible task. Sometimes the pressure to get started and make the endless decisions involved in

Volunteers were quick to respond to the tornado victims' plight.

cleanup is just too much for them. They want to be left alone.

Make sure that the most urgent needs are tended to first. If you have animal handling skills they may be needed. Pets and livestock will be frightened and difficult to round up. They will need water, food and shelter, as well as a firm and calming hand.

Work should be started immediately to safeguard what remains from further loss and damage. This includes protecting stored animal feed, tarping and boarding up damaged buildings, and gathering up salvageable items to shelter them from the elements.

Now the real work can begin: cleaning, sorting, burning, hauling, repairing, rebuilding– working, laughing and crying together as the community gathers around in support.

To the victims

You are going to need all the help you can get. Do not be shy to accept it. The people in your community need to be there for you as much as you need them. It is important to accept help in taking control of your circumstances. One of the victims we interviewed turned down many volunteers: "I guess I just thought that everything would fall into place automatically and the right people [officially designated workers] that were supposed to do the right things would be there to do them."

If you can involve your family in deciding how to start, how to take charge, they will all benefit from being part of the process. One of the families we interviewed gathered together on the night of the tornado to determine what they had to do first. Then they got on the telephone to some of their friends, asking them to co-ordinate specific tasks (e.g., clearing the lane, leading a bush crew).

Sorting through the rubble seemed like an impossible task.

One of the first decisions you will need to make is whether to live on the site or go elsewhere. You may be able to stay in your damaged home, but otherwise you must choose between a trailer, rental or other accommodations. Many people find that it is best to stay on site so that they can supervise cleanup and rebuilding, but also so they can protect what remains of their possessions from inconsiderate sightseers and looters.

continued on page 166

"You really gotta appreciate people who will come and help like that."

163

Tornado tourists

It is only natural for people to want to see the devastation wrought by a tornado for themselves. It is a rare demonstration of nature's power. But when thousands of cars line the roads– every day for weeks on end– innocent curiosity can become a dangerous nuisance to the victims and volunteers who must contend with the constant intrusion on their work and privacy. One victim echoed many when he said, "We should have had a dang box out there for donations!"

Imagine for a moment that, within seconds, everything you have built up in your life is shredded and strewn over fields for miles around. Imagine the shock and pain you would be feeling. Imagine how impossible it would seem to retrieve anything of personal value from the wreckage that represents the life history of your entire neighbourhood.

Then watch as hundreds of strangers go stomping about in what remains of your life, making it well-nigh impossible for you to continue your methodical search for the family photos, your wedding ring, your daughter's teddy bear. ... Many of them don't even bother to acknowledge your presence or ask permission before they wander in and out of your broken home. Some come up and make comments like, "Don't tell me someone lives in that dump!"

Grin and bear it as the umpteenth stranger asks you to tell the story of what happened, responding with an astonished shake of the head, but no word of compassion. Most of them just nose around and then drive off. Most of them don't even offer to help.

As one victim told us, "I wanted to say, 'The nerve– going through my house, my stuff. If you're not here to help, get lost!' But I was in too much shock to do anything about it then."

Many victims understand the curiosity; they just long for some respect and compassion, some ordinary consideration. As one victim explained, "Sightseers should ask, 'Do you mind if I walk back?'– like, I don't mind. I'm amazed by it too. Go and have a look at it, because you're never likely to see it again in your lifetime. But don't just stomp right over my land, then totally ignore me."

We would go further. If you want to look at the devastation, find a way to be helpful, not hurtful. Unless you are prepared to pitch in and help, unless you are ready to spend a few hours slogging through the mud searching for pieces of people's lives, unless you are willing to be a shoulder to cry on, a steady and willing hand, a thoughtful and respectful neighbour– please leave these people alone. When your life is in shreds, when your heart is an open wound, a helping hand is far more welcome than a prying eye.

Some problems caused by sightseers

- Volunteers and heavy machinery had trouble getting to the scene because of the line-up of sightseers.

- The back country roads were badly chewed up by the heavy traffic.

- Their dogs were constantly barking to warn them of intruders, so victims had no peace.

- Parents were afraid to allow their children to play outside because of the heavy traffic.

- Victims felt they could not safely leave their homes, even when they were desperate for a break, because of the constant intrusion of curious strangers.

"If we ever drive by anywhere and see that there has been any kind of disaster, I'm not going to say 'maybe'– I'm going to be there for sure."

Volunteers (a celebration)

The people who suffered through the April 20th tornadoes were astonished by the outpouring of help and support they received from friends, neighbours and strangers. As one victim told us, "I know there's not enough recognition given to the volunteers– not only the ones that came and helped clean up ... also the ones that cooked the meals, the clubs and [other groups] that brought gift baskets. People came and they gave their hearts and souls to us. They are the unsung heroes. It's important to thank them so that people will realize that if it wasn't for them, we would be doing all this ourselves.

"The idea of everyone wanting to help really [builds up] your spirit. To know that they are putting their own lives on hold. Like, the weather was so crappy– and they were out there all day long, they were not complaining, 'Geez, I'm cold, I'm wet, I'm tired.' Nobody said one thing. And I know these people couldn't help but have colds after it was all over! Every day they'd come back and they'd work and work. They just seemed to know what to do."

Going through a tornado is a hard way to learn that we all need each other, but a lesson well learned by the survivors. As one said, "You can't do without your neighbours if something like this happens."

Another commented, "One neighbour was at our door even before we came out of the basement. Our neighbours were fantastic. It was very emotional, all the support that we've had. After the tornado I thought that I wanted to move, but when you see the support that you have, you can't move."

Friends, neighbours and strangers took the important first steps that helped victims start the process of rebuilding. "We hadn't notified anyone, and about 6 o'clock the next morning people started coming, and by that night the majority of the fields were cleaned up." Another victim commented, "You could never turn down help because there's never enough. Without the hundreds of people cleaning up we'd be at the job for two or three years!"

It's hard for the helpers too, at first: "All through Sunday people would come up and just start crying. They just couldn't believe that anybody survived [or how] your life can be changed in a minute. ... It takes everybody awhile to get their bearings."

And the help came from all over. "The community pitched in, but, you know, 90 percent of the help came from outside. ... Just the fact that people came along and said, 'We really feel for you,' and gave you a hug, or, 'It could have happened to me. I want to help'– it means so much, just to be there. At that time you need support from friends and other people, because it seems that your world has crashed and you need somebody behind you."

"This one man just showed up the very first day. He came walking up the driveway– no bus, no ride, nothing– he just came walking up the driveway with a little wooden ladder and a hammer and a bag of nails. He just looked around, and then he was on the roof of the chicken coop, nailing away for four or five hours. He just started working. And the same way he came, he left."

Often, when we asked the tornado victims what they most wanted us to do in this book, their first thoughts were: "Let all the people who helped us know how much it meant. Let them know that we will never be able to thank them enough."

Cleanup companies

Most people don't know that there are companies whose business it is to help victims clean up, organize, repair and store their possessions after a disaster. They can take a load off your mind. As one victim said, "If I didn't have them I would have been lost." They tarped her roof, boarded up the house, took her furniture for storage and/or repair, sent her appliances to be checked, called in an upholsterer for the couch, bagged clothes and sent them to the cleaners, cleaned up the outside debris, listed everything they stored by boxes for easy retrieval and would have moved her.

Another victim, a seasoned veteran of the 1985 tornado outbreak, used a cleaning and restoration service too. "It was so much easier when we moved back to have everything organized like that."

It is easier, but you may want to consider carefully how much of this service you want to pay for. You will likely have many willing volunteers to do the cleanup work, and accepting help from your community can forge bonds of friendship and shared experience that last a lifetime.

If you will not be living on the same site as your home during rebuilding, you may feel the need to use one of these cleanup services. That way, your home's contents can be salvaged, cleaned and in storage while you aren't able to stand guard over them.

Your insurance company may cover the cost (although it will probably be considered as part of the settlement you receive on personal property), but you will need to obtain their agreement in advance to make sure there are no disputes later.

Remember, however, that this means that you are living with a constant reminder of the devastation. You will feel every wind in a trailer, and may spend a few sleepless nights wondering whether a storm is brewing.

If you live beside the skeletal remains of your home for long, it can be a very haunting experience. We (the authors) will never forget the eerie howling and creaking inside one ruined home. Nor will we forget the overpowering stench we encountered in the few cases where homes and their contents were left exposed to the elements long after the tornado hit. Even if nothing of value can be retrieved, you will not enjoy living beside the rotting remains. Make sure that your home is tarped and all contents are cleared out as soon as possible.

The prospect of all the work you must do to clean up and rebuild is unnerving. One victim advises, "What you need more than anything is tunnel vision. If you allow yourself to look at the whole thing, you'll never get through it. You have to focus on what needs to be done right now."

You may feel rushed to do everything right away, but concentrate on doing the necessary, labour-intensive cleanup and rebuilding first, while volunteer labour is available. Take your time in making long-term decisions. You can get contractors in for other buildings later.

Sorting, building and burning after the tornado.

"I take my hat off to everyone that came out."

They rolled up their sleeves and gave us their hearts

We can learn a lot about responding to disasters from the Mennonites. They have long experience in coming together to help others, both through the Mennonite Disaster Service and through local Mennonite congregations. There were Mennonite communities nearby both of the tornadoes on April 20th (indeed, several of the victims were Mennonites), so these local congregations were quick to respond, lending many willing hands to cleanup and rebuilding.

As one victim told us, "It was just amazing to us to find all the different people that came– especially the Mennonites. They came in bunches, they came in busloads. They were all cleaning up ... And it took them exactly seven days to put a complete barn up from nothing."

Another watched them take down her heavily damaged house. "That, too, was something to see! It isn't something you want to have to see, but when you do you won't forget it, because the way they go at it is so amazing. We asked them about how they were so highly organized. They said, "Oh, we just see something to do and do it," but I know there's more organization than that behind it."

Yet another exclaimed, "Oh, my, if it weren't for the Mennonites we would have been in trouble. They work hard and it gets done."

The Mennonite response to disasters grows out of a central theme of their faith and culture: "mutual aid", or, sharing your neighbours' burdens. The Mennonite Disaster Service's motto is: "Bear ye one another's burdens, and so fulfill the law of Christ." A pamphlet for disaster victims says, "We may be strangers to you, but you are our neighbours."

Their support is offered simply and quietly, with no strings attached. They recognize that it is sometimes difficult to accept help. One Mennonite Disaster Services co-ordinator offers this advice to those who want to help: "It's a lot easier to give than to receive. ... We persevere and keep in touch, since some people who have a loss might initially refuse our help, even though they need it. Then later they accept it. You have to put yourself in their shoes– you've just lost everything and here comes this stranger wanting to help for free. It's natural not to be able to accept help right away."

He also reminds us that emotional support is just as important as pitching in to clean up and rebuild: "Sometimes for a disaster victim, the biggest help you can give them is just to sit down and let them talk."

Volunteers for the Mennonite Disaster Service (MDS) are told that they are there "to help restore a sense of normalcy to a chaotic situation and to help individuals regain a feeling of personal dignity in the face of overwhelming loss. We are here to give moral support through our presence."(See *Day of Disaster*, by Katie Funk Wiebe, for more details on MDS.)

They also recognize that disasters are often opportunities for communities to grow stronger, and the best and most important help comes from within the affected community. "We never stay until everything is completely finished. It's a matter of moving in, helping, getting things going and seeing that everything is well under way. It's hard to decide when to stop, but you have to be open to encourage local help to [pitch in and take over]."

The most precious help any of us can offer in a disaster is to jumpstart the daunting process of beginning again. As a victim of massive floods in Rapid City, South Dakota, back in 1972, said: "We were at the end of our rope. [The Mennonites] tied a knot in the end of it, and we were able to hang on. All they did was roll up their sleeves and give us their hearts." (*Day of Disaster*)

"I've never seen a community come together so fast in my life. For so much hell it brought so much good– it was unbelievable ... It restored my faith in humanity."

Organized like never before

You will have to be organized like never before, and you will likely be creating that organization from scratch– with no familiar desk or kitchen table, and none of the structures that have normally given shape to your life. Here are a few pointers to get you started.

As soon as possible:
- Go through the house room by room, itemizing all the details of damage and losses. Scan for cracks and other signs of lifting or twisting If you can, videotape every room, making commentary as you go. If you have any receipts intact save them for dealing with insurance.

During cleanup:
- Keep a pen and notebook or a microcassette recorder with you at all times to list items (for proof of loss to your insurance company) and work notes as you think of them.

- Always have one or two people at the site to tell others what to do. Otherwise you lose good volunteers because there is nobody available to direct them.

- Don't be in such a rush that you end up in a worse mess (for example, ruining items which might have been worth salvaging, bagging salvageable with unsalvageable items, thus contaminating the entire lot with glass, insulation and mud).

- Separate what can be saved from what can't as you clean up, and colour code or tag bags so they don't get mixed up.

- Pack things for long-term storage and earlier use in separate places (such as trailers) and have someone in charge of making sure they are put in the right place. If items are being taken for storage in more than one place make sure that you note down what is going where. As one victim told us, "One of the hardest things to deal with is not knowing where stuff is and then it's all over the place."

- If someone says they will do something for you, particularly if it is a special job, write down their name, phone number and what they offered to do in your notebook. People sometimes offer help in the heat of the moment, but don't get back to you about it. If you don't know who they are you can't follow up, and you are not likely to remember all the details in the post-tornado mayhem.

For the long haul:
- Take your time in making major decisions with long-term impact. You will likely end up paying more for less if you rush, and you may have to live with a too hasty decision for a lifetime. As one victim advises, "You can't make wise decisions under stress."

The debris was spread high and wide behind the foundation of what was once the Greers' home.

"People just bent over backwards. We had people coming all the way from Toronto to help. And all the neighbours were out."

Getting started on cleanup

In the house

- If you are not staying in your house, remove plants, freezer contents and valuables, and safeguard other contents from weather damage (using tarps and boarding).
- The wrenching effects of tornadic winds can create invisible hazards in your home. Watch for possible dangers from damaged wiring, furnace ducts, plumbing and venting. Ducts and vents may also be clogged with dirt and insulation, so have them thoroughly checked before you use the heating or ventilation systems.
- Be on the lookout for potentially lethal fumes or soot from your furnace or fireplace. Your house may have so many gaps after a tornado that when a wind blows past it the air is sucked backwards down the chimney and spreads through the house. If a poorly designed fireplace can create smoke problems in a house, imagine what a tornado stressed house, riddled with gaps, can do.
- Check out-of-season equipment such as air conditioning or heating (depending on the season).
- Screen the attic if the roof has been lifted. Insects and birds may get in if you don't.

Carpets, upholstery and floors

- Be sure to clear mud, debris and glass splinters from flooring before too many people tromp through the house. Otherwise salvageable floors can be ruined very quickly.
- Do not bother trying to clean and retrieve carpets in any parts of the house where there is broken glass. If you do, you will probably be picking glass out of your children's feet for months afterward, and it is unlikely that any carpet cleaner can guarantee success in getting rid of it.
- Upholstered furniture may also be unsalvageable if it has glass in it.

Machinery and appliances

- Check for safety and for packed in dirt, insulation or glass before operating. A family who huddled in the basement as their house was blown apart told us, "We cleaned dirt and insulation out of our ears for a long time. It seemed like being inside a vacuum cleaner." Insulation and dirt finds its way into even the smallest openings. Be especially cautious about the safety of microwaves, gas or propane appliances, and refrigerators.
- Look for any sign that appliances may rust on the bottom. Even with the roof tarped, water may seep in.

Outside

- Establish a food station for volunteers.
- Clean up glass and other debris.
- Retrieve and store salvageable items.
- Tear down any dangerous structures that are beyond repair (salvaging what you can).
- Cut away tree debris.
- Collect steel.
- Sort wood (salvage or burn).
- Check everywhere (feed bin, seed grain, fields, driveway) for glass, nails and other hardware that can pose risks to your animals and machinery. Many tornado victims find nails in their cows feet for months after the event, and endless glass in the driveway and fields. Some animals died from "hardware problems" (ingested nails, etc.) later.

Looking out on the devastation...

It seemed that nothing was immune to the tornado's force.

How can I help?

We encountered a number of people who said, "I would have liked to help more at the time, but I just didn't know what to do." Don't be shy about offering to help. There will be plenty you can do, especially in the immediate aftermath, when tornado victims are too overwhelmed to get started without support from the community.

At times it may seem that the victims are distressed by the pressure others exert on them to get started on cleaning up. As one said, "I was wishing they wouldn't bother me, but thank goodness they knew enough to keep going."

It may seem tough to push the victim in the first few days after disaster strikes, but if you can keep their involvement to a minimum by shouldering some of the burden, providing emotional support, and shielding them from strangers who invade them in their own private hell, they will thank you later. The hardest part of cleanup is getting started, and homes and personal possessions that are left to the elements very quickly become unsalvageable.

You might be tempted to leave victims alone with their grief, but their families still depend on them, some key cleanup tasks can't be done without consulting them, and, most important of all, if they are not nudged into action they may spiral into depression. Getting busy is the first step toward getting back into stride, emotionally and physically.

So what can you do? One victim puts it simply: "Just chip in and do what needs to be done."

If you turn up and quietly go about remedying a specific problem, it can be very helpful without placing demands on the victim. One victim told us that a friend showed up, saw that there was glass inside the house that should be cleared up, and quietly set about doing the job. He didn't talk; he just worked. Another man walked into a farmer's lane carrying a ladder and nails to repair the chicken coop. Once he had finished the job he disappeared back down the lane. This kind of humble, silent generosity is very much appreciated. It ticks a task off the list with no demands on the victim.

If you know the victim, one of the most helpful things you can do is be there to listen, talk and pitch in as needed. But it is important to be sensitive to their emotions. Don't talk about the tornado all the time with them unless they want to (and they may). Just showing interest in their welfare helps a lot.

It is equally important to make sure that your help is truly helpful, and that your offer of help is realistic. Don't wash the unwashable, stack retrievables with irretrievables, promise and not come through, or be more trouble than help (for example, trying to clean up glass with young children in tow). Tornado victims need loving care, not further disappointments.

The rush of volunteer help often dies down to a trickle after the first week or two of cleanup, but the work goes on much longer for the victims. As one told us, "There was a time when I felt quite forsaken. Everyone was doing their own thing, and there was still a lot of stuff to be done

Can I do something special?

There are so many tasks and decisions facing tornado victims that they need all the help they can get. If there are areas where you can offer particular expertise, don't hesitate to offer it.

Here is a checklist of a few skills which are likely to be helpful.

- medical/first aid
- childcare
- cooking
- emotional support
- farm, livestock management
- veterinary skills
- organization/co-ordination of work
- cleaning
- moving/packing
- woodcutting
- repair (appliance, clothing, furniture)
- engineering
- building/contracting
- electrical/plumbing/gas
- insurance
- law/advocacy

"J'll tell ya right now, J live in the best neighbourhood in the world."

172

here. There are so many small things that carry on for a long time." If you can, continue to offer your help after the first flush of community of support has waned. As one victim said, "It's been four months non-stop work, dawn 'til dark."

The official emergency response

Although most communities have official emergency plans, how the response is carried out can vary widely. The April 20th tornadoes put three very different styles of emergency reponse to the test.

The officials on the track of the northern tornado (in Grey County) were responding to a tornado for the first time. Although they had an emergency plan they were learning as they went.

Those on the west end of the southern tornado track (in Wellington County), responded with a flexible and intuitive leadership in a community that had suffered through the tornado outbreak of May 31st, 1985. The people in charge of the response lived in the heart of the affected community, and many of the victims had been involved, directly or indirectly, in the 1985 event too.

And on the east end of the southern tornado track (in Dufferin County), the response was directed by an established office in charge of emergency planning and co-ordination, but the office and its co-ordinator were miles away from the affected communities and the track of the tornado was north of the area affected in the 1985 outbreak.

We will not indulge in a detailed discussion on emergency planning and co-ordination in this book. (There are many other sources for that information.) However, there are a few insights from these three very different experiences that might be helpful.

"You could tell they had done it before."

The combination of experience, flexibility and intuition that Jack Benham, the co-ordinator of the response in the Arthur area (the west end of the southern tornado track), brought to the task seems to have been most successful. Not only was there an established emergency plan, the community was responding to a devastating tornado for the second time in 11 years.

As one observer commented, "I think Jack Benham's way of doing things works a lot better. For one thing, he starts at 6 o'clock in the morning and works until 10 o'clock at night, whereas bureaucrats rarely do quite as well. And he has a lot of experience because he co-ordinated the response for the 1985 tornado in this area. He knows everyone, which has its advantages– he can understand where they are coming from, what their reactions are likely to be and what responses will be most helpful. And he had Council support. Jack could go to the Reeve and say, 'Listen, I need trucks,' and [the Council

Can I bring something?

Aside from bringing food and drink for the victims and volunteers, (which is in itself very helpful) there are many other items which you may be able to lend or donate to the cleanup effort.

Here is a checklist of a few suggestions.

- tarps, plywood
- tools, nails
- bins, garbage bags
- boxes, packing materials
- gloves, (many many)
- pens and masking tape
- cleaning supplies and equipment
- lumbering tools and equipment
- ladders
- all terrain vehicles
- heavy equipment
- moving and storage trucks and trailers

"The community spirit was overwhelming ... it was even more overwhelming than the twister itself!"

☞ Getting powered up

There are many easy-to-spot hazards from downed power lines in the aftermath of a tornado, as discussed in **Chapter four**. But there may also be less obvious risks (for instance, underground lines), and it is wise to trace all power lines in your mind to verify that they are safe and intact. If you think there may be a hazard, make sure that the power authorities know about it before the power is turned back on.

If your home or outbuildings have sustained damage which may have left unseen problems behind the walls, it is imperative that you have the wiring inspected before power is restored, whether through the main power line or through a generator. There is a heightened risk of fire from breaks in power or gaslines following a tornado.

It may be difficult to reach the power authorities by telephone. They are busy day and night, tending to emergency repair work along the length of the tornado's path. Many people were amazed at how quickly their power was restored in the aftermath of the April 20th tornado. This was possible only because Ontario Hydro workers were on the job throughout the night. If you have special needs or requirements for how new lines are laid, you may not be able to expect the power authorities to bear them in mind. They are trying to get the job done quickly. You may have to take the initiative of hiring independent contractors to do the work. This may be particularly true if you are a farmer whose livelihood is at risk, or if you are trying to safeguard those few trees on your property that have survived the tornado.

would] say, 'Hey, whatever you want, Jack, you got it.' People trusted him. They knew that he was not going to take advantage of anything. He seemed to know what he was doing. He seemed to do a very good job."

Learn as you go

On the north track, the official response was great at its best, but uneven overall. Arnold Rosenberg, the Clerk of Holland Township, learned the in's and out's of co-ordinating the response to a community disaster very quickly, and the outpouring of community support was tremendous. Most of the problems people encountered could be attributed to inexperience and occurred in the area most prone to failure: communications.

The biggest shortfall was felt by the victims on the east end of the path. As one victim told us, "It must have been a couple of hours before we saw the OPP (police). We didn't see any officials– nobody seeing if we were all right."

It is easy to understand how this could happen. The most concentrated devastation was along the west end of the tornado track. All of the primary responders (the OPP, fire departments, hospitals, and the Holland Township office) were also concentrated in that area, as was media attention.

"The highschool kids deserve a lot of credit. They worked like army ants."

Once the co-ordination for the cleanup was under way, help was more evenly available, but even then there were some victims who fell through the cracks. Specifically, the co-ordinators contacted property owners (some of whom were nowhere near the scene) rather than the tenants who were directly affected. As a result, some tenants were unaware of what help was available to them. And some victims commented that it would have helped to have someone check up on them occasionally to see if they needed help or advice.

The professional touch

In Dufferin County the overall response was very professional, but less personal and flexible than at Arthur. The greatest confusion occurred at the outset, and was probably due to poor communication between emergency responders. Fortunately, the result was an excessive official presence, not an inadequate one. Many people commented that they had repeated visits from fire, ambulance and police– sometimes five or six visits within a few hours.

However, the disaster co-ordination (under the leadership of Darrell Keenie) soon settled into an orderly rhythm, marked by a degree of organization and thoroughness that left little undone. Efforts were made to anticipate and respond to the full range of needs victims might experience: information, counselling, safety, housing, food, cleanup, rebuilding, insurance and problem resolution.

 ### If you can't be there …

There are endless possibilities for helping out after a tornado strikes– on the scene, from your own home, or through community actions. If you cannot help out on site (perhaps doing one of the jobs listed in *Getting started*) consider one of the following:

- Victims often need food. Everything is gone or packed away, and there is no time to cook or eat out with the dawn-to-dark work that confronts them. As one victim commented, "A friend organized the meals for a week. This was very useful because everybody was tired and starving. She just appeared like a magical angel– wonderful meals. It was a godsend." Other people brought coffee and sandwiches, which was welcomed because "you can't ask for it yourself."

- Provide easy eats (coffee, juice, sandwiches, doughnuts) for the many volunteers who are working day in and day out. This helps the victims, too, because they want to be able to extend hospitality to the people who are helping them, but have no way of providing this food and drink themselves.

- Provide childcare or special comforts to children, or quiet comfort and conversation to victims too old or disabled to be involved in the cleanup.

- Send a gift box of the kinds of items that everyone reaches for in daily life– simple things like tools, scissors, tape, openers, etc, or personal items like soap, toothpaste, bandages, washcloths etc.

- Donate clothing or furniture as it is needed.

- Provide a quiet place to retreat to for victims. This would most likely be helpful after the initial cleanup rush is over.

- Donate to the disaster fund or get involved in fundraising community events.

"I'd say that out of 100 people that were here I'd be lucky if I knew 10 of them."

One possible downfall of co-ordinating the response from the county level is that it was probably less personal than it might have been coming from people at the municipal level. As one township employee suggested, "People are more comfortable dealing with a familiar face. They are more likely to ask for things if they are not dealing with strangers or a large umbrella organization." Local officials and employees can often anticipate needs and respond with greater understanding of the circumstances and reactions of the victims; and the bonds of community may be strengthened by involving them more directly in the response.

Tree cleanup

When we asked people what brought home the power of the April 20th tornado most forcefully for them, many said it was the trees. In the heavily wooded countryside hit by the northern tornado (and in the Luther Marsh on the southern track) people saw large tracts of woods reduced to twisted wasteland. Forests of maples, elms, pines, spruce, and cedars that had graced the countryside for many generations were mutilated beyond imagination.

And other people, who had chosen their country properties for the mature trees lining the laneway or screening the view from the road, were left with a macabre queue of shredded stumps. What they valued most about their homes was gone.

As one owner of a large mature forest commented, "We're all quite devastated. It was my hope that this would all be a park." He figured that only about 17% of the mature trees could be salvaged from his woods. Many of the trees were twisted, and that loosened the annular rings. They looked all right at first glance– the bark was still on– but, inside, the twisting had separated the wood into layers and strands. When cut, they disintegrated into a heap of strands, unsuitable even for firewood.

Cleaning up tornado damaged woods presents special challenges. Many of the woods damaged in the 1985 tornado outbreak in Ontario are still a twisted mess. It is difficult even to walk amongst the confusion of uprooted, twisted and broken remains, let alone get in with the heavy machinery required to clean it up.

It took one couple 15 minutes to walk and crawl about 50 metres (150 feet) to their cabin after the tornado left their tall trees in a tangled ruin. The walk would normally have taken less than a minute. The trees were snapped off, uprooted and blown over, or ripped off, leaving "very jaggy edges." Cleanup on their land was a treacherous business (see picture below), even though they had experienced volunteers with heavy duty equipment at their disposal.

The cleanup of tornado damaged woods is too dangerous to be undertaken by inexperienced volunteers. It takes experienced woodcutters and the proper equipment. Fortunately, on the northern track of the April 20th tornado many people could offer this expertise; and, on the southern track, help was forthcoming from local conservation authorities.

"People came from all over. It was amazing how people pulled together."

6
Rebuilding lives and spirits

Watching the remains of your possessions being gathered and burnt is hard on the spirit.

When tornado victims climb out from under the wreckage, they are soon brought out of their initial shock and numbness by the energetic and caring responses of friends, family and strangers. They are inspired and comforted by the hard work and generosity of spirit others extend to them during the first few weeks after disaster strikes.

But soon, those willing helpers are called back to "life as usual" and the victims are left struggling to rebuild their shattered lives and spirits. It can be a very lonely time. They are cast adrift in a storm of nitpicking but necessary details, battered by a constant barrage of questions and decisions. And they have no way of anticipating all the problems they may encounter.

Moving forward in the glow of the compassionate support they have received from the community, they sometimes end up being doubly victimized. They have trouble sorting out the helpers from the hucksters, the volunteers from the vultures. They have come to trust that others have their best interests at heart, so it comes as a jarring shock when they encounter the hard reality of unscrupulous contractors, unfeeling and inflexible government officials and unco-operative or unfriendly insurance representatives. They are probably still suffering from post traumatic stress, and will be for some time, so it is particularly difficult for them to have to fight every step of the way toward rebuilding their lives.

We hope that by itemizing some of the decisions, problems and stresses they may encounter we can give future tornado victims an edge in facing these challenges. We also hope that others– friends, neighbours, onlookers, officials, tradespeople, insurance and other service representatives– will be able to walk a few steps in the victims' shoes, and respond acccordingly.

Stressed to the limit

The emotional stresses disaster victims face are normal, healthy responses to an abnormal event. They are to be expected, even desired. We need to grieve for what we have lost, and with an event as devastating as a tornado, victims may have many losses to grieve. It takes a long time.

On top of that, much of what normally anchored them in tough times has been scattered to the winds. The patterns of their lives have been obliterated. They can't restore their spirits over coffee in an old familiar chair– the chair is atop a tree in the back forty. Even if the whirlwind in their minds would settle down for a few hours, the books and hobbies they normally relax with have been burned or carted to the dump. For weeks they don't feel that

Rollercoaster to recovery

As with grieving, there is a common pattern of emotional response to disaster, which we have outlined below. This pattern is not rigid, however, and tornado victims will move back and forth through various reactions at their own speed and in their own ways.

- **Terrified,** but sometimes mesmerized too, as the tor– nado approaches. Slow motion experience of time. (This distortion of time sense may play into later feelings of guilt.)
- **Dazed and numb** immediately afterward. Emotional shutdown. (May be short period of elation due to thankfulness for surviving.)
- **Anxiety or fear** surfaces a few days or weeks later. May be tearful or shaky when confronted by losses or reminded of close call with death.
- **Confusion of emotions**– anger, fear, frustration, confusion, grief, anxiety. Rage against disaster may be misdirected elsewhere. (Possible problems at work or with relationships.)
- **Nightmares and flashbacks,** possibly accompanied by self-doubt. May have problems remembering simple things.
- **Guilt and depression**. Survivor guilt if victims feel they have suffered less than others; self-criticism if labouring under the mistaken belief that they had time to act more heroically.
- **Taking positive steps**. Re-establishing relationships, establishing new ones, making positive changes, reaching out and redefining what matters in life.
- **Acceptance**. Although nothing will ever be the same, constructive changes show that victims have accepted and adapted to life as it is.

they can escape the disaster scene, even for a day's respite, because a constant stream of gawkers makes them fear looting of what little they have left.

Everyone in the family responds differently to the stresses, and they may find themselves fighting when they need each other most. If remodelling a house can strain many marriages, imagine what rebuilding your life– house, contents and mementos– can do. Families can come out of disaster stronger than ever, but that is a testament to the quality of their love and commitment to each other. It is hard work under difficult circumstances.

To begin with, tornado victims are usually dazed and confused by the devastation that confronts them. The first helpers to arrive often find them wandering aimlessly through the wreckage, unable to talk or answer questions. They are at a loss to know how to begin the overwhelming task of sorting through the rubble, and they need the practical "let's roll up our sleeves" attitude that friends, neighbours, and strangers can offer. Alone, they wouldn't know how to start, but once they see others combing the fields for cherished objects– bringing back a wedding photo, a ring, a child's toy– they begin to gain the courage they need to begin again.

Then, the unending work, the constant assault of details and decisions, intervenes, and this is both a blessing and a curse. Physical activity and the presence of many helpers– who can lend an ear and a shoulder, not just a hand– help victims begin the process of grieving for their losses. But there is also a risk, especially for those who want to remain strong for their families, that the grieving process will be arrested, only to resurface many months or even years later, when friends think no more help is needed. (See *Rollercoaster to recovery*, left.)

Each in his (or her) own way

It is important for friends and helpers to bear in mind that we all have our own ways of dealing with stress. The executive who has always been in control may seem brusque and unappreciative to volunteers. But he is devastated by the fact that, suddenly, his life has been ripped apart by something completely beyond his control, and he responds by barking out orders and then fleeing the scene. He cannot allow himself to be seen out of control, but he knows he won't be able to bear the pain of sifting through the rubble.

People who are physically unable to participate in the cleanup and rebuilding process, due to age or disability, may suffer particularly. It is difficult to sit on the sidelines with no physical outlet to help you deal with your losses. Younger victims may learn to see a tornado disaster as an opportunity for a new beginning, but older folks can see only that they have lost what took a lifetime to build. They have neither the time nor the energy to begin again. No new home can take the place of the family homestead in their hearts. And they may have lost the things that mattered most to them– family photos and memorabilia, or a forest they lovingly tended as a bequest to the future. Some of the greatest sadness we encountered in our conversations with victims was in people who had lost large tracts of old forest. They had expected those trees to outlive them by centuries, providing joy and solace for future generations.

Climbing out from under

Although tornado victims are usually dumbstruck when they first confront the ruin of their homes, some feel a surge of elation when they realize how fortunate they and their family are to have survived, and this elation carries them through the first few days. As one man told us, "We were all in absolute wonder and shock when we knew that our pets were okay and we were okay. I had a profound feeling of joy. That kept me elated for a good week. I was just on top of the world." Another said, "I was really happy for a few days and then crashed right down. We couldn't even look outside. It was just so depressing to look out there."

Those who have experienced deaths or severe injuries in their families are not likely to benefit even from this small edge of elation. All tornado victims need people around them who will support them and listen to them as they struggle to come to grips with their losses.

☞ Emotional aftershocks

Tornado victims may be confused or worried by physical and emotional symptoms they experience afterwards. These symptoms may be physical (e.g. nausea, tremors, heart palpitations and dizziness), cognitive (e.g. confusion, memory problems and poor concentration), emotional (e.g. fear, anger, depression and anxiety), or behavioural (stumbling over words, inability to rest, withdrawal, erratic behaviour). If you experience any of them, remember that they are normal responses to an abnormal event, and will most likely pass with time and the care and support of those around you.

If, however, symptoms persist or get in the way of your efforts to recover from disaster, do not hesitate to seek help from your doctor, minister or a clinic. You have been through a very traumatic event, and these professionals may be able to help you through it. Here are some symptoms which may become problematic.

- Flashbacks
- Traumatic dreams
- Memory disturbances
- Persistent intrusive memories of the tornado
- Excessive drinking or drug use
- Anger, irritability, hard to control hostility
- Persistent depression, withdrawal
- A dazed or numb appearance
- Panic attacks
- Unreasonable fears (phobias)

"I lost my bearings ..."

Most people are disoriented and in shock when they first stumble out of the wreckage. As one victim said, "We were scared to come up. I lost my bearings because the porch was gone and the drywall was sucked out and I couldn't figure out why I saw daylight when I came up the stairs. I was really disoriented." Another couple were found where their house had been, "white and shaking, standing there without any shoes on."

Victims struggle with the loss of a sense of place. "It took about three days before it all sank in. For the first few days we just walked around with our mouths hanging open. It was hard to take in– the amount of destruction. What we've seen out our window for the past twenty years just suddenly, in a matter of seconds, isn't there any more. That was the hardest part."

Without familiar surroundings to anchor them emotionally, they find it difficult to establish a rhythm to carry them through the difficult days ahead. One woman told us, "I forgot so many things until later. It takes a long time to come back. There was a heifer having a calf in the barn [before the tornado struck], and I had joked [to my city friends], 'Oh, I'm goin' to make farmers out of you. You're goin' to help me pull this calf, but we'll give her an hour to see if she has it on her own.' But we never got back to the barn because the storm passed through. And then after the tornado there was a new calf and I couldn't figure out where it came from. It took me two weeks to remember about her having a calf."

Survivors of the 1985 tornado outbreak in Ontario have said that it took one to three years to bring back a sense of place. "It's hard to lose what you are used to and what you made."

One man who lost his treasured forest said, "It really changed my outlook. I used to look forward to retiring. I had it all landscaped around the forest - bush trails, nice walking trails. It's just flat now. So I don't think I'll ever go there again. I don't want to look at it. That was sort of my salvation back there. It's just a helluva mess now."

One of the most important things that victims and their friends can do to help them through the earlier stages of disorientation is to **find ways to bring back a sense of home as soon as possible.** One woman planted a garden and found teacups so that she and her husband could sit down and relax over tea– a familiar comfort. She advises, "As soon as you can, try to get back to normal. For me it was cups and saucers and little things. You have to have a couple of nice moments, even in all that chaos."

There's no escape, no time to grieve

Many tornado survivors reach a point where they want to be alone but can't. There are too many people around. Because helpers and workers are there every day, from dawn until late at night, it is hard for victims to take a break. To leave the property, to leave everything– even for a short while– seems impossible, especially when there is a constant parade of sightseers walking through their property.

Sometimes grief reactions are delayed because victims cannot afford to divert their attention from the busyness that crowds their days. Or there may be other factors– the birth of a child or the hospitalization of an injured family member–which delay the process of grieving. Many victims don't begin to show the emotional impact of their losses until

Proving that you own it

How on Earth can you remember everything you owned, let alone prove it, after your property has been scattered to the winds? You may have been asked to fill out inventory sheets when you bought your insurance policy, but it just seemed like too much work. As one insurance representative told us: "I've probably got 1,000 homes insured, and I'll betcha I got maybe three inventory sheets back. But then, when people have a loss, they have to make it out and they get angry." As one victim said,"It's easy to say, hard to do."

At the very least, you should take photographs or a video of your possessions, room by room, when you buy insurance. There are companies that will do this for you and have the documents sealed. Whether you use inventory lists, pictures or videos, store any documentation you may need to prove a loss where you won't lose it with your belongings (perhaps a safety deposit box).

months after the tornado. It is important for friends to be there to support them when the grieving begins.

How to cope

One victim we interviewed talked a lot of sense when she said, "I think it's really healthy to talk about it. At that time you need support [from friends and other people], because it seems that your whole world has crashed and you need somebody behind you. Somebody described it as a bereavement– and you just have to let it out. They say that if you don't talk about it and let it out it's [still] going to be there, and it's harder on you. ... Sure, everything has died down now. Everyone is gone and they figure you are on your own. They keep saying, 'You're pretty well settled now?' I say, 'Just ask me in a year from now.' You just don't get over it overnight."

But some people find it painful to talk about the tornado. As one victim explained, "I had a hard time discussing it for a long time. I didn't want to relive that feeling I had of total helplessness." The best advice for friends is probably to **be there, be willing to listen, and be alert for signs that the victim is having difficulties.**

Difficulties may surface gradually (through depression, for example) or suddenly, through extreme anxiety. One victim seemed to be coping well until her family left, but once she was alone she had a panic attack. "I couldn't breathe, I got dizzy. I had to go outside and take deep breaths."

Sometimes the healing process is complicated by insurance struggles. If rebuilding is stalled by an insurance dispute, victims don't want to live with constant questions about why they haven't started yet. As one victim said, "What we are going through now is really hard on our spirits." They need emotional support, not impatience, from family and friends. When rebuilding is stalled, the stress can reach dangerous levels, because the victims cannnot get on with life until things are settled. And, if time is the best healer, it walks hand in hand with "getting on with life."

Decisions, decisions

It is unlikely that any other life experience will require more organizational and decision-making skill than surviving and rebuilding from the devastation of a tornado. But disasters also bring forth an outpouring of community support that is rare in these days of tattered human bonds. Victims should not be shy to accept the help they are offered. The task of rebuilding needs many hearts, minds and hands; and the lives of the volunteers and the community will be greatly enriched by their involvement.

How is the tornado victim kept busy?

First, of course, victims must find shelter and a place from which to wage the cleanup and rebuilding campaign. As one survivor told us, "All I want is my kitchen table, a cup of coffee and a cigarette. All the stuff that I would do, all my paperwork, I would do at that kitchen table. You try to make a decision sitting in somebody else's house, everything's all over the place. There's no spot for anything."

And what needs doing?

- lists, endless lists, of losses and decisions to be made

- cleaning up/repairing anything and everything

- tending to the needs (equipment, food) of a constant stream of volunteers, friends and hired workers

- putting up with the media and non-stop sightseers (gawkers)

- arranging, organizing and co-ordinating work

- making decisions on repairing/rebuilding, salvaging/trashing, cash value/replacement value, for everything that has been destroyed or damaged

- pricing and replacing things as they are needed

- eventually, replacing and rebuilding the accumulations of a lifetime

- and this is all on top of the normal demands of daily life

Repair or rebuild?

The complex wind and pressure patterns in a tornado can produce severe structural damage that is hidden at first, but sneaks up on you in time. It often takes a structural engineer to determine whether a building should be repaired or rebuilt. For this reason, owners of homes that are not obviously destroyed or irretrievably damaged often experience the greatest difficulties in rebuilding their lives.

In some cases they must suffer through periodic upheavals for years, while yet another structural defect is unmasked and corrected. Many people whose homes were hit in the devastating tornadoes that went through Ontario on May 31st, 1985, were still opening up walls to do further repairs years after the event.

In other cases, victims may begin to repair the damage, only to discover, once a few walls are opened up, that they have to rebuild. As one victim of the April 20th tornado told us, "There were cracks through the walls. Over time they got worse and worse, and when the workmen started opening them up to do repair work, they realized that the structure was not sound enough to be repaired."

Any decision to repair rather than rebuild a tornado-damaged building must be made with great caution, careful assessment of the damage, and an insistence on having the success of the work guaranteed by the contractors and/or your insurance company.

Assess the damage carefully

If you are nervous about the structural integrity of your home after it has gone through a tornado– and you should be if you have bulges in your walls, cracks that spread, signs that the roof has been lifted and dropped, or signs of twisting– get a building inspector and possibly a structural engineer in as soon as possible. Your family's health and safety may depend on it. (You may run the risk of fire or carbon monoxide poisoning due to wiring or heating system damage.)

Do not assume that you can trust to a single assessment from your insurance adjuster. It may be a tough call and it is wise to have a second opinion at the outset. The adjuster may be encountering tornado damage claims for the first time. Your local emergency response co-ordinator may be able to send the building inspector over, or recommend an independent structural engineer for the job. If your insurance adjuster recommends repairing your home, you will be in a position to present your concerns about his determination much more convincingly if you have had an expert assessment done right off.

Get a guarantee

"The adjuster came in. I expected him to tell me what was wrong, like a doctor, only he didn't. So then, I'm seeeing all these cracks and they're telling me they are going to patch it. I said, 'It doesn't look good. What's the guarantee?'"

If contractors will not guarantee their work because they do not believe that the approved damage appraisal is thorough enough to solve your home's structural problems,

Making a list ... and checking it twice

If you have not done a written or video inventory of your possessions before disaster strikes, you may feel pressured and frustrated by your insurance company's requests that you fill out Proof of Loss forms as soon as possible. It seems such an impossible task, and there are so many other things that seem more urgent. But you will be better off if you start this process as soon as possible. Once you have made out an initial list you will need time to discover what has been left off; and if you don't start early you will end up being too rushed to do the job justice. Give yourself time to take it step by step.

As soon as possible:

Have someone video or photograph your home, room by room, looking into every nook and cranny. If you are videotaping, look for signs of damage to the structure (cracks, bulges, water seepage, etc.) and video your possessions before cleanup begins. Talk while you video to record your comments on the damage.

Gather together any receipts or proofs of purchase that have survived the tornado and put them where you will be able to find them easily. Make sure any salvageable items are protected from the elements.

Within the first week

Get your family together to think through what has been lost, room by room, activity by activity, (not forgetting seasonal or occasional activities). List everything you think of and put the list in a safe place where they can all find it to make additions.

For the next while

Keep pen and pad in your pocket at all times so that you can add to the list as you remember more losses.

Is it complete?

Once you think you have remembered most items, go back through your home (in your mind, if necessary) to see if anything more comes to mind.

No matter how thorough you have been, you will probably remember something else after you have submitted your Proof of Loss forms. Ask your insurance representative how and if you can claim on items you remember after you have submitted the forms. Some insurance companies will allow a small extra amount for "miscellaneous." Some may have a buffer period during which you can add more.

don't allow the work to begin. Discuss the issue with your adjuster and come up with an agreement for repairing or rebuilding that can be guaranteed.

If the insurance company advises to repair, and problems crop up later, they are liable for the costs of further work; but it is better by far to fight this battle before settling your claim inadequately. You will not enjoy the upheaval of repeated repairs over the years, no matter who pays for them.

Getting the work done

In the aftermath of a community disaster it can be doubly difficult to get what you want when you are repairing or rebuilding your home. Some victims complained, "We had difficulty getting people to come and give us quotes. It was almost like the community didn't have enough repair people."

Builders and contractors may be slow (because they are overbooked and overworked) and you are dependent on a great many building suppliers and tradespeople coming through on schedule, so there are bound to be glitches. Expect things to take longer than planned.

If you can use local contractors/tradespeople, do. Or, if there are Mennonite contractors available in your area, their experience in working quickly to rebuild from disaster can be very helpful. **You have the right to choose which contractors you use**, and local contractors or Mennonites are more likely to do the work in a helping community spirit.

Watch that contractors and suppliers don't compromise on quality. (Since they have had a quote accepted by your insurance company they may have the opportunity to substitute inferior materials to boost their profits.) To safeguard against this, you can have the quality level specified in the quote.

Am I covered?

Now we come to the single most important factor in determining how painful and problematic the rebuilding process will be– insurance. How many of us even think about tornado damage when we buy insurance? It seems so unlikely that we will ever need it! But that is exactly what insurance is all about– protecting ourselves against losses that we hope never to experience.

Tornadoes are covered under wind perils on insurance policies. They don't fall into the black hole of "Act of God," that uninsurable no-man's-land that can leave flood and earthquake victims weeping long after the event. **Tornado damage is insured in the standard policy.**

But tornadoes leave their victims with more wide-ranging needs for insurance coverage than other more common perils do. Their impact on buildings, their contents, property and human lives puts insurance to the test. It's wise to choose a policy that is up to the test. It will serve you well on lesser claims too.

What should you be looking for when you buy insurance, or what should you be checking your current policies for? How do you make sure you have the best company and policy for your needs?

First, you need to know what to insure, for how much. When deciding on insurance needs or reviewing your policy, place yourself on the scene of a disaster. Too often people enter into insurance naïvely, assuming that it will take care of them without thinking through what that might entail. They may have extra expenses for temporary accommodation (sometimes for many months), cleanup, storage and repairs, plus the cost of replacing just about everything they own, including their home and outbuildings. They will have to absorb any losses that cannot be covered by insurance (e.g., fencing, tree and landscape damage), so they will want to have other losses covered as fully as possible. As one victim of the April 20th tornadoes told us: "Most people just buy insurance, and they don't know what they are getting it for." It is important to understand what the various levels of coverage mean (see *Types of coverage*, opposite). Inadequate coverage can spell ruin.

Yet, the most common mistake people make is to underinsure. If you underinsure your home, you may fall into a "catch 22" that few of us know about. Not only do you have too little insurance to cover the cost of rebuilding, you cannot even claim the full value of your insurance. As one victim advises: "If you're underinsured and nobody tells you [before disaster strikes], you're wasting your money. You might as well throw it in the ground or put it in the bank and take your chances!"

Choosing insurance

Once you are clear on what you want from insurance, how do you choose a company that will be responsible and responsive to your needs when it comes to the hard reality of making a claim?

The cheapest quote may not offer the best deal on insurance. You need to be able to count on the agent/broker and the company to serve you well. For the few dollars saved on the lowest quote, you might be buying yourself a painful struggle. Make sure you ask for the insurance you will need should you have to rebuild or relocate. (See *What do you need?*, page 187.)

Basic areas for which you will need coverage are temporary accomodations, cleanup and debris removal, house, outbuildings, machinery, vehicles, personal property and any special items not covered under personal property.

 ## Types of coverage

The type of coverage you choose for your home and personal property makes a big difference to the value you will be able to claim on a loss. You have a choice between three levels of insurance.

Actual cash value: (most likely on vehicles or personal property) You can claim the amount you paid for an item at the time you bought it, subject to depreciation. You will end up with much less in your settlement than if you had **full replacement cost**.

Full replacement cost: (on house, outbuildings, personal property or vehicles) If you have full replacement cost on your home, you must be sure that it is insured for at least 80% of what it would cost to replace it, in which case losses are covered up to the insured value. If you are underinsured (less than 80% of replacement cost) you may fall into the "catch 22" described above.

You may choose to have full replacement cost on personal property and vehicles too. (Many tornado victims were unable to replace their vehicles with the actual cost settlements they were given.) Remember that, even with replacement cost insurance, if you choose not to replace an item, it will be valued at actual cost, subject to depreciation.

Guaranteed replacement cost: (on homes) Your home must be insured for 100% of its replacement cost; but, if you are claiming for replacement within one or two years after valuation and the true cost of replacement is higher, guaranteed replacement cost insurance will cover the difference (e.g., if you were insured for $100,000 and it cost $105,000 to replace, the insurance would pay you $105,000).

We feel that the best advice is to insure your home and contents for full replacement cost, and make sure that your home is not insured for less than 80% of what it might cost you to replace it within the next couple of years. You should also reassess the value of buildings and contents every three years (or whenever you make significant changes) to make sure that they are adequately covered.

It is helpful to look at the track record of a company before you choose it. Remember that the agent or broker is not the company, and important as it is to get along well with him or her, you need a company that will stand behind you, too.

"Which do you prefer— beef or pork?"

However, bear in mind that claims for tornado damage are more complex and stressful for both the claimant and the insurer than are run-of-the-mill claims (loss, theft). If you know anyone who has suffered tornado damage or other pervasive losses (such as fire), ask them whether they felt they were fairly treated and, if so, who insured them.

There are many issues which arise in tornado damage claims, and even the most responsive and responsible company may not be able to meet all of a claimant's demands. But it is usually quite easy to differentiate between those who drag their feet or argue every step along the way and those who treat their policyholders with respect, compassion and fairness. Most companies want to do right by their customers– treating people well is good for business. But, as in any other enterprise, there are always a few bad apples (and a few good apples having a bad day). If you get stuck with one of them, you may end up thinking you suffered more from your insurance dealings than from the tornado.

Making a claim

One of the first things you will need to do after a tornado strikes is contact your insurance agent/broker. Some companies have 24 hour emergency lines, and may even be on the scene before you have a chance to call them. They may be able to give you a cheque on the spot to cover your immediate expenses in finding shelter. In the confusion of the moment they may not mention (or you may not remember them saying) that you should keep receipts for expenses you pay out of that cheque. You are probably covered for temporary living and relocation expenses, which are insured under "additional living expenses", as a percentage of the value for which you have insured your home. (Additional living expenses are separately insured, not deducted from the value of the settlement on your home.)

From this moment on you should keep records on everything that relates to losses or expenses you may be claiming. Impossible, you say? Probably. But the better your documentation is, the smoother your claims process is likely to be. Some victims of the April 20th tornadoes kept pencil and pad in their pockets at all times so that whenever they remembered or encountered anything relevant to their claim they could jot it down.

As soon as you are able to, protect what remains from the elements (tarping, boarding up windows, getting salvageable items under cover). The fine print on your policy will tell you that it is your responsibility to "mitigate further damage".

Have someone videotape the damage site, documenting the devastation room by room before you start cleaning up. Once you have done this you can get right to cleanup without waiting for your insurance representative to arrive.

Retrieve any receipts or proofs of purchase that may have survived and put them where you can find them when you are making out your claim. If you haven't done a written or video inventory of your possessions, you will be facing the daunting task of remembering, listing and pricing everything that you owned. Anything you can do to simplify this process is a priority, because it will speed the processing of your claim.

What do you need?

What follows is a list of some specific expenses and losses you may experience with a tornado. All of them have been derived from shortfalls and disputes experienced by the April 20th tornado victims.

Cleanup and debris removal– Usually part of building insurance coverage (and these costs are taken off your building settlement), but you can purchase extra debris removal coverage.

Living expenses– Most policies pay for trailers, rent or other temporary accommodations up to a percentage (e.g. 10%) of the valuation on your home. You may be given a cheque up front to cover immediate expenses. Keep all receipts and remember that you might be in temporary accommodations for many months. You may also be able to claim for payment for friends who have provided temporary accommodations.

Contents– Even if everything is destroyed your insurance company will not simply setttle for the full amount of your contents insurance. They will want you to list and value specific items that you have lost, although they should be flexible about providing proofs of ownership. They will also expect you to protect anything which survives the tornado from later damage (from the elements).

Food– Any food you lost in the tornado is covered under contents.

Trees, fences, lawns– Ask your agent or broker whether any or all fences are covered. Farm fences usually aren't. Occasionally some compensation is given for foundation plantings. If a tree falls on a building, the cost of removing it is covered under debris removal.

Power poles and lines– Some insurance companies cover these on their standard policies (and some cover inspection costs and GST, too) but others don't. Ask your agent or broker.

Building up to code– Some insurance polcies do not cover extra expenses due to changed building code standards, but they should be covered under "all risk" policies.

Antennas and satellite dishes– Some policies include this as standard coverage, but it may have to be specified. Check with your agent/broker.

Boats and like objects– These may be covered on an all risk rider on your homeowner's policy, whether they are in shelter or not. If they are covered under named perils (specified), they may only be insured if in an enclosure.

Animals– To get full value out of your livestock floater, make sure that you maintain insurance on at least 80% of the value of your animals. This probably means reporting changes in your livestock population at least twice a year. Be careful if your agent recommends a "more or less" clause to allow for fluctuating livestock populations during calving. One farmer we interviewed had his losses prorated, even though the policy stated "more or less."

Vehicles– Generally, vehicles are covered for wind damage on car insurance policies. Some (but not all) victims found that their vehicles were not covered if they were damaged inside the garage. Insurance will not cover car rental, since the claim is not due to collision, so make sure that when repairs are done you find a garage that offers a courtesy car.

Specialty items– If you have items of special value (coins, jewelry, artwork, furs, specialized equipment), especially if the value exceeds $500, check whether they need to be put on a special rider. You may not be able to claim them otherwise.

Tenants– Coverage you can ask for includes personal property, improvements (tenant upgrade) and possibly moving expenses.

If you decide to hire a cleaning and restoration company, get your insurance company's approval and verify that any damage the cleaning company causes will be covered.

Set aside time with your family to do an initial inventory of losses, and discuss the options you have for repairing, rebuilding and replacing what you have lost. Add to the inventory of losses as you remember things, and try to bring to mind items associated with activities you do irregularly or seasonally (e.g. Christmas). (See *Making a list ... and checking it twice*, page 183.)

When problems arise

Everyone involved in a tornado-related insurance claim is likely to be under stress. It is sometimes difficult to keep the claims process on an even keel. The fact remains, however, that even though the agent/broker, the adjuster and the company may be swamped with claims, the victim is under the most stress by far, and should be treated with respect and compassion. The onus is on the insurance professionals to pave the way for a smooth claims process.

That being said, if you are making a claim, you can anticipate a more sympathetic and timely response if you are co-operative and respectful too. If you expect the worst from your company you are more likely to get it. Nobody wins when insurance claims degenerate into an antagonistic relationship, and the strain of having to fight every step along the way is too much to heap on top of the post traumatic stress you are already experiencing.

At the same time, victims should feel confident and fully justified in getting verification (inspections, second opinions) on issues that worry them. They are the ones who will have to live with the results of the repair/rebuild decisions. No reputable insurance representative should object to this, and if they do it may be a harbinger of future problems. One victim told us, "He seemed quite fine ... so friendly, joking, sharing stories. But when I started questioning, his back went up. I thought they were awfully legitimate questions to be asked. He was upset that a building inspector had been called in. Why?" Once an adjuster is on the defensive there is a risk that the claims process will suffer. You may want to ask your agent or broker to help rebuild a relationship of trust. If that doesn't help, you may need to have someone else intervene on your behalf. Some claimants are left with no other choice, but in most cases it is possible to settle down to a more productive interchange after tempers have cooled.

If you feel pressured by the adjuster (for cash settlement, specific repair/rebuild decisions, Proof of Loss forms) explain that you don't feel it is wise to decide in a rush, and give yourself the time to review all your options. As one victim said, "It's unfortunate you can't just say, 'Geez, let's just stop time here. Give me 24 hours.'"

But perhaps that is exactly what you should do. Delegate continuing cleanup to a trusted friend for a day, and give yourself an island of undisturbed time to sort out how to proceed on your insurance claim. The claims process is far less likely to run off track if you start firmly seated on the rails.

Getting back to normal

It takes a long time to get back to normal after disaster strikes– and things will never be the same again– but most victims of the April 20th tornadoes found that their insurance companies were responsive and helpful as they struggled to rebuild. Without insurance they would have been devastated. (Indeed, a few were, because they had inadequate or no coverage.)

Victims, stunned by the enormity of their losses and the endless work ahead of them, find that they are able to start taking the first steps out of despair when their insurance company sends a sympathetic representative to the scene, sometimes within hours. It can make the difference between a fresh start and descent into depression.

As painful as disputatious claims may be, they are the exception. You wouldn't want to find yourself facing disaster without a responsible insurance company standing behind you. You might have to walk away from a lifetime's work, starting again with nothing.

7
Helping kids cope

Children react strongly to tornado events, even when they have not been directly affected. One mother told us, "These guys were terrified for months after. ... I'd say there was a couple of months where they did not want us to go out or they wanted to come with us. So there seemed to be a fairly good [pronounced] effect from having been a part of this– and then all week helping people clean up and seeing first-hand."

Another woman, who was helping out at school, said, "Some of these kids are fairly hooked on tornadoes. These kids [are] out in the portable and it's dark, and the kids are saying, 'There's going to be a tornado! There's going to be a tornado!' and they are all panicking. They didn't even see the tornado and they are panicking. I'm sure a lot of them saw the damage, but still, that's all they hear about. They see the pictures."

For those who have been directly involved the panic may be more extreme. One child, whose home had been destroyed, was out on her bicycle when the wind started to blow. A neighbour told us, "She just panicked. She dropped her bike, she ran out of her shoe, and she never stopped." As one mother told us, "I think that, through all this, the kids are most affected. It will be a long haul for them."

Children who see the aftermath of a tornado may need help dealing with their fears.

Every time the wind blows ...

Children become very sensitive to changes in the weather after a tornado strikes. One young boy explained, "Everytime there was a wind or anything after that, I just freaked, because of the tornado. And every night we'd all think there was going to be a tornado– even if there was a little draft of wind and one or two dark clouds, or anything."

As one teacher said, "I know it's on everyone's mind, especially the little kids in this area, because they're getting sick to their stomaches– when it starts to rain, or heavy wind, lightning or anything that's not normal– like high winds without rain is scary for them, because it was such a nice day that day."

These fears may be generalized to include any and all natural disasters. One spirited young fellow told us, "I used to be scared of dogs. Now I'm scared of storms, earthquakes and tornadoes– and dogs. ... When I look at a black cloud, then I'm worried because I think there's going to be a tornado or thunderstorm or something. And there might be a pouring rain. That might make a flood."

Or they may be specific to aspects of the weather they remember from the day of the tornado.

When the tornado came the cows were okay. The hay thing's broken. The glass is broken in our van. The Mennonites are coming to help us today. It was scary. Lots of people are helping us. My Mom cried at the dance but Daddy said it was good no one was hurt and everyone's okay. Tippy is okay too but he bit the insurance man. We're in our trailer now. I like it.

Charlie Bryan

One nine year old became fearful whenever there was heavy rain or wind. She woke her mother up early one morning, saying, "Mommy, come on. We gotta get up, there's a tornado," because the rain was so heavy she thought it was the wind. Although the most common fear associations are with dark clouds, wind and thunder or lightning, children may also be fearful of hail, rain or any sudden change in the weather.

Some children devise plans to help them take control of their fears. One mother told us, "To this day, my daughter– whenever it's thunder and lightning– she has her emergency tornado kit. She has her stuffed animals and she has her hamster. So whenever it gets dark and she knows that it's raining she puts her kit by the basement door– she's ready!"

The imagination runs wild

Younger kids may think of the tornado as a living creature, and worry that it will come back to get them. One father realized his boys' fears and took steps to deal with them quickly. "We went on the tornado tour the next day. I wanted to show them and just tell them, 'This is what happened when the tornado went through. It's not coming back. It's done with.' Because they kept on thinking, 'It's coming back.' All night they were waiting for it to come back. [I said], 'No, no, it's gone. It's way way far away. It's not going to come back. It's done with. It's gone back into the clouds and there won't be another one.'"

Touring the damage may help some children whose fears are not based on direct experience, but it may also be upsetting for them, especially if they know the victims. As one young boy said, "I saw the Henry house inside ... and every time we were coming outside I started crying, and every time that Mommy started talking I started crying, and when we started walking I started crying again."

What worries kids most is that a tornado might come at night, when they cannot see it coming. This is a natural expression of their fear of the unknown, and in Canada and parts of the U.S. parents can reassure them with some confidence that tornadoes rarely strike at night. (People living in the south and east parts of the U.S. "tornado alley"– particularly in Mississippi, Alabama, Arkansas and Louisiana– have more reason to fear nighttime tornadoes.) Nonetheless childrens' nighttime fears are very real to them. As one teenager said, "I'm always scared they'll come at night, 'cause you don't know what's coming."

Night terrors disturb many households after a tornado strikes. One mother told us, "One night [my

Frank
Maletta

Guidelines for parents

There are a few general guidelines that parents should consider when helping children cope with a tragedy such as a tornado. Bear in mind that many children who have not been direct victims may nevertheless need help in coping with a community disaster.

- Help them stay in touch with family and friends. They need to know that they can still count on these relationships.

- Give them plenty of supportive, physical contact (hugs, etc.), especially if they are young.

- Encourage them to express their feelings in their own ways, e.g., play, drawing, diaries and stories. Let them know that their feelings are okay.

- Encourage them to talk about what happened. Discussions with young children may come in fits and starts (because they have a short attention span), but adults and children alike benefit from talking about traumatic events.

- Children of any age may act babyish or younger for awhile. This is a normal reaction because they have been scared. Give them the comfort that they need, especially at bedtime.

- Help them learn something about weather and storm safety so that they don't start fearing every dark or windy sky. Information helps them regain a sense of control.

- Talk through what the family should do in threatening weather. Children will be reassured if they know that you have a plan of action and everyone knows what to do.

- Engage them in activities (baking cookies, fishing, planting a garden) that will help them experience success and greater confidence. Familiar activities also help them feel that things are getting back to normal.

- Try to build hope by reassuring them that the future is promising.

- Take care of yourself. It will make it easier for you to help your children get back to normal.

Some of these guidelines have been adapted from advice given by Dr. Ron Fischer in a book that was published by The Counselling Center of Butler County (Kansas) in 1991. You can order it from the counselling centre, at 217 Ira Court, Andover, Kansas, 67002. Ask for, *Tornado: Terror and Survival*, edited by Howard Inglish, Connie White and Dr. Ron Fischer.

daughter] just got up and was running down the hall screaming, "tornado!" In her mind she was so scared." And the noises in an unfamiliar temporary shelter can aggravate these fears: "At nighttime [I] could hear through the windows and it was so loud, and I just ran for my mom's bed because it was hailing so loud I was crying. ... I hate them. I can't sleep during storms anymore at night."

For children who have suffered losses during a tornado, these fears are compounded by grief, disruptions of their normal routines, and possibly relocation (losing contact with their friends), deaths or injuries. Their parents are also struggling with these losses and disruptions, and it may be difficult for them to provide the calm reassurance their children need.

Tornado are very dangers no one should go near them. because they can hurt you bad. route windows and wood

Charlie Bryan

The very young (up to 6)

When young children are overwhelmed by events or emotions that they cannot understand, they are likely to show their needs and feelings non-verbally. They may cling to their parents, become whiny and go back to habits they had outgrown (bedwetting, thumbsucking, security blankets, fear of strangers). Their fears our likely to be generalized to anxiety at being separated from their family, and if their parents go away they may think, even expect, that they will never see them again.

Bedtimes can be particularly difficult. They struggle against sleep, which plunges them into the unknown, where they may be assailed by nightmares. (These nightmares may serve a positive purpose, however. They bring anxieties and conflicts out into the open so that parents can talk about them and help their children work them through.)

What these children are expressing is a craving for love and reassurance. They need to regain confidence that the world is a safe place for them. It is best not to fuss, punish or nag them about their emotional neediness. Teasing or ridiculing them will make matters worse. Rather than reacting against inappropriate behaviours, parents can help their children by acknowledging and encouraging appropriate behaviour with praise.

Give them what they need

If parents give their children what they need– the extra time (especially at bedtime) that can help them feel special and loved– they will regain their confidence much more quickly. Children who are allowed to accompany their parents as they go about the many tasks of cleanup and recovery will be reassured by their inclusion.

Young children need help in expressing and venting their feelings. They may play it out in games that allow them to re-enact the traumatic experience. Parents and teachers can encourage this play, allowing them to express their feelings– even if it means throwing a toy across the room– with no intervention except to listen when kids want to talk out their feelings. Vigorous play and exercise can help children work off the tension, and may make it easier for them to sleep at night.

Creative activities such as drawing and writing stories also bring out feelings and tensions that children need to express. Art can prevent the denial, alienation or repression that sometimes occurs when children are overwhelmed by feelings that they cannot understand or express.

Very young children (under three) may not be affected at all, except by their parents' reactions. While hiding in the basement, one mother noticed that although her older children reacted with fear to the tornado, her two-year-old daughter "just looked from one person to the next with big eyes, and she was probably smiling. The whole time through she probably figured it was funny."

What you do affects them

It is important, especially at the time of the tornado, for parents to be aware of how their actions and reactions affect their children. As one mother said,"I found that it helped– that if I'm calm and I'm not panicking or running around, then she is sort of taking that as an example of what to do."

Kids who were forced down to the basement while their parents took photos or videos of the tornado, expressed the terror they felt. One boy said,"I was scared because I thought [my dad] was going to die. He was taking a video! He was right by the window!" When we asked his younger brother how he felt, his answer was, "Lonely."

A father who stayed upstairs to video said of his children, "They were scared. Yeah, I guess we had them pretty scared when we started to move. We were screaming at that point. They were scared because I had them huddled down in the basement underneath the front step– in the cold storage. And they were blocked in there. I blockaded it with plywood."

A mother who stayed inside with the children commented, "My youngest son was absolutely terrified. He saw *The Wizard of Oz* years ago and the tornado in that. He hated the movie. ... And of course, I think when he saw the tornado he was just going back to that movie– to the house being picked up, thrown in the air. He started to scream. He was just shaking and screaming and the tears were pouring down his cheeks and he kept saying: 'Mommy phone 911, phone 911. We're going to die.' [My husband's] out there snapping pictures and I'm holding [my son] as tight as I can."

Children have very active imaginations, and if they are left alone with their fears they may be overtaken by them. One mother told us, "We have a four year old daughter and she was quite upset because she didn't know why we were acting the way we were. She didn't understand what the tornado was. She thought it was some kind of animal."

Old enough to understand (6-12)

Older children are likely to have a better understanding of what a tornado is and, as a result, their fears are more specific. Some even come to see it as an adventure after awhile. The mother of one eight-year-old girl told us, "It doesn't bother her [the way it does her younger brother]. I think now she's at a point where it was actually kind of exciting– like this is something that happens once in a lifetime and you actually had the privilege of experiencing it."

But others become terrified by the weather. They may "go crazy" whenever there is a storm and insist on going down to the basement. Even children who were not directly affected may need to work or talk through their fears. One mother said, "My [eight-year-old boy] is in grade three and he talks a lot about [the tornado]. He helped a lot

Frank Maletta

with the cleanup. He's very concerned when the weather starts to turn, or if it gets dark cloud or anything– he's just right on the window. Some of the younger kids are more talkative than the older kids."

Talking helps, as does respecting a child's fears. One mother told us,"Well, we just did a lot of talking. I'm not sure whether there's any real way to assure them or not. I'd tell them, 'If you feel that there might be another tornado, get to the basement and stay there.'"

Look for the signs of trouble

Six to twelve-year-olds may act out by being irritable, disobedient or depressed; or they may have physical symptoms such as headaches, nausea, vision or hearing problems. They need the same patience and understanding that younger children do, but they may not be able to ask for it. They are old enough to be sensitive to their parents' problems after the disaster, and may be afraid to burden them further. For this reason, it is particularly important that they get back to school as soon as possible, because there they have access to friends and teachers who can help them work through their feelings.

But they may be afraid to go back to school, or they may have problems concentrating or disrupt the class with their behaviour. This could be due to their fear of leaving their parents (separation anxiety), but they may also be worried that they will not be able to keep up their normal level of performance. However, renewing their connections with friends at school can help them get back to normal. As one mother said, "When my daughter went back to school, she said she didn't know what to do the first day. But then her class gave her a bunch of stuff and that helped her get back into normal living."

Don't play it down

Most of all, it is important to acknowledge the trauma these children have experienced. As one mother said, "I know what didn't work– and that was trying to make light of it. Their father really tried to make light of it and tell them 'Oh, everything's fine, don't worry about it.' And everything's not fine. The main thing I tried to get across to them that might have been a good thing was that when they were [at their destroyed home] the next day, the last couple of animals were found. Because we had to leave Saturday night and there were still two cats missing. ... And then we found the last one, the little house kitten they got at

It's ok, Toto... just a little wind and rain.

Christmas– so that made them feel better. The only thing I told them was– all those things can be replaced, but at least I was still there and they were still there, and we had done it before– made a house and gotten everything fixed up for us– and we would do it again."

Her children were not at home when the tornado struck, so they needed help in making the disaster real for them. "I had made sure that they came on Sunday, because I wanted them to see it, first of all. And because their bedrooms had been so demolished, like walls and everything, I wanted them to go up there– I mean, what looks like junk to me and you in a kids bedroom means the world to them. ... So it was a good thing that they came to go through [the rubble and debris] because they found special little things that meant a lot to them. Because it was dangerous to move around, an adult went into the rooms and the kids stood

Bethany Power

at the top of the stairs and directed their search. That made them happy."

Pets and special objects are very important to children whose homes have been destroyed, and restoring these small comforts can help them along the road to recovery. Writing about their experience and losses also helps. This mother told us, "I had my daughter [writing out her thoughts], because she was really really upset about losing everything and her pony being injured. She sat down and wrote stories– [once] she had her computer back– about the tornado and [her pony] and how she felt when she first saw the house ... about her feelings and emotions and how it felt and what she was thinking at the time and whether it was sadness or happiness."

Carrying their weight (12-18)

Once children get into their teens different issues arise. Disaster may threaten their growing independence because they are forced to pull together to help the family, and they may be isolated from friends by relocation. Teenagers have a strong need to appear competent and may not be able to express their pain or fears to anyone in the family. They may also be forced into an adult role, shouldering responsibilities too great for their age. If there have been deaths or injuries amongst their family or friends they may need counselling.

Parents and teachers may have to be alert to signs that teenagers are suffering and need help. Signs to watch for are withdrawal and isolation; physical complaints such as headaches, stomach pain or loss of appetite; depression, sadness, tension or suicidal thoughts; antisocial behaviour such as stealing, aggression or acting out; school avoidance or disruptive behaviour; and sleep disturbances (sleeplessness, nightmares, or withdrawal into sleep). These problems are usually temporary. They will disappear in a short time.

Being confronted by something they cannot control at an age when asserting control over their own lives is of paramount importance, teenagers are sometimes enraged by their losses. One mother told us, "Because it was [my fifteen-year-old son's] room that [the tornado] entered into, and his room was damaged– he's very angry. Really angry. Ooh! He wouldn't move back into the house."

"We fought back!"

Teenage victims of a tornado can work through their trauma with involvements and activites that help them reassert their control and independence and maintain their ties with friends. They look mainly to their friends for support. After the 1985 tornado outbreak in Ontario, peer support was a key element of the Barrie community's response to young people's needs. A self-help group of young teenagers was formed, calling themselves "The Tornado Community Volunteers," and operating under the motto, "We fought back!" They met three times a week for nine months, and through a variety of activities moved from powerlessness to control.

They had regular social events (to reinforce the bonds of friendship), participated in creative activities such as drama and art (they held a creative art contest to promote the expression of feelings about the tornado amongst other community youngsters); and served as a core of volunteers (helping the elderly and other victims and conducting a tree planting campaign).

The tornado that wreaked havoc on our county

It happened in a matter of seconds! That is the way I would describe the tornado on Saturday, April 20th, 1996. A thunderstorm was passing through and my sister Kelsey and I were playing in our basement, when I noticed our horses were racing up and down their fields. I thought nothing of it and was just turning around to talk to Kelsey, when my older sister Erin screamed "Look at all the stuff flying in the air!" I looked out and saw our roof shingles and other things blowing in the air. I think it was probably instinct because I wasn't even thinking of a tornado but whatever it was I ran for shelter behind a big counter and covered my head. However, as I ducked down I saw Kelsey standing in front of the window. A few seconds later I got up, I went to the sliding glass window. Kelsey, who had been in front of the window when the tornado struck, had a big bump on her forehead, which came from when the window shattered, but that was all. Erin was beside me when I looked out, we saw the roof blown off our barn and immediately ran outside, for our one horse, Kahlah, had been in the barn. When we got up there I looked around. Everything was total destruction! Just about all the windows in the house had been broken, our garage was wrecked, one of our horse's fields was totalled, the horse's shelter was gone, the barn roof was gone and a wall was down. Absolute destruction in a matter of seconds! Our horse Kahlah was all right, along with the other four. Our dog was fine but our cat was missing. We found him later, though. Through this ordeal people have constantly asked me what it was like and if I was afraid. All I can say is that I didn't have time to be scared, it all happened so fast! The tornado was just really, really noisy! You couldn't even hear the windows all breaking. I never knew this tornado was coming. If I did I might have acted differently, but I didn't. I just hope I will never have to go through another tornado again.

Kristen Butler

Young people who witness other people's losses may feel guilty and upset. One father told us, "My son suffered because he saw damage across the road, and he just couldn't justify why it missed us and got them. He just couldn't handle that– he really suffered with that. So he finally went across the road and started to help everybody and I think that made a difference to him."

Guys and girls react differently

In the teen years there is often a sharp differentiation between how boys and girls who have not been directly affected react to a tornado. One highschool teacher told us, "Something that I found talking to the kids at the highschool ... these young women said they were absolutely terrified of the tornadoes ... it was like a nightmare, and they hope that it never comes back again. The boys were, 'Ooh, that's totally awesome, that's fabulous.'"

One man told us about his own fascination with the chaos following the 1985 tornado outbreak: "We were so amazed by it that we spent the next few days cruising around. It was, like, the thing to do. As a 16 year old kid, you were with your buddies and you'd have a couple of beers and then you'd be driving out to check this out. It was almost like a party type of atmosphere, in a way. You know, for an adolescent it seemed like a really interesting thing to do rather than sitting at home in the basement listening to Black Sabbath records." When we asked about whether girls reacted differently he said, "Teenage girls normally [are] a little more responsible about that kind of thing. They semed to be a little more sympathetic to the people who were affected. Whereas, we were sympathetic and everything– it's just, you were out more to see the chaos that was going on."

The first glimpse I took of her my eyes filled with happy tears in relief that she came out with no serious injuries. It has been a little over a month now since my only pony, Magic, was swept up inside the horrible tornado that ripped through the area destroying our entire property.

Magic was found just minutes after the tornado running down the highway with live wires sparking in the dark just below her feet. Luckily, with the help of our great neighbours we were able to catch Magic before she sustained deadly injuries. Just after we caught Magic the vet came running and gave her a shot of steroids to relax her since she was obviously in shock. The vet also cut a large piece of hanging skin from her leg. Magic had a deep wound on her front pastern, and five puncture wounds on her gaskin .... Magic got two shots a day for almost three weeks to prevent infection and kill pain. Every day I scrub Magic's legs with an antibacterial soap and then wrap her leg with layers of bandaging. It takes hard work and lots of patience, but when I think of how much I love Magic, I'm willing to do anything!

Mandy Swallow

The Tornado by charlie

There was a Tornado. I was scared. Mommy said I'm not kidding. Go to the basement now! Stephi and I went down and stayed til mommy came back with Daddy. Then we went to help our neighbors

Charlie Janke

A TEENAGER'S STORY

Melissa Dobson (then Roberts, but now married and a teacher) was sixteen when she wrote this true story about her experience with the 1985 Grand Valley tornado. When we spoke to her in 1996, we asked her how long it had taken to recover emotionally. Her answer was "about eight years."

It is often difficult for teenagers to let their families know that they are suffering. They don't want to burden their parents, who are suffering from the same trauma; and they are at a stage in life when it is of paramount importance to be seen as independent and capable. Writing and journal-keeping can provide a much needed outlet.

We hope that this excerpt from her story will give a flavour of what it was like to be there. We pick up her story as she and her mother scramble back home after abandoning the car (from which they had watched the tornado pass) a block away.

"The rain ceased suddenly and the sun began to shine as though it was just another fine spring day. People began to emerge from their homes to survey the damage. Although the damage around us was extensive, nothing could have prepared us for the scene that greeted our eyes as we rounded the corner onto our street! I looked towards our turn-of-the-century, two-storey house, but it wasn't there! In its place was a fifteen foot pile of garbage.

At first it didn't register; I was too stunned by the enormity of it all. Suddenly I realized what had happened and all I could think about was my little sister trapped somewhere beneath the wreckage.

I ran with speed I never thought possible towards the remains of our house. Behind me I could hear my mother crying. I couldn't remember ever having heard her cry before.

I climbed onto the pile of rubble that ten minutes before had been our comfortable old home.

"Jacquie! I screamed, horrified. "Oh my God, my sister!" I shouted hysterically. My body shook and sweat poured from me.

"Jacquie!"

My mom caught up to me and took my arm.

"It's no use, Melissa," she said quietly. "Jacquie's gone."

"No!" I cried. "Jacquie! ... JACQUIE!!!"

"Get her the hell out of here," my mom cried.

Paul, a neighbour from across the street, obeyed my mother and helped me down from the

The Tornado

I'll never forget the time when the 1996 tornado came through it was on April 20th, 1996.

I was so frightened because it was around 5:10 pm on Saturday and Jesse and I were watching Forest Gump. And our parents were in the kitchen reading the newspaper and talking about the weather outside.

Then my dad said well it looks like there might be a tornado so he went outside and you could hear him swearing then he said Oh my God there is a tornado. So we all ran to the livingroom and since we just live in a mobile home then we just laid on the floor with the couch on us.

Then the tornado went by and two more came by, and then we all ran over to my Grandpa's house because it is safer.

When my dad saw the first tornado it just came by and it just rounded us and it also hit stuff all around us. That night we all praied.

Courtney Belford

mess. I crossed the road with Paul and went into his home. Compared to ours, his house looked untouched by the storm.

I watched through the window as neighbours gathered to help my mom with her search. They lifted boards, bricks and rubble, searching for my little sister. My mother had faced reality and now took on the task of recovering the body of her youngest daughter. It was then that my first teardrops came. I wept for Jacquie. I loved her so much.

"No," I caried to myself. "NO!"

Just then, my older sister, Dawn, came running to me. She knew what had happened and tried to comfort me.

"It's okay," she said."It's okay."

"NO!" I screamed back at her. "Leave me alone!"

I didn't want her to touch me and when she tried to embrace me I hit her.

"I want Jacquie!!"

"Jacquie will be all right," she said gently. " She's a fighter, and you know it." It was true. My sister was a fighter. That last year she had been hospitalized several times with serious medical problems. She had recovered from all those illnesses, but I knew deep in my heart that this time she wouldn't recover.

Seeing just how upset I was, Dawn went to get me a drink of water. Despite how awful I'd been to her, she didn't give up trying to help me.

Paul guarded the only door to the room so that I couldn't get out, but seeing my chance, I climbed out of a smashed window and into the now warm and sunny fresh air.

I couldn't control my weeping. I cried so hard that I would soon be sick. I lay down in the wet gravel of the driveway and sobbed. I loved my sister dearly and couldn't cope with the thought of her death.

A neighbour lady came and grabbed my arm roughly, causing me pain. "Can't you see what you are doing to your mother?" she scolded.

I glanced across the road to where my mother was still searching. More people had gathered to help her.

"Now you just calm down and be quiet!"

I hated that lady with passion so intense that I felt like hitting her.

Suddenly, Dawn ran over and grabbed my arm.

"Here she comes, Miss!! Jacquie's coming up the road!"

My heart leapt. Could she really be alive?

Together, Dawn and I ran through the remains of Amaranth Street and I saw my sister. Jacquie's head was bleeding and her eyes were swollen and red. She, too, had been crying. Just when my tears should have stopped, I began to weep all over again.

I ran to her and hugged her tightly.

"I'm so glad you're okay!" I squealed.

"I thought you were dead!" cried Jacquie, "I couldn't find you."

"We're fine," I told Jacquie, trying to reassure her. "We thought YOU were dead."

Mom came down the street from where she had been digging and hugged all of us.

"It's all right girls," she said. " It's all over now and we're all okay."

Jacquie's back had been injured when the house collapsed and needed medical attention. While we waited with her at the cenotaph, where the injured had been assembled for transportation to the hospital, I reflected on the day's events. Today had been the worst, and yet the best day of my life, and somehow life seemed more precious and more delicate to me than it ever had before.

BUILDING CONFIDENCE- A PRINCIPAL'S STORY

Ken Topping was one up on most school administrators when a tornado swept through just south of Shelburne on April 20th, 1996. He had learned from being on the job in Grand Valley after the tornado that devastated that community in 1985.

The Grand Valley school had carried out an extensive program for the school and the community. They identified children who were experiencing different levels of difficulty–damage to property, injuries, family members injured or killed (on a scale of least to worst affected)– and followed their ups and downs systematically over the next year. Every month the school administration asked teachers to comment on how well the children were coping, and this information was used to develop responses, either through school programs or individually.

But as helpful as this was, Ken Topping commented that it wasn't enough in itself. "In order to make kids feel comfortable, we found that we had to do something else, and that was to show that [we had] plans to deal with the potential of a tornado– for the students and the community, but also for the staff."

Most schools now have emergency plans that include tornadoes (in Ontario they are required to do so), but administrators should attempt to provide more than a bare bones emergency plan: they must inspire confidence in students, staff and the community that everyone's needs will be understood and attended to. For example, at the time of the 1996 tornado there were two teachers at Mr. Topping's school who had been teenagers in Grand Valley during the 1985 tornado, and others on staff were also affected: "So they [wanted]– as adults, even– to know that we are prepared for this type of event if it happens." Melissa Dobson was one teacher who had suffered through the Grand Valley tornado as a 16 year-old, and she stressed how important it was to her (as a teacher) to feel confident that her principal knew how to respond to severe weather. Soon after the April 20th, 1996 tornado, (on May 1st) her class was on edge because of an approaching storm. But she was able to calm their fears (and hers) by saying, "We'll just remain calm. Don't worry, Mr. Topping's looking out for our interests and he'll let us know if we need to move anywhere– and we don't, so feel good about that. There's no problem right now."

Frank Maletta

That May 1st storm damaged a couple of buildings and was thought by some to be a tornado (on analysis, the damage was more likely caused by downbursts on a gust front). It caused quite a stir, following so soon after the April 20th tornadoes. As Mr. Topping said, "When that little tornado [the May 1st storm] went through it was a very strange day around here. A number of the kids were really excited. You couldn't keep some of them away from the windows! As the storm went through they were both frightened and enticed by it, and the teachers couldn't keep them on their work, couldn't keep them from the windows– and then they are worried, 'What's this?– another tornado coming?'"

It was still early in the severe weather season, and this experience underlined the need for all the staff to think through how they would handle the fears they and their classes were harbouring. Mr. Topping said, "The people who I felt were the most successful in this situation were the teachers of the younger kids. They would use that time to read stories out loud to the kids to distract them. With the older kids– grades seven and eight– it was really hard just to keep a lid on things. They got really excited and agitated by it.

Charlie Bryan

"We assessed the situation after that storm and said to the teachers, 'Look, you know that the kids are more excited now because of these situations. You've got to have a plan, knowing that,' and I've asked [all the teachers] to think about it in terms of their classrooms and their comfort level. For instance, 'If you are in a class and you are worried about storms, and the kids are all wanting to go to the windows and watch a storm– like, it's a kinda fun thing to do! If you are really uncomfortable with that, then close the windows, close the blinds. Take a different activity that will calm the kids down at that time, by design. It has to be sort of a match of what the collective of the class feels and what you as a teacher feel will be comfortable.'

"In most schools– and in my school particularly– we have tornado drills like we have fire drills. Not as frequently. We have what we consider the safest places in the building identified, and the children will move from their classrooms to those safe places– primarily the inner halls of the school. And we have a few rooms in the school without doors and windows. ... We have kids face the walls and even turn off the lights to simulate power failure. We simulate using an old handbell as a warning, since the PA [public address system] may be out. We also have an emergency team identified for the school– five or six people that I can count on to help me.

"For ten or eleven years [between the 1985 and 1996 tornadoes] it was sort of, 'Ho, hum, here's another tornado drill.' We had to do our best to keep them serious about it ... 'til this year. But, now it's really hot! What really shocks me about it is ... some schools are doing thunderstorm drills. If there's a severe weather warning they'll bring the kids into the school, out of the portables. In an area where a devastating tornado has happened, it may be appropriate for schools to be overly cautious, just to set the community's mind at ease ... but I've tried not to do that. We're here to do school, and thunderstorms are a fact of life. It is an unnecessary reaction to normal weather situations."

One of the reasons that Ken Topping's staff and students have confidence in him is that he is willing to listen to their concerns and take them into account. For example, he told us, "The main thing that changed after [the tornado scare was that] the staff said, 'We don't think that the procedures we have in place right now are the right ones.' They thought we shouldn't have kids on the second floor, even if they were in the centre hall, so everyone goes downstairs now. It's more crowded, but the teachers are more comfortable." He is having an assessment done to make sure they are going to the safest places, but, whatever the engineers advise, he is prepared to set up procedures that accommodate the feelings of the staff and children. They deserve that respect.

Very few schools are actually hit by tornadoes, but many are struck by the fears that severe storms may set off in both staff and students. Ken Topping's recipe– of equal parts weather awareness, emergency preparedness, sensitivity and respect– builds confidence and security for the entire school community.

A TEACHER'S STORY

Teachers have a broader view of how children respond to tornado events than most of us, and they know that tornadoes can traumatize even those children who are not directly affected. As one put it, "My feeling after that April 20th tornado was, even if the children weren't involved, they heard enough about it. For some children it was kind of a funny windstorm and for others it was a frightening experience. This one little girl just became very, very quiet– very tight. You can tell their bodies are tightening. Kids are more likely to react when an adult makes a decision that is out of the ordinary, like ending recess early to come into the building."

When another storm went through after the April 20th tornado event, Melissa Dobson– a teacher who had been a tornado victim herself in 1985– commented that "a couple of kids were less able to look out the window– it caused some panic with other kids. This one child in particular was very agitated and I could tell he was really not doing well with the whole thing. I insisted that he come away from the window. I tried to reason with him [that they would be alerted if there was any danger] ... and that yes, it is scary. 'I know some of you are scared, and that's okay to feel scared, but we're going to continue with what we are doing right now, with this lesson.' We did that to the best of our ability.

"I had one child (who I don't think was directly involved with the tornado) and she was under her desk, and she was hanging on to her chair. I got an educational assistant to take her as well as the boy and had them removed from the classroom, because their reaction was upsetting me that much more. [They] were taken to a quiet place where the other kids wouldn't be affected or tease them."

Once a tornado has struck in a community, children tend to be agitated by every passing storm for awhile. One teacher commented that "recesses are very interesting, because if you have someone going around saying the sky looks like it did on the tornado day that can cause havoc. Other things trigger fear– thunderstorms and any discolouring of the sky." Another teacher said, "After the April 20th tornado, a couple of kids had actually seen it and they were fixated on it for weeks. Their pictures were all tornadoes. I remember the one child– we were doing the three pigs and I said 'I see only two' and she had drawn this thing and it was a tornado and the other pig was in the tornado."

A child's swing set lies mangled beside the house.

When one or several of the children in a class have suffered losses in a tornado, all of the children are likely to share in the trauma. It takes patience, sensitivity and wisdom for a teacher to guide the class through the days ahead. A teacher in Shelburne had all these qualities.

Lynn Topping knew that she would have a challenge on her hands when she heard that one particularly sensitive boy had been in his home when it was destroyed by the April 20th tornado. He did not return to school until awhile after the tornado, so she took that time to contact his mother and find out exactly what had happened. She then set about preparing her class for his return. "I just couldn't imagine what it was going to do to him because he's a real family-oriented little fellow, and I knew he would be real upset."

Bethany Power

First, she gave every child in her class a chance to talk about the tornado, "because they needed to tell [their stories]. If not, they were going to goof [off] for a week anyway."

She discovered that somebody in another classroom had taken pictures of the damage at his home, and asked if she could show them to the class. "I didn't think the boys and girls had any idea. I figured in their heads it was like the *Wizard of Oz*– it spun up and it was gone. [These were] actual photos of the storm, and his home. Their little faces just dropped."

"And we talked about: 'How would you feel if [this] was your bedroom?'; 'Well, where are all his toys?'; 'What about his clothes?'; and I could see them really starting to think. And they wrote letters to him, telling him that they really missed him, and that they hoped that he was okay and that he would be back to see them soon. They didn't mention anything about the house (we talked about that) and the loss of his toys or clothes. We went on the positive side as much as we could– and talked a lot about that."

When he did come back to school his classmates were prepared. He didn't recount the details of his experience, but he thanked them and said he was glad to be back.

But recovery is a long haul. "We had so much windy weather after that, and very grey weather. Even if the wind started to blow, he was beside himself. And of course the mobile home [where his parents had to live after house was destroyed] moved in the wind. He used to say to me, 'Is it going to be a tornado day?' [I answered] 'No,' and we went through the drill with him."

But when a particularly dark and windy storm came through, the young boy responded with terror. When he came in from recess he was shaking. Lynn Topping talked him down by using reason and letting him talk through it. She asked, "If this [were a tornado] did you do the right thing?'" And he answered, "Yes, I came in the building." So she went on, "Did you go looking for help?" He replied, "Yes," and so on. It gave him the chance to confirm that he knew what to do, and this built his confidence.

Lynn Topping said: "The class discussed whether these were the right steps and could anything different have been done, to help [him] feel he was reacting properly. He wanted to go under the desk. I said if that made him feel secure, then fine." By handling his fears with calm and sensitivity, she affirmed his decisions and gave the class a chance to support him. They all learned from the experience.

Getting professional help

In most cases, changes in behaviour and emotional or physical problems are relatively short-lived. Kids of all ages move back toward life as usual with the help of their families and friends. If, however, symptoms of emotional difficulties persist or endanger the stability of a child's life at home or at school, parents should not hesitate to seek counselling for them. The child has gone through an extremely traumatic event, and it may have stirred up deep-seated fears and insecurities that need to be worked through. Children who have had previous traumas or losses may be in particular need of help, because any new trauma can rekindle past emotions. Remember, for adults and children alike, the emotional stresses that tornado victims experience are normal responses to an abnormal situation.

Knowledge is power

Tornadoes bring home humankind's essential powerlessness before the forces of nature. The best way to reassert our power and control is to learn more about how the weather works and what we can do to ensure our safety. Weather awareness helps tornado victims and witnesses regain control of their lives. If we can't beat it, we can find out as much as we can about how to relate to it.

When children see that their parents are taking control– developing their weather smarts and working out a tornado safety plan for the family– they can start feeling more secure again. As one young girl told her parents, "I think it's a good thing that you guys are really aware of the weather."

One parent told us, "I think if you prepare yourself a little bit for it, then you're not as frightened. We need to be educated about it and have a plan ready, just like for a fire." Some parents even thought that information was more important than counselling support. "I don't know even if having a psychologist come in [to school] would do a whole lot of good. It would be better with a tornado expert, who can describe to children exactly what it is."

Children are keenly interested in finding out about severe weather after a tornado strikes nearby, and the event provides a rich opportunity for parents and children to learn the joys of weather watching. As one father said, "The kids are still terrified of thunderstorms– any dark clouds. I've never seen kids pay so much attention to weather!" A teenager told us, "Now my dad says that I'm a bit paranoid every time there's a storm. Like, I go outside and look at the clouds. ... Usually when we start getting thunder, automatically its a reaction for me to go outside and just sit out there and look at the clouds."

Fear can be transformed into wonder and respect for the glorious power of nature. As one father told us, "All [my boys] need is someone to be there and say, 'It's not really that bad,' and explain it to them, saying, "This isn't tornadoes. It's not what you are seeing. It's just a thunderstorm. ... And I want them to grow up and have respect for [weather] and see the beauty of it– because, you know, storms are beautiful. To watch nature is amazing. Nothing is better than nature."

8
It can't happen here

Most of us have never seen a tornado first-hand or been affected by its destructive power. We think of the possibility as a long shot risk, a very unlikely event that's more of a curiosity than a concern. Tornado victims have another view. They once shared these sentiments, but now wonder why they were the unlucky ones, why their lives were disrupted by this freak of nature. Many feel "chosen" by the tornado they have experienced, as if it had plotted a deliberate path through their place instead of through the next block or another community. For them, the long shot came in and they became the unlikely victims that the rest of us only hear about on the news. We all think it will happen to somebody else– and most of the time it does. But when it happens to us, the tornado risk takes on a personal dimension and we can never again see it as the stuff of fantasies and folklore. The risks in general may be very low, but they have already been fulfilled, and we are now ever-wary and watchful for the next tornado.

Audiences watching Twister *at a drive-in in Ontario were surprised to be treated to the real thing.*

What are your chances?

Where, when and why tornadoes happen

Tornadoes occur throughout the mid-latitudes in many different countries around the world. Their frequency per land area is roughly equal in the affected parts of many countries, but by far the greatest number happen in the U.S. where about a thousand touch down each year. The U.S. also has the most intense tornadoes on the planet.

The concentration of tornadoes in the middle of North America results from the position of the Rockies and the proximity of the Gulf of Mexico. The mountains accentuate the favourable weather patterns which lead to instability, while the Gulf provides the fuel. Warm, humid air is drawn up into the Plains and is overrun by drier and colder air aloft. The mountains prevent this favourable air mass from being easily swept aside, allowing time for ideal conditions to build up. The result is the repeated formation of intense weather systems and explosive storms, especially in spring.

Severe storms capable of tornadoes depend on strong winds aloft. In theory, they can occur anywhere, as long as sufficient heat and moisture are available. Mountainous areas are less affected because storms are forced into existence "prematurely" by the land elevation and sap the atmosphere of these ingredients too early. Places along the coasts are less favoured too because of the cooling influence of the water. The cool Great Lakes also decrease tornado activity, but not enough to offset stronger weather systems which track through them from the southwest. Farther north, in Canada, even though the jet stream is energetic in summer, lower temperatures and moisture levels lessen the likelihood of tornadoes.

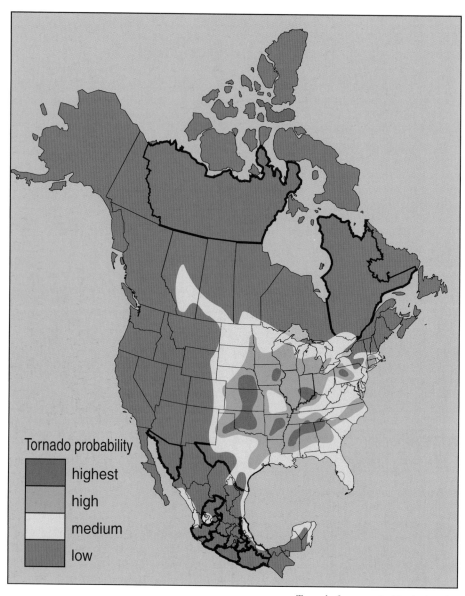

Tornado frequency in North America

The stronger tornadoes accompany large-scale weather systems which, in turn are carried along by the jet stream. The position of the jet stream shifts from the southern U.S. in winter to central Canada insummer, and there is acorresponding northward shift in peak tornado activity. States near the Gulf, for instance, have their maximum in March-April, the Midwest in May-June, and the northern states and Canada in July. Things are much quieter in the fall, except for a second, smaller maximum in the Southeastern States in late-fall. Along the West coast, themaximum is in winter, but results mostly from waterspouts that come onshore with cold fronts.

Most of the tornadoes reported each year are weak and occur in late-spring through summer. They depend less on organized weather systems and occur everywhere that strong convection is likely. They make up a sizable proportion of all tornado events, especially farther north and west, where clear visibility makes them easier to see. Strong tornadoes happen mainly in spring, and the most intense ones occur relatively early on. On average, they become weaker after late-March through April and begin decreasing in number after May-June.

A zone of higher tornado incidence stretches from Texas northeast through Indiana, where all the right conditions repeat most often. This "tornado alley" is a region of rich soils, a pleasant climate– and frequent storms! It peters out in the Great Lakes region, where the influence of the Gulf of Mexico wanes and unfavourable atmospheric conditions are more prevalent. A second, smaller tornado alley crosses the Southeastern States.

These two zones are only modestly apparent in the statistics and the use of the term "alley" is largely subjective– it's adopted by anyone who thinks his or her own region is tornado prone!

What's the trend?

When we talk about trends we have to talk about numbers– and that's where the problems begin. If all tornado sightings followed the same standards (how and what we see and report)– and all tornadoes were reported– we might be able to trust the numbers. But we are far from that degree of standardization. Even the definition of "tornado" varies from time to time and from place to place. Inconsistencies in the record of reported tornadoes point out this problem. Since 1980, the number of tornadoes reported has gone up significantly, but the death rate has been decreasing for many decades. Does this mean that tornadoes are getting weaker or are we just paying more attention to them? Improved weather warning systems and public awareness are clearly responsible for a big part of the change, but then, what is it that we are responding to now that we didn't years ago? Until tornado identification and reporting is stable and reasonably objective for a good long time, we can't expect to know what the true changes in occurrence, intensity, and location are. In a time of mass communications and twister-mania, the incidence of over-enthusiastic false sightings may be countering improvements in our knowledge and observations of true tornadoes. The low death rates in recent decades can't be explained by awareness and improved construction alone. It is possible that there is also a slight downward trend in strong tornadoes.

Some people have wondered whether global warming might be affecting tornado frequency. Weather patterns oscillate through high and low periods of every kind, over many time scales. Each shift in conditions alters the balance globally and changes the expected weather in a given area. The change isn't always what we would expect. If present trends in global warming continue, we will definitely see more thunderstorms. But will we see more severe ones and more tornadoes too? That is less clear, because it takes the right contrast between cold aloft and warm down below to support a severe storm. Some of the recent warming trend has come from prolonged spells of warm, dry weather under a stable atmosphere– conditions that do not favour tornado development. It **is** possible that the timing and location of tornadoes will shift as the climate changes. They may come earlier, farther north, and more in groups in the future. Stronger tornadoes may become more frequent in the spring, while summertime tornado frequency decreases. A warmer climate may carry the jet stream farther north, slightly increasing tornadoes in Canada but greatly decreasing them in the U.S. Nobody knows. What we do know is that we don't have enough information to make anything more than a wild guess.

There are far greater risks

As disasters go, tornadoes are way down the list of most deadly and most damaging. Even when compared with the other hazards from severe weather, they rank well below flooding and lightning deaths. Your risk of becoming a tornado victim is extremely low, even

Do two incidents make a trend?

If a particular family or community is struck once by a tornado, that's a fluke of nature. But when it happens a second time, as it did in the Arthur area, is that a trend, a recurring pattern that we can expect with certainty? When you look at all the tornado paths plotted on a map together, most areas are untouched but a few places have intersecting paths. Where two tracks cross, there's at least one small spot that experienced two events. In some cases it may even be three. If a house was standing exactly in that spot, the family there will certainly feel that fate has chosen them. Statistically, we know it has to happen to someone once in a while– but when it does, we can't help but wonder if there's an element of destiny attached to those events.

The community of Codell, Kansas had their brush with destiny too. For three consecutive years– in 1916, 1917, and 1918– a tornado came through town on May 20th. You can bet that everyone was outside looking at the sky on May 20th, 1919 for what must have certainly seemed like a "guaranteed" return visit! Tornadoes do recur, but although some regions can expect more of them on average, the long-term distribution is fairly uniform and random within any local area.

South-central Ontario has had a recent history of memorable tornadoes (1985, 1996, and a brief one in 1988) but we still can't label it as tornado–prone on that basis. However, public perceptions will not be changed in the near future, because every tornado that skips somewhere through the broader region will be remembered and adopted as another piece of proof. We may go a generation before the next big tornado in the area, or it may happen this year. Either way, most of the numbers will balance out in the longer run.

For those affected, there's no statistical cure. They were the victims of coincidence and random selection as much as anything else. For them, one or two incidents have already made a trend. For the rest of us, we've been sensitized to expect more tornadoes too. Our perspective has been warped by fresh memories and our expectations will remain exaggerated for a while. After years of inactivity the memories will fade. Those events of the past will look like an exception again– until the next time.

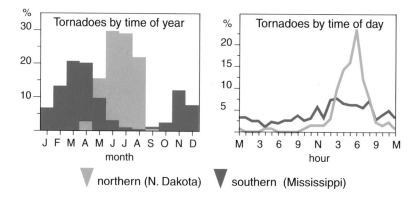

A north-south comparison of strong (F2-F5) tornadoes
Peak tornado activity progresses northward from spring to summer. The hourly distribution is quite uniform in the Gulf States region but farther north a pronounced late-afternoon peak is evident, with nearly none at night. The northern example is representative of all regions north of tornado alley, including the Prairies.

Tornado trivia

- a typical tornado— is less than 45m (150 feet) wide, lasts a few minutes and travels at 50kmh (30mph)

- the largest tornado— can be over 1.6km (1 mile) wide, lasts over an hour, and can travel at 96kmh (60mph) or more

- worst outbreak— April 3-4, 1974 – 148 tornadoes, over 3,800km (2,400 miles) of damage over much of the eastern U.S.

- longest tornado— March 18, 1925, the "Great Tri-State tornado" – travelled 350km (219 miles) across Missouri-Illinois-Indiana at 60mph – 689 killed and 1,980 injured

- in the U.S., tornadoes occur on about half the days of the year – the average (reported) is 748/year, 23 of which kill someone

- in Canada, tornadoes occur on about 20 days a year – the average (reported) is 40/year, with no fatalities in most years

- more than half of all tornadoes have wind speeds of less than 160kmh (100mph)

- largest number of tornadoes per 10,000 sq km— Canada: 2 (Southwestern Ontario) – U.S.: 20 (Oklahoma)

- largest number of F5 tornadoes by area— Canada: none – U.S.: Kansas, Iowa (about 1 every 10 years)

- F3 or greater frequency— Canada: less than 5% – U.S.: 7%

- peak locations— Canada: Southwestern Ontario, from Windsor-Sarnia; south-central Saskatchewan – U.S.: central Oklahoma; also north & northwest Texas, and central Florida

- highest ratio of strong to weak tornadoes— Tennessee and Kentucky

- highest risk to life— Mississippi (the birthplace of the term, "twister")

- king of the numbers— Texas, averaging about 125 tornadoes a year (compared with 25 in Ontario)

- peak time of day is 5-6pm local time (varies by location, generally earlier farther north)

- peak month— Canada: July – U.S.: May

- thunderstorms per year (estimates)— Canada: fewer than 5,000 – U.S.: 100,000, of which 10% are severe and 1% produce tornadoes

in the most prone areas. The risk of being involved in a traffic accident is much higher– yet we rarely give driving a thought or worry. We don't need to lose sleep over the tornado. In fact, we are more likely to be affected by damaging straight-line winds or fires from lightning.

While our chances of being directly affected by a tornado are next-to-none, there may be one or more nearby. For those who were hit, these words probably sound far too optimistic! But when you consider the total number of affected people or the total damage area and compare it with all the unaffected persons over alifetime, it's a surprising and realistic fact. Nowadays we hear about every significant tornado, see them on TV, get the full force of all the misery and destruction flashed at us as if we were there ourselves. It's easy to become too sensitive and too worried about our own vulnerability.

There's no doubt that some places will have more tornadoes than others. But most of the variability we perceive is due to two things which are both independent of the actual risk at a location. One is our recent experiences– having lived through a recent encounter in an area puts us at a disadvantage because the normally rare statistical chance has already come true for us. The other is the difference between being hit by a tornado and having seen one. A tornado can be seen by many more people than are directly affected by it. If you can see it for, say 10km (6 miles), then a 100 metre path width with a 400 metre reach only impacts directly on about 2% of the people there, assuming that the tornado is on the ground for the entire stretch. This means that while many people feel they have experienced the tornado, only a small fraction of them actually suffered first-hand.

How likely are you to experience a tornado? Probably not as likely as you think. Based on a rough risk calculation, the very highest risk of any one place being hit is about once in 2,000 years (central Oklahoma). But since nobody can predict or control exactly when and where tornadoes will happen it is best for all of us to know what to do, no matter how unlikely it seems. (They certainly did not expect a tornado in Williamsford with snow still on the ground, and the Eden family would not have bet on being struck twice.)

Although we can't use the past to judge the future, it's clear that the public's increasing awareness and responsiveness to the tornado threat has helped to bring death tolls down to only about 50-100 a year in the U.S. We are more aware, benefit from better communications, and are building sturdier houses– all of which are working in our favour. Most of the deaths today are with very strong tornadoes which, fortunately, are rare. But if and

 Exploding a myth

There was a time when experts thought that the low pressure in tornadoes made buildings explode. However, this idea was based on two mistaken assumptions:

- that buildings are still structurally sound after they have been through the area of strongest wind in a tornado (which gets to them before the core of low pressure and pummels them with vicious winds and flying debris),

- and that the buildings are so tightly sealed that the pressure differential cannot be equalized.

Have you ever seen a house, let alone a barn, that was so tightly constructed that it was inpenetrable by wind or flying debris?

A close look at video footage of a barn that "exploded" in the April 20th tornado outbreak clearly showed that the explosion was an illusion created by the speed with which the structure disintegrated from sheer windforce. Tornadic winds have been measured to be as high as 287mph (459kmh). Winds less than half that strong can destroy some buildings. The results may be explosive, but the damage is done by brute force combined with structural weakness.

when that rare threat comes your way, your safety still depends on how attentive you are to the weather and whether you take the right action when it's time.

Building to withstand the wind

The likelihood that your home will be damaged by a tornado is very small, but it is worthwhile making sure that it has been built to sustain strong winds. It doesn't take a tornado to destroy poorly designed and anchored buildings. In fact, most wind damage to conventional structures occurs at wind speeds of less than 200 km/h (125mph), and damage can occur with winds as low as 120 km/h (75mph). The many non-tornadic storms that regularly march through the countryside can wreak havoc with straight line winds;

downbursts can cause localized wind damage; and the occasional derecho storm can cut a wide swath of straight line wind damage. (The storm which caused heavy damage in Goderich, Ontario in 1995 was an example of a derecho storm.)

So, although no structure is likely to withstand the immense force of an F3 to F5 tornado unscathed, there are things we can do to minimize damage from the much more frequent F0 to F2 tornadoes, or the straight line winds of non-tornadic storms.

Appearances are deceiving

Contrary to popular belief, houses do not "explode" because of pressure differences within a tornado (see *Exploding a myth*, opposite). The picture to the right demonstrates what usually occurs. First the force of the wind lifts the roof; then the walls collapse because the roof no longer provides bracing for them. The windward wall falls inward (the wind pushes it in) and the other walls fall outward. This splayed appearance may be partly why people think that houses have exploded, but many years of engineering analysis has established that it is a combination of windforce, construction, orientation and structural geometry that determines the wind-worthiness of a building.

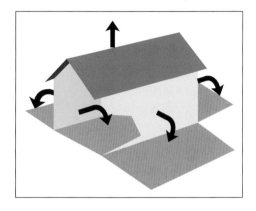

Appearances can be deceiving in another aspect of wind damage, too. When damage to a house seems to be due to twisting, it is more likely to have happened because of variations in the strength of the foundation anchoring than because of rotational

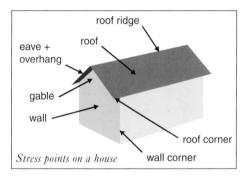

Stress points on a house

winds, even in a tornado. The scale of rotation in a tornado is larger than the scale of twisting damage in a home. The explanation for the damage pattern is that the structure pivots on its foundation around its strongest anchoring point (often the bathroom, with all its plumbing).

The greatest deception we are likely to fall prey to is the belief that our homes and buildings are solidly built and cannot be damaged easily. They look so solid– how could they fail us?

How buildings fail

A quick look at how engineers classify buildings will help pinpoint what we should be looking for in our homes and businesses. Buildings are ranked (from most to least wind-resistant) as follows:

- **Fully-engineered**– individually designed by architects and engineers. They usually withstand extreme winds very well, even when buildings around them are destroyed.

- **Pre-engineered**– planned (as a group) by engineers before construction and marketed widely as units (components are used). They may fare well with careful attention to on-site construction practices, but they fail more often than fully-engineered buildings do.

- **Marginally-engineered**– commercial buildings, light industrial buildings, schools, motels and apartments that are built with combinations of masonry, light steel framing, open web steel joists, wood framing, wood rafters and concrete. This is the largest category of loss during windstorms. Combinations of these materials **can** be engineered to withstand strong winds, but they are often carelessly assembled and provide only minimal resistance.

- **Non-engineered**– single and multiple family residences, some apartments and commercial buildings. They are usually wood frame and offer little resistance to the wind.

It is clear, then, that all buildings are not created equal. Small increases in the degree of attention given to engineering a structure can produce large dividends in improved wind resistance. But not all of us can afford to hire architects to individually design our homes, so what should we be looking for when we build or buy?

The main factors affecting wind resistance are construction, orientation, house geometry and shielding from adjacent structures.

Construction

Most buildings are damaged when a connection or anchorage detail fails (see diagrams, opposite). Structures need to be properly anchored at two main junctions: from the roof to the walls, and from the foundation to the walls. If they are not, the roof may easily be lifted by strong winds, and once it goes the entire structure may collapse like a house of cards. Wood-framed buildings that are not properly roof-anchored or have porches or large overhangs (like those over motel walkways) are often destroyed at winds of less than 200km/h (125mph). If there are not enough anchor bolts or concrete nails anchoring a building to its foundation, much of it may simply disappear in strong windstorms.

It is not enough simply to use strong materials in constructing your home. Even they can fail if poorly assembled. The structural integrity of a building– the absence of weak links– is its strength.

Although many people assume that masonry walls are strong, they may fail if the hollow block cells are not grouted and the walls are not reinforced with steel. In fact, masonry buildings are particularly susceptible to windforce, often sustaining severe damage from winds under 200km/h (125mph).

Another factor which should be borne in mind in choosing building materials is how resistant they are to missile impact– damage from flying debris. Brick and stone, even brick facing, are more resistant than many other exterior finishes.

Orientation

How your home (or parts of it) is oriented in relation to the wind direction in a storm will play a large part in how much damage it sustains. In many areas most severe storms approach from the west through southwest, so particular attention should be paid to structural features on the west side of a house. Structural features which may contribute to the failure of a building (if they face the wind) are attached garages, porches or large overhanging eaves, and gables.

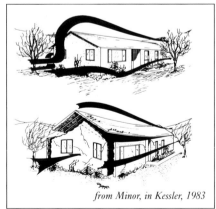

from Minor, in Kessler, 1983

House geometry

The main feature of a building's geometry which can affect its ability to withstand strong winds is the roof design. Flat and gable roofs are more susceptible than mansard and hip roofs, which have better anchorage and are shaped to handle the wind better.

Shielding by adjacent structures or trees

Trees or other buildings (in close proximity) can provide some shielding from violent winds. The houses on the windward side of housing developments usually sustain more damage.

Whether or not you are in a position to determine how storm-worthy your home is, it helps to be aware of where the weaknesses may lie. What is even more important, however, is to make sure that **you** are not the weak link that prevents you and your family from riding out a tornado in safety. Your greatest strength comes from knowledge of how to read the stormy sky and what to do if a tornado approaches. We hope that this book has provided you with the reinforcement you need to recognize and respond appropriately to dangerous storms.

What to watch for when you build

Integrity: The overall integrity of the structure (anchoring and openings in the walls (doors, windows) should not be weak relative to the strength of the walls.

Roofing: Hip and mansard roofs are best. Otherwise, roof systems that are more than 7m. (20 ft) wide should be built of roof trusses. Be careful that the trusses and roofing materials (battens, shingles) form an integral unit.

Roof anchoring: The roof should be firmly attached to the walls. This is best done by framing the walls so that they are integral with the roof (so the wall studs form part of the roof trusses). Hurricane clips are superior to toe-nailing.

Walls: Stud walls should contain missile (flying debris) resistant sheathing, such as brick veneer (which should be anchored to the walls) or metal panelling. Windows and doors should be storm quality or protected by wind (and missile) resistant screens.

Foundation anchoring: Anchor bolts should be used, with a substantial number of anchorage points. Foundations should be at least 60cm (2 feet) into the soil, and concrete block foundations should be reinforced with vertical reinforcing steel.

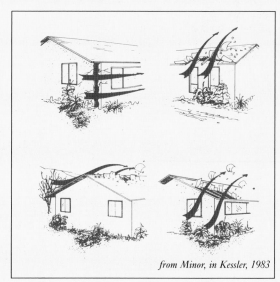

from Minor, in Kessler, 1983

Where the wind does its damage

But things have changed ...

Since the first edition of this book much has changed in the way people relate to severe storms and tornadoes. *Twister* initiated a frenzy of interest in storms and storm chasing which has been both a blessing and a curse.

Insofar as people have become more engaged with the sky and weather it has been an exciting change. We love to see more and more people open their eyes to the glory of our atmosphere. It's bound to enlarge their vision of life and make them more alert to the dangers the weather may present. But we worry that too many people are looking for a quick fix, a momentary thrill to divert them from an otherwise humdrum existence.

The sky has the potential to engage you fully, giving your thoughts and imagination room to roam, room to rediscover what you value most in life. If you reduce your interest in it to a few dramatic moments near a tornado, you are missing out on its greatest gifts. You are grasping for a one night stand (and chances are you won't even get that lucky!), whereas you could be building an enduring and enriching relationship which will challenge your imagination and capacity for wonder until the day you die.

Storm chasing should never be approached as an extreme sport. It must be motivated by curiosity and fascination with the mysteries weather presents, and carried out with responsibility and concern for the people who happen to be in the path of storms or chasers. Otherwise it descends into a reckless pursuit that may endanger lives and hamper the efforts of those chasers and researchers who are trying to make positive contributions to understanding and warning people about severe weather threats.

Serious chasers have been dismayed by the increase in "chaser convergence" over the past few years. Many of these new enthusiasts are fully and productively engaged with the weather, but some put themselves and others at risk, with little understanding of what they are doing or how close to catastrophe they are venturing.

We can only hope that they will soon be discouraged by the frustrations, hard work and single-minded dedication required of a true storm chaser. As the following story demonstrates, a successful storm chase doesn't come easy – even to chasers who have been at it for decades!

Catching the big one

After the snowiest winter in recent memory here at home, we yearned for a taste of summer. The spring of 2001 had teased us with several fast-moving weather systems that had swept severe storms across the Midwest. By late May, we were itchy to feel the warm winds and hear the thunder of a good storm chase.

With plenty of work still calling, we decided to chance a short trip– only four chase days– in hopes of seeing a few good storms and relieving some of that "itchy" anxiety. It was a big gamble. An uncertain weather pattern, a very long drive from Ontario, and high expectations (our usual unrealistic optimism) all suggested that this effort was just a crazy impulse likely to fail!

A long hard two–day drive landed us in Liberal, KS early on the 27th of May. We soon realized the town was full of chasers– some old friends, a few others we knew, and many more we didn't. It was like a big party, with everyone waiting for the guest-of-honour to appear in the sky nearby.

By mid-afternoon, storms developed rapidly and we drove out to meet what became a raging squall line. Winds up to 100mph blasted us with a wall of dust as the line passed. We tried to outrun the storm but it was no use. A few brief photos and a wild windstorm left us in awe of Nature's power and hungry for more. Not too bad for our first day out!

The next morning we took our time, enjoying a quiet breakfast, looking at data on the internet, and watching the Weather Channel. The day's target was less clear, but most of the other chasers headed south to wait for action in Texas. We left later, heading mainly west. We wanted to stay north of a large cloud deck which was refusing to clear farther south. We thought it was better to see **something** than wait for a long-shot storm in a boring overcast.

We drove into northeast New Mexico (beautiful countryside!), then spotted a storm anvil far to the northwest. A quick check revealed that Colorado was now under a tornado watch. "What!?", we thought, "Way up **there**? All the storms were supposed to be in the other direction!" But, ... it was ok because we'd have an excuse to see the mountains and that crystal-clear sky, even on this short chase.

A few hours later we arrived in Trinidad, Colorado, where a line of persistent storms drifted off the mountains to the west. Each storm looked better than the last, until one became larger and began showing supercell features. Its base lowered and became nearly circular before a gusty wind undercut the inflow and slowly choked it off. Close call, but not quite enough! There was one more, but it looked weaker.

With dusk setting in we decided to park with a view to the west and shoot lightning. We waited as the light faded and distant lightning bolts became more prominent. Meanwhile, our last storm had slipped by us and was followed by a rush of air and a brightening sky. I should have been thinking about this, but I was preoccupied with shooting into the distance. I began to wonder, though, and I glanced back to the north and saw something whitish hanging in the air. Was it a chunk of low cloud, or...?

In my usual joking manner I turned to Jerrine and said, "Hey, check out that tornado." (I do this with every pointy piece of cloud.) But the joke was on me! While we had our backs to the storm, it had tightened up and formed a ragged wall cloud and then a long ghostly funnel. It was hard to tell if it had actually touched down as a tornado, but it was obvious that we had been much too careless and presumptuous about that storm. We wheeled around and got a better view for one photo before the funnel vanished.

I was in shock, and depression gnawed at my feelings. We had done everything right, except at the very end when it counted. Never turn your back on a wall cloud! The bitter lesson of missing an opportunity so close at hand accompanied me to bed, but faded the next morning as we learned that there had been no storms elsewhere. And, besides, an even bigger storm day was taking shape.

We had decided to stay in Trinidad because the next day might be good in Colorado. After reviewing morning forecasts, a pronounced severe weather "bullseye" was staring at us from the Texas Panhandle. We left mid-morning under sunny skies. A pleasant drive brought us to Clayton, New Mexico, where we dropped in on a few other chasers at a motel in town. The lobby was filled with bustling chasers and an air of nervous anticipation. After exchanging a few excited words we all left for Texas, each of us with slightly different ideas and interpretations about where to be. The chase was now on, but where to?

I had originally thought of heading south, to stay near a dryline coming out of New Mexico. But an attempt at a data update along the route failed, so we decided to head east to Dumas instead. There, the local library could offer us one last look at conditions around the region. We normally don't worry too much about data on the road, but this day was cloudy (hard to see distant) and the stakes were high. It was one of those serendipitous decisions you later recognize as crucial to the day's outcome.

In Dumas the clouds began to bubble into taller towers here and there. We got a brief update (which didn't help much) and headed south toward Amarillo. I was carefully watching the wind direction. It had been southeast but was now south– not good. That meant that the area behind us (north) had better convergence. I was already a bit nervous because the one thing the data stop did suggest was likely severe weather in southeast Colorado. But we were now committed to our Texas target and the only thing we needed to do was find a storm. Once formed, they would quickly go severe.

As lower cumulus cleared out en route, we spotted long thin anvils shooting up from the southwest like cloud spears. Wow! The first storms had fired and were racing toward us! We rushed into Amarillo for gas and headed east to the edge of town for a better look. Those anvils were zooming overhead on 100mph winds but the bases were still small back to our west. The extreme growth rate was obvious from the thunder– constant cloud-to-cloud rumbles even in the thinnest parts. A bit of rain and the storm was past us. But another came up behind it. This one had a larger inflow base and a darker rain curtain. "They're pulling together rapidly." I thought.

We went east and north a little to get into position for the approaching storm. But after a short while we noticed it remained well to our west. It was now "backbuilding", such that new growth on its south end was so rapid that the storm's strongest updraft remained in almost the same place. We searched for a road going west to get closer, and found one. After a few miles, it turned north then ended abruptly as a red mud dirt path. Oh no, a dead end just when we needed to get closer!

We decided to stay there to watch and photograph the evolving storm. Its base lowered and widened, then a brief wall cloud appeared silhouetted against the bright sky underneath the base. Our longest zoom lens caught that on film, but just. "What if that thing puts one down now!?" I agonized. We thought of leaving– of driving back east (away from it), going back south, back through the city and up the freeway. Tempting, for short-term gain– but what if the storm then passed us? With no road options on the map, we were trapped where we were. It was down to waiting until the storm got closer, and hoping nothing important popped out before then!

Our storm approached, becoming larger, with dark sky passing to our north and continuous high thunder above. In the meantime, other storms had fired farther south. (We later found out that most chasers that day were down there.) One of these southern cells sent a shower over us, and for a short time we could no longer see cloud detail around us.

The urge to leave grew stronger, and when the sky cleared again to the southwest, we saw a magnificent boiling thunderhead down there, brightly sunlit. Should we pass on the grey mess to our north and go for the obvious power and clarity of this churning beauty? Decisions, decisions! This was really tough– one storm clearly visible but farther away versus another, less obvious but closer.

We did the usual see-sawing about whether to go that way, but we agreed to stay with what we had. It's far too easy to be suckered by "greener pastures syndrome" but we managed to resist. We also remembered one of our rules: "Don't leave what you're near unless it is definitely dead!" and laid the temptation to rest with a few photos.

We left our spot and returned to the highway, then headed north. Our original storm was on the move now and was to our north-northwest, just about to cross the road! We raced north, then stopped beside the now large, low wall cloud as it neared the road. We took a few wide-angle shots. There were now a number of other chasers parked along here.

The cloud came closer so we backed off to the south a bit. As it crossed the road, a rush of air turned the southeast wind to westerly and the sky immediately brightened. "Hmmm, this reminds me of something ..... oh, yes, last night!!" Another strong RFD (rear-flank downdraft) was plunging down the backside of the wall cloud. This "cascading RFD" not only opened up the sky but also tore away at the back edge, causing the cloud material there to descend like a waterfall. This was a good sign for possible tornado formation because now the storm had its updraft-downdraft couplet in place, ready to tighten up the flow.

The RFD swept forward, pushing the wall cloud well east of the road and quickly away. With low clouds, even a few miles steal your view! We got more photos, but were now nervous that the storm was readying for a touchdown just when it would be out of range. I felt a twinge of panic. The sudden realization that we might be watching our hopes disappear with the storm was enough to get us moving. But that fear also clouded my better judgment, and I opted to go north to the next east road. Bad idea. Within minutes, a fine rain filled the air as a developing "hook" came sweeping around the backside of the mesocyclone.

We wheeled around and headed south again. The next east road was closer than we thought. We went east to Panhandle, all the while eyeing the darkish area in the distance. In that thirty-minute period of driving, the storm put down two brief tornadoes, we found out later.

At Panhandle we joined highway 60, a long road through nowhere angling to the east-northeast. That would put us on a gradual but certain intercept course with the storm. Along the way we saw a few other chasers, but not many. There were several media vehicles though. Later we found out where the real chaser convergence was– down on the second

A large cone tornado a few miles to the north becomes slowly lighter as it reflects the bright western sky

storm to our south. There, hundreds of chasers swarmed another impressive storm but one that only managed a brief dusty tornado. Perhaps Mother Nature was a little shy with all that attention?

The sky changed quickly with every mile, and soon the large wall cloud was plainly visible to our north. As we drove, Jerrine spotted a brief funnel cloud, then another. It, too, disappeared but this was a good sign of things to come. We often see these high, thin funnels come and go before a larger tornadic funnel forms. Then, she noticed a dirt whirl on the ground to her distant left. Touchdown! We seemed to be the first chase vehicle in the vicinity to spot it. Above it was a still small funnel but only seconds later it was already widening up near the cloud base.

She was now on alert for a cutoff to get us across the divided highway for a better view. Of course the north side of the road was littered with wires along a railway line (much too ugly– we needed a pristine view!). She zipped into the left lane and put the pedal to the metal, searching for a crossover to get us past the tracks.

There was our chance! We crossed over the hump of tracks and screeched to a halt just short of a red mud road surface. Whoa! Those red mud roads are deadly when wet, turning to "snot" which gives absolutely no traction! Jerrine lept out with a camera and zoom lens, ran up to the fence line and started clicking. She yelled to me, "tornado on the ground!" as the dust whirl/funnel cloud spun down into a nice cone-shaped tornado.

My moment of truth must now be told. As thorough and organized as I am on all other aspects of chasing, when a tornado forms I'm all thumbs and generally useless to her. The intense excitement seems to occupy every brain cell I have! I'm lucky if I manage a few shots, a few glances, or a change of film when needed. Alas, my secret is out! Luckily our partnership includes someone who is the complete opposite– cool, controlled and efficient in the face of any crisis or danger.

Minutes seemed like years, and yet passed by as if time were being sucked silently from us by the ever-growing vortex. The large tornado was now due north of us and gradually changing appearance, from a greyish backlit cone to a pale white one *(see above)*.

Then, out of nowhere, some idiot (oops!) videographer wheeled in beside us and set up his tripod just as Jerrine's camera jammed (probably that dust storm in Kansas!). Well, if that

A gigantic wedge tornado emerges from wind-driven rain less than a mile to our left!

wasn't Murphy's law! She ran back to the car to get another camera from me, but in the heat of that moment I handed her the 1600 ASA film one because I wasn't sure if our slower films could take in the dark sky. (Too bad! 1600 ASA film is bound to be grainy– but it's better than nothing. **I knew** I should have loaded the spare camera!!)) On the way back out, Jerrine excused herself to the crouched guy beside our car, but thought, "Sorry,... but hell, **I was** there first!"

Moments later, he whisked up his tripod and drove off. Jerrine took a few more shots as the tornado developed a beautiful black skirt of debris at its base. The tornado glided across the green landscape. There was some wind, but no other sound. It was too quiet, too strange to see a thing of beauty and destruction move so gracefully– so **effortlessly**– before our eyes! It was now quite clearly visible, and impressive!

Meanwhile, I managed to locate our fastest lens (a 50mm, which makes the tornado look unreasonably small) and took a few test photos. They were fine, but we were beginning to run out of time. Another "hook" of fine rain was sweeping in from the back of the storm and quickly obscuring our ghostly marauder. It was time to move forward, hoping to retrieve a clear view.

We were very excited and tense as we gunned it east on the highway. I knew our chances of another view were slim: once wrapped in rain, tornadoes rarely reappear. Within a minute we began passing various chasers parked along the road. We kept going, looking for an open stretch and a glimpse of our shrouded marvel. The only thing on Jerrine's mind was, "I've got to get past the rain so I can see that tornado!" I was trying to assess our position and the risks we might face.

In the desire to get another view, we didn't pay too much attention to the fact that all the other chase vehicles (mainly news crews) were dropping by the wayside. Obsessed by getting a view, we were not thinking that we were on a collision course with the tornado. With low cloud bases it's easy to overestimate distance, so I thought we had room to spare as we drove.

Suddenly ... it was as if the curtain had lifted on an epic drama. There it was– right, I mean **right beside us**– a humungous wall of tornado! *(See above.)* We screeched to a halt, and Jerrine reached for the camera (100 ASA this time). I was not sure what she saw, but it didn't matter. My attention was transfixed by the very strong, increasing wind outside! The rain had eased, and Jerrine's excited remarks did not temper my fears. Outside, the wind howled, but inside the car it was very quiet. I said, "I think we're too close" in a **very** quiet voice. My abnormal tone shifted her attention onto me and away, briefly, from the massive tornado to her left. She thought, "I've never known you to speak so quietly and plainly during a tornado– its usually more like 'Holy shit!!!' " We were definitely too close. I thought, "How did I get myself into this mess?"

Jerrine sensed my extreme apprehension and started to back up. There was no one in sight behind us, but we couldn't see far that way because the wind was wrapping rain in at 80-90mph at our backside. We didn't get more than 20-30 ft back before she realized the tornado would pass in front of us. (But when we initially stopped she thought we might end up in the middle of it.)

She stopped, but at an angle to the road so she could shoot out her window. It would have been impossible to get out of the car– the winds were too strong to stand up against them. We had stumbled into the inner edge of the hook echo region (which is the outer edge of the tornadic circulation) and were experiencing the intense stream of air which led straight into that vortex now less than a mile from us!

My worries eased as she began shooting but I don't recall what I was doing during the first minute. Probably more of that "all thumbs" business! The silence was punctured by each camera click and framed against the ever-present howl outside. Neither one of us said a word until she stopped shooting about five minutes later.

Hurricane-force winds with rain were blowing against the back of Jerrine's head as she leaned out the window to shoot. First she used the 24mm leans– but this tornado was too close and too huge to get a good shot with that wide-angle lens. So she switched to– believe it or not– our widest lens, a 15mm (110 degree) to shoot a **tornado!**

"I still can't believe we needed practically a fisheye to take in a tornado! Were we really that close?! Were we really **that** foolhardy? ... thank God we were!" It wasn't a decision I would have made on purpose, but I, too, was glad for the results afterward. We **were** pretty reckless driving right up to a monster wedge tornado. But then, sometimes it takes a mistake to expose the opportunity of a lifetime!

Jerrine clicked away, with only the sound of the wind and the feel of the horizontal rain driving into the back of her head. But it was no problem keeping the camera steady because

The tornado may not look very close here but it filled the sky in this 110° view.

Update on tornado research

Recent studies have teamed up professional chasers and researchers in field experiments, intercepting severe storms to gather detailed data and observations. As a result, we are learning a great deal about supercells and tornadoes that is challenging older notions. It appears that any neat and tidy cause-effect relationship is unlikely. There are many supercells but few produce tornadoes– and those that do are not necessarily typical or obvious examples. Put another way, the distinction between tornadic and non-tornadic supercells cannot be made using our current technology.

A few surprising results have emerged too. It now appears that outflow undercutting the mesocyclone does not impede tornado formation and may, in fact, be a necessary influence. In particular, the rear-flank downdraft (RFD) is being looked at with great interest. This downdraft at the back (south to west) of the storm may be more important than the updraft because it acts as the final "kicker" to a tightening-up of the rotation. A sustained updraft is required, too, but how moist the downdraft is (which varies with the day's environment and the height from which air descends) and how much vorticity it contains (spin) all contribute to rotation as this air moves down, around the mesocyclone, and then back into the updraft. Tornadoes don't seem to depend on obvious factors like high instability or a strong updraft, but rather on small scale effects with subtle changes making very large differences to the outcome.

These changes are adding complications to forecasting and warnings too. We are still a long way from predicting tornadoes. A mesocyclone on radar or a well-built intense supercell do not imply more than a slight chance. Tornado formation is so complex that it will take many years and hundreds of detailed storm intercepts before we begin to improve our current predictions. Each storm we chase and document provides an opportunity to further the science and unravel the tornado mystery!

the wind was completely constant– absolutely no gusts. It was not until a couple of days later that she realized the reason that her neck was sore was that she had braced her head against the wind as she shot the tornado.

As she shot, she thought, "I can see the fine, almost delicate texture of the horizontal rain sheets and the darker dust skirt wrapping around the huge trunk of a tornado– beside, then in front of me. There is no large debris here because there are no structures nearby." (It was fortunate that there was nothing along the road that could become airborne, or we could easily have been injured.) You hear people talk about "elephant trunk" tornadoes. But what we were looking at was the "elephant's leg"– so close that we could see all the wrinkles in the skin! *(See previous page.)*

As the tornado moved toward the road *(see photo on title page)*, and started crossing it ahead of us, a couple of cars came up and passed us from behind. I stepped out for a couple of final shots. What a wind! The tornado faded from view as rain obscured it again. We took off, leap-frogging other chase vehicles as it plowed ahead, veiled in rain.

We stopped with a few other cars where the tornado had crossed the road because there were heavy duty wires down across it, but within a minute or so we spotted emergency flashers coming up behind us and we and the other cars drove over the wires slowly, knowing that help was right there if things got dicey. Power poles lay along the highway like slain giants with their arms outstretched. Pieces of debris lay here and there, strewn along the road for almost three miles.

I thought about this and speculated that the tornado might have circled the mesocyclone's outer edge– first to the south and east as we stopped the last time (that may explain why it seemed to be nearer than expected), and then curving more east-northeast along the highway. We didn't have a chance to survey the results in more detail because a heavy deluge of rain, hail, and increasing wind enveloped our route. Later analysis suggested this was another dangerous moment. The increasing wind occurred as the tornado briefly became stationary just to our southeast. A storm's rebuilding phase can sometimes cause a tornado to back up before resuming its regular course. We were trapped on the highway by bouts of heavy hail and rain, and near-zero visibility.

We never saw the tornado again– it was rain-obscured. We made our way down the next highway to the interstate and headed east to Shamrock before dark. That town has become a favourite hangout for chasers because it has a gas station with data access and Weather Channel on. Maybe we'd run into some chaser-friends there, we thought. After all, how can you live though such an adventure without telling someone? Sure enough, Jerrine walked in and spotted old friend and veteran chaser Dave Hoadley surveying the drink cooler at the back of the store.

They exchanged a few excited words and breathless (with awe) stories. He had filmed it too, but from further back. Jerrine sent him out to me and we shared a few minutes of laughter as we teased each other and shared the joys of our fantastic catch. By the time she came back out to the car he'd already bid me farewell.

Seeing Hoadley was a fitting way to end the day. We'd run into him before Trinidad too, so it was like touching home base. We had caught the "big one" for sure! It was the largest, closest, most awesome tornado we had ever encountered, and the memories of this day would inspire our dreams and chasing fantasies for a long time.

The next day, we toyed with a nice storm in Texas for awhile before breaking off for home. Behind us, as we sailed east through Oklahoma, we watched the sky sparkle with lightning. The light show lasted hours, bidding us farewell and teasing us to return again someday soon.

Our short chase was a fantastic success– and not just because of the tornado. The whole experience was time-out-of-time, a wild ride on Nature's coat-tails, the perfect remedy for a chaser's itch.

The sky is always there

We will always be skywatchers first and storm chasers second. Even if we were motivated mainly by a desire to get under the wall cloud, cheek to jowl with a tornado, we would not have much success if we were not willing to stay engaged with the sky even in its quieter moments. Once you know it intimately, as we do, you, too, will want to delight in its infinite and varied beauty whenever and wherever you can.

And although you will probably never have to take cover from a tornado, you are now free to start enjoying the magnificence of the stormy sky. Now, you know enough to respond with exhiliration, not terror, to the many manifestations of wind, water and electricity that paint glory in the heavens. Happy skywatching. Perhaps we'll see you out there, eyes to the sky!

Acknowledgments

We would like to thank the following people for the insight and information they provided in personal communications and telephone consultations:

Harold Brooks (Researcher at the National Severe Storms Laboratory, Norman, OK)
David Etkin (Researcher on risk assessment at the University of Toronto)
Tom Grazulis (Tornado historian and author)
Tim Marshall (Structural engineer and editor of Storm Track, a magazine for chasers)
The staff at the Ontario Weather Centre, especially Mike Leduc. Thanks also to Environment Canada, Commercial Services for the use of the base map on page 130.
Paul Markowski (Researcher, Department of Meteorology, Penn State University)
Erik Rasmussen (Researcher, Cooperative Institute for Mesoscale Meteorological Studies, NSSL)
David Dowell (Researcher, Advanced Studies Program, NCAR)

We also thank T.T. Fujita (now deceased), Professor Emeritus at the University of Chicago, for permission to use some of his diagrams and research.

References

Publications which were particularly useful in our research (and some of which have been cited in the text) are:

Brooks, Harold E. and Doswell, Charles A. III, "A brief history of deaths from tornadoes in the United States", submitted to WEA.Forecasting.

Church, C., et al., editors, *The Tornado: Its Structure, Dynamics, Prediction, and Hazards*, Geophysical Monograph 79. Washington: American Geophysical Union, 1993.

Doswell, Charles A. III and Brooks, Harold E., "Lessons learned from the damage produced by the tornadoes of 3 May 1999", submitted to WEA.Forecasting.

Etkin, David A., *Environmental Adaptation Research Group, Environment Canada*, Soren Erik Brun, *University of Toronto*, P. Joe, B. Archibald, J. Archibald, A. Coldwells, R. Cripps, D. Dudley, R. Fleetwood, P. Ford, M. Gaudette, T. Keck, M. Leduc, A. Lachapelle, R. Mandeville, P. McCarthy, J. Mullock, D. Robinson, G. Vickers, and A. Whitman, *Environment Canada*, and H. Brooks, *National Severe Storms Laboratory*, U.S.A., *A Revised Risk Analysis of Tornadoes in Canada*. Toronto, 1996.

Grazulis, Thomas P., *Significant Tornadoes 1880-1989*, Vols. I and II. St. Johnsbury, VT: Environmental Films, 1990.

Grazulis, Thomas P., *The tornado: nature's ultimate windstorm*, Norman, Oklahoma: University of Oklahoma Press, 2001.

Hammer, Barbara and Schmidlin, Thomas W., "Response to warnings during the May 1999 Oklahoma City tornado: reasons and relative injury rates", submitted to WEA.Forecasting.

Inglish, Howard, Connie White and Dr. Ron Fischer, *Tornado: Terror and Survival*. Andover, KS: The Counseling Center of Butler County, 1991.

Kessler, Edwin, *The Thunderstorm in Human Affairs*, 2nd edition, Volume 1 of *Thunderstorms: A Social, Scientific, and Technological Documentary*. Norman, OK: University of Oklahoma Press, 1983.

Lafond, Raymond, "Helping Children Cope With Disaster," *Emergency Preparedness Digest*, January-March, 1989.

Marshall, Tim, *Storm Talk*. Flower Mound, TX, 1995. (Sketches by Dave Hoadley.)

Minor, Joseph E. et al., *The Tornado: An Engineering-Oriented Perspective*, NOAA Technical Memorandum NWS SR-147. Fort Worth: NOAA/NWS, 1993.

Thanks to the people we interviewed

Our thanks to all the people who gave generously of their time to make this project possible. Their stories gave life and colour to the book.

Deedee Adams • Aubrey Alderdice • Phil Anderson • Bill, Lynne, Kelly and Scott Anderson • Larry and Linda Andrew • Tammy Andrews • Arnold Ashton • Michael Axford • Launce Bagg • Kim Bailey • Ray Baker • Laura Banks • Bill Barber • Maureen and Heidi Baufeldt • Emma Baumlisberger • Danielle and Paul Beckingham Courtney Belford • Ray and Velma Bell • Robert Bell • Nancy and Nick Belviso • Betsy and Jack Benham • Victoria and Adam Beverstein • Herb and Ilse Birkholz • Joanne Blacklock • Mike, Pat, Danielle and Michelle Boivin • Bill and Isobel Bospoort • Vince Bowen • Nick Bowie • Peter Bowie • Wayne and Wilma Boyd • Kim Brintnell • Teresa Brown • Grace Brown • Charlie and Liz Bryan • Cathy Bryan • Tim Burdick • Loren Burns • Eileen and Jack Burnside • Ann, Gary, Erin, Kelsey and Kristen Butler • Jean Cameron • Mary Ellen Caudle • Mark and Shelley Champagne • Doug Christian • Brad, Cathy, Carolyn and Telisa Clarke • Gary Clayton • Krista Coates • Len Coffey • Marlene Coke • Dina and Rudy Coleman • Jennifer Colton • Dave, Sue and Becky Comber • Archie (Vic) Comber • Bob and Freida Comber • Bob, Cynthia and Alex Cook • John and Yvonne Cook • Catherine Cooper Pam Cotton • Annie and Claude Coupal • Mark Courtney • Bob and Shirley Cox • Shawna Coxon • Archie Crawford • Gerry, Ruth and Kimberley Crews • Bill and Ruth Cruikshank • Jean Cuco • Fred, Linda, Anna Marie, Jody John and Salina Dakin • Betty Dale • Terry Darling • Vernon Davidge • Len Day • Randy Demorest • Bobby-Jo Denney • Cheryl Dennis • Pat Dinsmore • Melissa Dobson • Melissa Dobson • Jim Douglas • Ellen and Ron Dowling • George (Ted) and Sherry Draper • Jo-Anne and Robyn Dreyer • Ken Dumais • Ken Dunn • Leon Dutfield • Betty-Ann and Jim East • Judy and Stephanie Eden • Carol and Tom Egan • Joan and Rich Eldridge Robert Elms • Peter Elms • Tom Evans • Paul Evans • Francine Evans • Rick Eyre • George Farley • Eleanor Farrow • Irene Fell • Bobby Ferguson • Lynne Ferris • Dennis, Helen, Daniel and Margaret Fischer • Janice Fisher • Jim and Laura Franklin • Yvonne Frehner • David Fries • Darlene Frizzell • Elaine and Lloyd Galbraith • Edith Geffken • Greg Givens • Betty and Ralph Gorvett • Helen Gorvett • Colleen and Russell Gratton • John and Terri Griffin • Norman Grove • Graeme Hackston • Doris Hagarty • Paul Hald • Jacklyn and Les Halucha Howard Hamlin • Barb Hanley • Ellie Harder • Troy Harquail • Cindy, Janis and Josh Harrison • Janice, Philip, Angie and Christopher Hawkins • Earl and Robin Hawkins • David Hawthorne • Paul and Shirley Heimbecker Bruce Henderson • Sherry, Brittany and Jacob Henry • Mike and Wendy Heslop • Candy, David, Angela, Cameron and Jennifer Hill • Lila and Melvin Hill • Kathleen and Trevor Hill • Chris Hilty • Stanley and Susan Hogencamp Shaun and Tawana Holland • Betty and Robert Holman • Diane, Glen and Kevin Holmes • Michelle Holt • Gus Hostrawser • Bill and Hazel Hutchison • Jack and Karen Idzik • Les, Linda, Charlie and Stephanie Janke • Kirk and Laura Jeans • Christine and Lyndon Johnston • Susan Johnston • Guy, Diane and Roger Jolicoeur • Dyan Jones • Jackie and Wayne Jones • Marlies and Walter Kaelhi • Karl Kamermyer • Shawn Keating • Scott Keddie Darrell Keenie • Norm Keith • Joanne and Norman Kidnie • Karen Kimpel • Debbie, Ron, Aren and Josh King • John and Wilhemena Kottelenberg • Jack Kottelenberg • Bruce Krug • Diana Krul • Louisette Lanteigne • Barry Lazelle • Steve Leach • Mike Leduc • Irmgard Leimbrock • Arlene Leis • Joann Lewis • Carol and John MacDonald • Don MacIver • Gloria and John MacKenzie • Jim MacNamara • Karen Mahon • Saverio, Vedia, Chris and Frank Maletta • Marg Manto • Jack Marshall • Randy Martin • Roger, Sharon and Dale Martin • Mary, Jacklyn and Leeann Martin • Paul, Rose, Darcy, Derek, Dorothy, Laura, Reann and Shari Martin • Cheryl Mason • James Masters • June Maycock • Julie Maycock • Vivian McCauley • Pam McCauley • Lorne McCauley • Jeff McCullough • Bonnie, Darryl and Jeffrey McDougall • Phyllis McDowell • Pauline McEwen • Jerry McKinnon • Jane McKinnon-Wilson • Kate McLaren • William McMaster • Russell McNabb • Bill and Diana Metzger • Julie Meyer • Kathy Meyer • Jan Middleton • Donna, Fred, Anna and Chelsea Miller • Michelle Mitchell • Harold Moore • Kerry Moore • Greg Moore • Joan Morris • Richard Mountain • Melvin Muller • Angela Mulligan • Donna and Pat Murphy • Tony Murray • Audrey and John Neerhof • Eric and Heidi Neumann • Irving Newman • Dennis Novasad • Michael O'Halloran • Shirley Orr • Sharon and Terry Palmay • Rob Paola • Karen and Michael Penny • Mike, Nelson and Scott Phillips • Faye Phinney • Ernie Plant • Peter Ponsen • Ray Pool • Peter Poremski • David Potts • George and Bethany Power • William, Jeremy and Steve Prins • Charlotte Pritty • Cyril and Margaret Pritty • Dawna Proudman • Chad Purdie • Mike Queenie • Sgt. Dave Quince • Jerry and Kelly Radstake • Diane Ransom • Jutta, Paul and Cathy Reaburn • Christine, David, Jenna and Kevin Reaburn • Wayne Reid • Ron Reid • Rev. Merlyn Rensberry • Bill and Joan Richardson • Angela Ringrose • Gisele Robinson • Kevin and Sherry Robinson • Grace Rock • Arnold Rosenberg • Wanda, Jerry and Rhonda Ross • Carolyn Routenburg Jason Rusnak • Gary and Lynn Russell • David Ruttan • Geoff Ruttan • Kara Saba • Albert, Rosemary, Daniel and David Sandink • Jim Sannes • Brian Saunders • Ed and Eleanor Saunders • Marg and Stacey Saunders • Lloyd Sawden • Barry Scarlett • Gabe and Michelle Scavone • Janet Scheibler • Ann Schneider • Anna Scott • Chris Seabrook • Ed Seidle • Joan Shaw • Gisela and Henry Sieger • Andrew Sieger • Jim Simpson • Dave and Lorie Smith • R. Avery Smith • Susanne Soles • Velma Specht • Brenda, Wayne, Jason and Justin Specht • Tim Spencely • Don and Jen Stanker • Cheryl Ste. Marie • Brent Stevenson • Doreen and John Still • Shelley Still • James Stinson • Gail Stoddart • Barbara Stott • Audrey and Kim Straker • Lee, Corey, Jenine and Mandy Swallow Christa and Jesse Tait • Bruce and Susan Tait • Steve Taylor • Barb and Stan Theriault • Lynn and Ken Topping Laura Tovell • Martin Tovey • Laverne, Faye and Ross Trimble • Andrew, Diane and Mitchell Tripo • Don Turner • Bob Venables • Arthur Vernon • Cornelius and Faye Vlielander • Paul Waechter • Keith Wagler • Willis Wakes Joyce Walker • Robin Wallace • Laurie Waller • Chris Walsh • Luella Wark • Shari Ann Weber • Darrell and Miriam Weber • Linda and Sean Weisner • Jason Weisner • Ken and Sandra Wells • Ruth, Wayne and Todd Whitelaw • Ira Wilson • Leslee Winchester • Kim Winchester • Helen Winters • Frank and Brian Wood • Janice Wyville • Sam Yoder and family • Jim Zantinge • Wayne Zettler • Jim Zyta

Have we sparked your imagination, fired up your enthusiasm
for storms and sky?
Visit our website: www.skyartpro.com

You'll find loads of pictures, adventures, information and ideas
about chasing the sky, along with updates on upcoming books,
speaking engagements and projects.

Or check out some of the other products you can get from Skyart:

Full-color storm chart
US $15 (plus shipping)

Watching the stormy sky is a visual guide to storms and tornadoes.
This dramatic, 24" X 36.5" full-color poster displays a fascinating variety of
storm and tornado pictures in one stunning layout, complete with captions

Storm chaser screen saver
US $12 (plus shipping)

Electrify your screen!
Featuring 25 spectacular photos by the Verkaiks, this screen saver transforms your screen
into a riveting display of nature's awesome power and fury. Storms, lightning and
breathtaking skyscapes leap randomly from your screen every 10 seconds.
Compatible with both MAC and all Windows operating systems.

Contact us about these and other products at: Skyart, RR#3, Elmwood, Ontario, Canada   N0G 1S0

(519) 363-5785   e-mail: skyartpro@skyartpro.com